The Hidden Costs of Clean Election Reform

THE HIDDEN COSTS
OF CLEAN ELECTION REFORM

Frederic Charles Schaffer

CORNELL UNIVERSITY PRESS

Ithaca & London

First published 2008 by Cornell University Press

Printed in the United States of America

Library of Congress Cataloging-in-Publication Data

Schaffer, Frederic Charles.
   The hidden costs of clean election reform / Frederic Charles Schaffer.
     p. cm.
   Includes bibliographical references and index.
   ISBN 978-0-8014-4115-8 (cloth : alk. paper)
   1. Elections—Corrupt practices. 2. Elections—Corrupt practices—United States. 3. Voting. 4. Voting—United States. I. Title.
   JF1083.S34.2008
   324.6'6—dc22
                       2007048080

Cornell University Press strives to use environmentally responsible suppliers and materials to the fullest extent possible in the publishing of its books. Such materials include vegetable-based, low-VOC inks and acid-free papers that are recycled, totally chlorine-free, or partly composed of nonwood fibers. For further information, visit our website at www.cornellpress.cornell.edu.

Cloth printing   10 9 8 7 6 5 4 3 2 1

Contents

Preface

It was three o'clock in the afternoon when a crackling voice announced over tin-pot loudspeakers that the polls were now closed. I was sitting in the courtyard of Barangay Commonwealth High School, located in a poor and crowded section of Quezon City, the largest city in the Philippines and a part of Metro Manila. The school was serving as a polling place for the 2004 national elections, each classroom converted into a separate precinct, 117 in all.

All around me in the courtyard were people who had come to vote but could not find their names on the voters' list. In every election a certain number of voters cannot find their names, but the scale of exclusion in this election was different. I had been to this same high school three years earlier to observe voting during the 2001 elections. Then, about seventy voters could not find their names. Now there were a thousand or more.

Oddly, many of the people milling about the courtyard held in their hands receipts given to them by the Commission on Elections (COMELEC) a few months before when they had registered for the first time or had had their registration "validated." As part of its efforts to modernize elections, COMELEC had begun in 2003 to generate a centralized computer database—complete with digital photos, fingerprints, and signatures—of all registered voters. With 18 million dollars' worth of newly purchased data-capturing machines, the poll body had asked all registered voters to have their registration validated in order to purge the voters' list of ineligible, fictitious, and double voters. People who did not validate would still be able to vote, COMELEC had informed everyone, but they would be placed on a separate "watch list" and subject to possible exclusion. Voters trooped to COMELEC offices around the country and waited in endless lines to validate. By the end of the registration drive, about 6 million of the country's 37 million registered voters had validated their registration, and another 6 million voters had registered for the first time.

Problems arose, however, when COMELEC found itself unable to reconcile the old lists maintained by its field offices with the new centralized list generated by the data-capturing machines. According to COMELEC spokesperson Milagros Desamito (2004), the software used to manage the old list was incompatible with the software used to maintain the new list. When COMELEC tried to consolidate the two lists, a large number of names were dropped. Unable to work out a solution in its central office, COMELEC hastily advised its local officers, less than two weeks before the election, to generate their own voters' lists, using their own records.

In the ensuing scramble, the local COMELEC officer in charge of Barangay Commonwealth High School (one of sixty-eight polling places she oversaw) put many of the validated and new voters apportioned to the school into six newly created precincts. Her office prepared the voters' lists but in the last-minute chaos made no provisions for the physical precincts. There were no classrooms, no ballots, no ballot boxes. Almost all of the people waiting in the courtyard were assigned to one of these six ghost precincts.

Voter exclusion was not limited to this high school. Down the road, half of the voters assigned to the Payatas Elementary School were not able to vote. "They are turned off," said the principal on election day, "because they have their voter's registration record, they have been validated, and still they could not vote" (*Philippine Daily Inquirer,* May 11, 2004). News reports revealed similar patterns of exclusion in towns and cities across the country. An exit poll conducted by the Social Weather Stations, an academic survey research center, found that nine hundred thousand people—more than 2 percent of all registered voters nationwide—could not vote because their names were not on the voters' lists. In Metro Manila, the rate of exclusion was nearly 5 percent (SWS 2004). A newspaper captured the prevailing mood when it published a cartoon portraying disenfranchised voters as a raging dog ready to lunge at a very nervous COMELEC (see figure 1).

The scope of exclusion not only provoked anger but also put into question the very legitimacy of the elections. Among the offices up for grabs was the presidency, which pitted incumbent Gloria Macapagal Arroyo against a phenomenally popular movie actor, Fernando Poe Jr., and three other candidates. Arroyo was proclaimed the winner, but her margin of victory was modest—only 1.1 million votes out of some 32.3 million cast. In this context, the exclusion of almost a million voters seemed highly suspicious. Many people, especially

Figure 1. Cartoon from the *Manila Times*, May 12, 2004.

those who supported one of the losing candidates, believed the foul-up with the voters' lists was deliberate. The fact that the rate of exclusion was much higher in Metro Manila, where Poe ran strong, than in the rest of the country only added fuel to these suspicions. Poe refused to concede defeat. Rumors of coups, destabilization plots, and mass demonstrations filled the air.

Validation was supposed to assure voters that they would be able to vote on election day, but the opposite happened. An effort to prevent fraudulent voting not only kept the most responsible voters from casting their ballots but also undermined the very credibility of the elections. A measure adopted to enhance the quality of democracy instead damaged it. To borrow an analogy from medicine, we might call this unhappy outcome an "iatrogenic" effect of COMELEC's efforts to prevent vote fraud. In Greek, *iatros* means "doctor" and *genic* means "produced by." An iatrogenic illness is one induced by treatment. It was the very attempt to make elections better that made them worse.

It is not only in the Philippines that the iatrogenic effects of clean election reform have been felt. After the hanging chads and butterfly ballots of Florida 2000, reforming the mechanics of voting rose high on the American public agenda. Many local election officials hurriedly purchased the latest in election technology, direct-recording electronic voting machines, only to find that they had serious security flaws, left no paper trail of how voters cast their ballots, were difficult for ordinary poll workers to operate, and sometimes malfunctioned. In Mercer County, Pennsylvania, machine glitches during the 2004 elections caused at least four thousand votes to disappear, representing 8 percent or more of all that were cast. That same year, seven thousand people in Orange County, California, did not have their votes recorded—more than 1 percent of all votes cast—because ill-trained precinct workers provided them with incorrect access codes. By 2007, officials in Florida, Maryland, and Virginia already wanted to replace their newly acquired machines. Stopgap measures hastily adopted to forestall future electoral crises of Floridian proportions themselves generated irregularities and a loss of confidence.

Other countries around the world have not been immune to such ills either. In Venezuela, a bungled effort to automate the electoral process led to the exclusion of up to 5 percent of the electorate during the 2000 elections. In South Africa, tightened registration rules put in place for the 1999 elections prevented roughly 6 percent of the voting-age population from participating in the polls. In post-Soviet Georgia, the poorly handled computerization of electoral lists for the 2003 elections kept an estimated 10 to 15 percent of the electorate from being able to cast their ballots. And the list goes on.

I examine in this book the iatrogenic effects of clean election reform. I investigate the ways in which attempts to clean up dirty or sloppy electoral practices sometimes do damage to the very principles of democratic fairness and integrity that these efforts are intended to promote. One goal is to figure out why citizens—such as those who were unable to vote at the Barangay Commonwealth High School or those who lost their votes in Orange County—sometimes find themselves cut out of the electoral process. Another goal is to see whether lessons might be learned to help prevent such breaches of democracy in the future.

It is the unique contribution of this book to examine the pitfalls of clean election reform using evidence drawn from both the United States and other parts of the world, evidence that is both contemporary and historical. In the United States, it must be underscored, iatrogenic harm has not been confined to post-Florida electronic voting. Indeed, in this book I examine how an overzealous purge of Florida's voter rolls contributed to the disaster of 2000 in the first place. I also look at the damage done by more recent moves around the country to tighten voter identification requirements. I analyze, too, historical cases of iatrogenic harm in the United States, focusing on the advent of secret balloting in 1890s Arkansas, New Jersey, and New York, as well as the impact of registration procedures on Chicago voters in the 1920s. Nevertheless, the book is expressly comparative. I examine a historical case of harm abroad, specifically damage caused by efforts to insulate voters from outside pressure in nineteenth-century France. I also consider more recent cases of harm from around the world. Focusing on the 1991 to 2006 period, I look at iatrogenic damage not only in the Philippines, Venezuela, South Africa, and Georgia but in more than a dozen other countries as well. These varied instances of harm come from different times and different places. Nevertheless, they issued by and large from similar sets of circumstances. Thus we all have as much to learn from the experiences of other countries as from our own histories. Indeed, a major goal of this book is to make people both in the United States and abroad think about clean election reform—and its hidden traps—in ways that are a little less parochial.

To acknowledge that clean election reforms sometimes inflict damage should not, of course, be taken as an argument that such reforms should simply be abandoned. Left unchecked, fraud and error can compromise the quality of democracy. Most obviously they can override the will of the electorate. In the Philippines, an estimated 2 million spurious entries plagued the voters' list in the 1995 elections, and the vote padding that this allowed cost at least one senatorial candidate his seat (CSER 1995, 7). Fraud and error can also alienate voters and thereby depress voter turnout. In Mexico, for instance, a 1991 public opinion survey found that 59 percent of the respondents "said that they believed that many people did not vote in elections because the elections were not perceived to be honest or clean" (Domínguez and McCann 1996, 159). Widespread fraud and error, in addition, make it less likely that losers will accept electoral outcomes or the democratic rules of the game as legitimate. This loss of legitimacy may well undermine the credibility of elections and weaken people's commitment to the democratic process. It was not only the exclusion of voters in the Philippines that led Poe to contest the official election results and stirred fears of coups and uprisings but also a belief that the tallying was rigged. The need to clean up the registration and counting processes in that country is urgent.

It would thus be a mistake to frame the issue too narrowly as a choice between elections that are "clean but exclusionary" on the one hand and "dirty and sloppy, but inclusive" on the other. Both vote depression and election fraud or error depreciate the quality of democracy. The real goal should be to make elections both as clean and as inclusive as possible. For this reason, it is important to understand how and why clean election reforms sometimes go bad. I hope that such information will help legislators and election officials, or the activists in civil society who watch over them, find ways to achieve both goals simultaneously. While I do not believe that the "reform of reform" is simple or straightforward, to the extent that iatrogenic harm is preventable, those of us with a commitment to clean and inclusive democracy should try to prevent it. When there are inescapable trade-offs, we should, at a minimum, be aware of what has been traded away.

Why do clean election reforms sometimes go bad? It is tempting to assume that the key factors that explain iatrogenic harm have to do with the *properties* of the reforms themselves. That is, we might suppose that the secret ballot should have one type of effect, voter identification cards another type of effect, and so on. We might further suppose that certain types of clean election reform are inherently more troublesome than others.

At the beginning stages of this project I held these very suppositions. Indeed, in early outlines of the manuscript I imagined separate chapters being devoted to the secret ballot, registration reform, computerized voting, and the like. I came to see, however, that a focus on different types of reform as explanatory variables obscured more than it revealed. First, I found that the same reform had dramatically different effects in different places. For example, the advent of the secret ballot depressed turnout in 1890s Arkansas but increased turnout at around the same time in places like Michigan, Denmark, and Germany. Second, I found that similar outcomes could be caused by different kinds of reform. Very similar patterns of disenfranchisement, for instance, resulted from both the introduction of the secret ballot (in 1890s Arkansas) and the introduction of new registration requirements (in 1990s South Africa). Eventually I came to see that the key explanatory variables were not types of reform (secret ballot, voter identification, computerized voting), but the motives, knowledge, and capacities of the *actors* involved in crafting, implementing, or reacting to reforms. Thus, to give but one example, the consequences of the secret ballot have been very different depending on whether the motive behind its adoption was protecting the privacy of all voters or controlling illiterate voters who required the "help" of polling officials to read and fill out their ballots.

To be sure, certain types of clean election reform do possess qualities that make them more prone to damaging democracy than others. As I will discuss in chapter 1, particularly prone to doing damage are reforms that are by nature restrictive (for instance, those designed to ensure that only eligible voters cast ballots), reforms that are complex and thus difficult to manage (such as electronic systems to transmit election results), and reforms that are disciplinary (such as anti-vote-buying campaigns) and thus likely to provoke unanticipated reactions from voters, parties, and local poll workers. But these potentialities are hardly determinate. Not all reforms that tighten voter eligibility, introduce electronic systems, or combat vote buying damage democracy. Only under certain conditions do particular actors make these potentialities become real. For this reason, I organize the chapters of this book around types of actors, not types of reform.

Consequently, I do not identify which types of clean election reform are inherently more troublesome because—even if some reforms are more prone to doing harm than others—any type of clean election reform (secret balloting, computerized voting, voter identification, voter education, etc.) might become damaging under certain conditions or benign under others. It is the motives of those involved, the way reforms are implemented, and how parties and candidates react that I found to be determinate. It is primarily about these "actor-centered" explanatory variables that I theorize. In the conclusion to this book, I boil these variables down to "motive," "knowledge," and "power" and discuss the ways in which their different configurations do or do not result in iatrogenic harm.

There are four sets of actors who each play a crucial role in clean election reform: lawmakers, who craft the new rules; election officials and workers, who implement them; candidates, their agents, and party leaders, who play by them; and civic educators, who teach the public new ways to behave. Each type of actor can, intentionally or not, damage the quality of democracy. In the Philippines (2004)—as in Florida (2000), Venezuela (2000), and post-Soviet Georgia (2003), among other places—it was the ineptitude or connivance of election officials or workers that caused voter exclusion. In places such as France (1880s), Arkansas (1890s), Chicago (1920s), and South Africa (1999), it was lawmakers who crafted new rules that put up obstacles to electoral participation. In New Jersey (1890s), New York (1890s), Guyana (1997), Taiwan (1990s), and Mexico (2000), the demobilization of voters was caused by the shifting tactics of party operatives in response to new clean election safeguards. In Thailand (2000) and the Philippines (2001), clean election campaigns mounted by civic educators tended either to alienate more than educate or to reinforce the very behaviors they were designed to curtail.

The plan of the book is straightforward. I devote a chapter to each set of actors and the conditions under which their actions become damaging, while in the concluding chapter I examine various measures that might be adopted to prevent or minimize such iatrogenic harm. Before turning to this analysis, I take up in chapter 1 a few foundational questions: What is clean election reform? What kinds of damage to democracy can such reform cause? What makes clean election reform prone to doing damage? And finally, what kinds of methods and evidence does this study use?

I owe a debt of gratitude to many people and institutions for their help in writing this book. For research assistance, I thank David Art, Jessica Piombo, and Julia de Kadt. For teaching me Tagalog, I am ever appreciative of Paz Mendoza. For their thoughtful comments on early presentations or individual chapters of this book, I am grateful to Myrna Alejo, Suzanne Berger, William Callahan, Kanchan Chandra, Raymond De Vries, Jørgen Elklit, Jennifer Franco, Richard Katz, Ben Kerkvliet, Nancy Kokaz, Carl Landé, Chappell Lawson, Tony Moreno, Michael Pinches, Andreas Schedler, Richard Snyder, Ashutosh Varshney, and David Woodruff. I am also grateful to John Gerring, Tova Wang, and an anonymous reader for their detailed comments on the manuscript. For their ongoing support, I owe much to Dick Samuels, David Collier, and Roger Haydon.

For providing, or helping to track down, specific pieces of information I thank Alain Pelletier of Elections Canada; Mireille Loignon of the Directeur général des élections du Québec; Garth Stevenson of Brock University; Gregory Tardi, senior legal counsel, Office of the Law Clerk and Parliamentary Counsel, House of Commons, Canada; Elizabeth Danley of the Arkansas State Library; John Lantigua of the *Palm Beach Post;* R. Boyd Murphree of the Florida State Archives; Linda Howell, supervisor of elections for Madison County, Florida; John Groh, Election Systems & Software senior vice president of international sales; Terry Holcomb, former senior advisor, International Foundation for Election Systems; Miriam Kornblith of the Facultad de Ciencias Jurídicas y Políticas at the Universidad Central de Venezuela; Chin-shou Wang of the National Cheng Kung University, Taiwan; Yogendra Yadav of the Centre for the Study of Developing Societies in Delhi, India; and Paula Cossart of the École des Hautes Études en Sciences Sociales in Paris.

I collected much of the material on the Philippines from January through August 2001 while conducting fieldwork supported by the Fulbright Scholars Program. Funding for additional fieldwork in 2000, 2002, 2003, and 2004 was provided by the Center for International Studies and the School of Humanities, Arts, and Social Sciences at the Massachusetts Institute of Technology. I thank the Institute of Philippine Culture and the Political Science Department at Ateneo de Manila University for providing me with an institutional home. I am also indebted to Alfred Antonio, Marion Pantaleon, Jorge Alberto, and E-Anne Enriquez for their research assistance, and to Victor Lee, Maggie Baybay, and Beverly Ravinera for their transcription services. For their help and friendship I thank Gerry Lopez of the Parish Pastoral Council for Responsible Voting (PPCRV) and Telibert Laoc of the National Citizens' Movement for Free Elections. Others who helped include Alexander Calata and the staff of the Philippine-American Educational Foundation; Felipe Miranda of

Pulse Asia; Mahar Mangahas and Jeanette Ureta of the Social Weather Stations; Vilma Malumay at the National Statistics Office; COMELEC Commissioner Resurreccion Borra; former COMELEC chairpersons Christian Monsod and Harriet Demetriou; Ramon Casiple of the Institute for Political and Electoral Reform; Emigdio Tanjuatco, Jr., former chairman of the House of Representatives Committee on Suffrage and Electoral Reforms; Quezon City PPCRV organizers Johnny Cardenas, Tony Villasor, Angel Gahol, Sister Naty, and Rene Baylon; and in the national PPCRV office, Clifford Sorita and the late Apolonio Dionisio. I also profited immensely from my conversations with Aries Arugay, Father John Carroll, Grace Gorospe-Jamon, Eddie Nuque, Patrick Patiño, Mary Racelis, and Fernando Zialcita. I am, finally, deeply grateful to the people of Barangay Commonwealth for their openness and warmth.

I also thank the Taipei Economic and Cultural Office in Boston for organizing and funding a short trip to Taiwan in 2003. I am also indebted to Tsai Pi-yu, Horng Guang-sheng, Dan Chan, Ching Chi-jen, and Chou Huai-lien in the Ministry of Justice for their time and candor.

Parts of this book were researched and written during an idyllic year at the Institute for Advanced Study in Princeton, New Jersey. I am most grateful to Michael Walzer, Eric Maskin, Joan Scott, and the late Clifford Geertz for creating an environment so conducive to deep reflection.

For granting permission to reprint cartoons that originally appeared in their newspapers, I am grateful to the *Philippine Star,* the *Philippine Daily Inquirer,* and the *Manila Times.* Special thanks are due, too, to the editorial cartoonists themselves: Rene Aranda of the *Star,* Jess Abrera of the *Inquirer,* and the late Boy Togonon of the *Times.* Parts of chapters 2 and 4 appeared in Frederic Charles Schaffer, "Might Cleaning Up Elections Keep People Away from the Polls: Historical and Comparative Perspectives," *International Political Science Review* 23, no. 1 (2002): 69–84. An abridged version of chapter 5 and a small portion of chapter 4 were published in *Elections for Sale: The Causes and Consequences of Vote Buying* (Boulder: Lynne Rienner, 2007), which I edited.

Finally, I have been moved deeply by the patience and support of my family during too many long absences. To them I dedicate this book.

Abbreviations

HAVA	Help America Vote Act (United States)
HSRC	Human Sciences Research Council (South Africa)
ID	Identity document
IEC	Independent Electoral Commission (South Africa)
IFES	International Foundation for Election Systems (United States)
INEC	Independent National Electoral Commission (Nigeria)
KMT	Kuomintang [Nationalist Party of China] (Taiwan)
NAMFREL	National Citizens' Movement for Free Elections (Philippines)
NAQ	National Assembly of Quebec (Canada)
NNP	New National Party (South Africa)
NSO	National Statistics Office (Philippines)
OAS	Organization of American States
PPC	People Power Coalition (Philippines)
PPCRV	Parish Pastoral Council for Responsible Voting (Philippines)
PRI	Partido Revolucionario Institucional [Institutional Revolutionary Party] (Mexico)
SNTV	Single nontransferable vote
TBVC	Transkei, Bophuthatswana, Venda, and Ciskei (South Africa)
VMV	Valid multiple vote
VRA	Voting Rights Act (United States)
VVPAT	Voter verifiable paper audit trail

THE HIDDEN COSTS
OF CLEAN ELECTION REFORM

1

When Good Reforms Go Bad

Poll fraud and error take a variety of forms. Ineligible voters can register illegally. Eligible voters can register in more than one locale. Spurious voters can impersonate registered ones, often those who died recently or are out of town. Campaign operatives can intimidate voters, buy their votes, or commandeer polling stations. Poll workers can stuff ballot boxes or miscount votes. Election officials can doctor or incompetently maintain the voter registry. Canvassers can intentionally pad or shave vote totals or make inadvertent tallying mistakes.

Such forms of fraud and error afflict many post–World War II quasi and emerging democracies. In some places, instances of fraud and error have been sporadic. In other places, the scale has been large to massive. More than 150 people were killed in India during the 1989 parliamentary elections; much of the blood was spilled by armed partisans who raided polling stations in order to stuff ballot boxes, a widespread practice known locally as "booth capturing." The incidence of fraud in Nigeria's 1999 presidential election was, according to the country's main election watchdog organization, "great enough to completely distort the election result" (Transition Monitoring Group 1999). In Thailand, 30 percent of household heads surveyed nationwide said that they were offered money during the 1996 general election (Pasuk et al. 2000). In Venezuela, election results in four and then five of twenty states were declared void in the 1992 and 1995 national elections, respectively, as a result of alleged vote rigging.

Poll fraud and error vex established democracies as well. In Australia, some fifteen thousand multiple votes (more than one vote cast per name on the voters' roll) were recorded in the 1993 election (McGrath 1996, 7). In the 1983 municipal elections in France, more than twenty-five hundred appeals were filed to overturn the results of individual races; among the most common charges were ballot box stuffing, the falsification of election returns, and the fraudulent use of voters' cards (Maligner 1986, 7–20). In the United States, absentee ballot fraud was wide enough in scope to alter the outcome of the 1993 state senate election in Philadelphia and the Miami mayoral election of 1997. Georgia had more than fifteen thousand dead people on its voter rolls in 2000, while New York had as many as seventy-seven thousand in 2006.[1]

Many quasi, emerging, and established democracies find themselves, as a result, under domestic and/or international pressure to make polling more honest, accurate, and protective of individual freedom. In response, many governments have put in place reforms to reduce poll fraud and error, what we might call "clean" election reforms. The number of clean election reforms implemented since the early 1990s is large. Here is a small sampling: Nigeria, Zambia, Lesotho, Malawi, Mexico, and Bangladesh computerized their voter registers. Israel, Italy, and the states of Florida and Kentucky undertook extraordinary registry purges. Senegal, Bolivia, South Africa, and the Philippines adopted new procedures to verify voter eligibility. Ghana, Mali, Malawi, Mauritania, Yemen, Macedonia, Guyana, Mexico, Costa Rica, and the Dominican Republic introduced new forms of voter identification, while Indiana, Arizona, and South Dakota, among other states, tightened voter identification requirements. Brazil, Belgium, India, Germany, Quebec, Costa Rica, Ecuador, Paraguay, parts of Australia, and many jurisdictions in the United States began using electronic voting machines. Poland, Kyrgyzstan, Venezuela, and Mozambique switched to computerized vote counting or tabulation.[2] Mexico, Thailand, and the Philippines mounted voter education drives to discourage vote selling, while Taiwanese prosecutors cracked down hard on vote buyers.

It is often assumed that such reforms will enhance the quality of elections. The reality, however, is that sometimes this is not the case. The history of clean

---

1. "Even Death Can't Stop Some Voters," *Atlanta Journal and Constitution,* November 6, 2000; "Deceased Residents on Statewide Voter List," *Poughkeepsie Journal,* October 29, 2006.

2. Election experts distinguish vote "counting" (adding up individual votes) from vote "tabulation" (calculating vote totals based on polling station or polling center vote counts). Thus while Venezuela computerized both counting and tabulation, Kyrgyzstan continued to hand-count votes and computerized only tabulation. For most discussions in this book, it would have added unnecessary clutter to repeatedly make the distinction between counting and tabulation. Consequently, in the remainder of the book, I use "counting" in its broad, everyday sense to encompass both counting and tabulation—unless the context indicates otherwise.

election reform teaches us that simple changes in the administration of elections can have a profound and detrimental impact on, among other things, voter turnout. In the late nineteenth and early twentieth centuries, one of the most important electoral innovations was the secret ballot, championed by reformers as a means to reduce bribery and intimidation. But it had less salutary effects as well. In the United States, Democrats in the South deployed it to depress the turnout of illiterate voters and thus keep Republicans and Populists from power.

I identify in this book some of the conditions under which reforms designed to clean up elections today (with a focus on the period from 1991 to 2006) also keep potential voters away from the polls or damage the quality of democracy in other ways. For clues into which conditions are most important, I also look to the experience of late-nineteenth- and early-twentieth-century reform in Europe and the United States, about which much interesting, and I believe pertinent, scholarship has been produced.

I focus specifically on three questions. The first is descriptive: how has clean election reform actually damaged the quality of democracy in various countries around the world? The second is analytic: what conditions prevailed that allowed harm to be inflicted in some places but not others? The last is prescriptive: are there any safeguards that can be put in place to reduce such damage in the future? Before we turn to these questions in chapters 2 through 6, a few preliminary issues must be addressed.

What Is Clean Election Reform?

The reforms that are the subject of this book are all designed to reduce fraud and error in the casting and counting of votes.[3] They are all intended, more precisely, to ensure that only eligible voters cast ballots, that they cast them freely, and that the ballots are counted accurately. We might think of these reforms, respectively, as efforts to authenticate voter *eligibility* (to prevent spurious voting), safeguard voter *insulation* (to prevent the buying or coercion of voters), and strengthen vote *integrity* (to prevent the miscounting of votes).[4] An array of measures have been adopted to achieve these goals.

---

3. Additional information about the definition of "clean election reform" can be found in the appendix.

4. I adopt these categories, with some modification, from Schedler (2002, 39).

VOTER ELIGIBILITY

Reforms designed to ensure that only eligible voters cast ballots include the following:

- Adopting registration procedures that facilitate the detection of spurious registrants
- Purging dead and ineligible voters from the registry
- Remapping precincts to help poll workers detect fraudulent voters
- Requiring voters to dip their fingers into indelible ink to prevent double voting
- Electronic mechanisms to suspend voting when ballot box stuffing occurs

VOTER INSULATION

The following reforms are designed to protect the privacy and freedom of voters:

- The secret ballot
- Disqualifying ballots with extraneous writing or markings on them (such ballots can be used to identify voters in various vote buying or intimidation schemes)
- The vigorous prosecution of vote buyers
- Education campaigns designed to convince voters not to sell their votes

VOTE INTEGRITY

Other reforms are designed to safeguard an honest and accurate tallying of votes:

- Allowing contending political parties to name poll workers to each polling station
- Electronic voting machines
- The automation of ballot counting and tabulation
- The electronic transmission of vote counts

There are, it should be noted, other kinds of electoral reform that fall outside the scope of this book. Not included, for one, are reforms designed to generate *fair competition* among parties and candidates, such as laws that impose term limits, regulate access to the mass media, or limit the total amount of money that election campaigns can spend. Also outside the scope of this book are reforms intended to make the electoral system more *representative,* such as laws to prevent gerrymandering, the creation of minority-majority electoral districts, and the adoption of proportional representation. Also excluded are reforms meant to make elected officials more *accountable* to the electorate, such as party primaries (to increase the responsiveness of officeholders to the party rank and file) and bans on certain kinds of donations (to reduce the influence of special interests on those who get elected).

There may well be iatrogenic effects produced by these other types of democratic reform, but such ill effects have, historically, been well studied. The simple casting and counting of ballots has been, in contrast, an area too often neglected by those of us who study democracy, at least until the controversy stirred by the 2000 election in Florida. In the past, when we asked how democratic an electoral system was, we tended to think first of big constitutional or representational questions—who is allowed to vote, how votes are translated into seats, the relative merits of a parliamentary versus a presidential system, and the like. A few scholars, to be sure, did examine the impact of election mechanics— voter registration in particular—on the quality of American democracy prior to Florida 2000.[5] But most of us did not, until after that momentous election, think enough about the nitty-gritty of carrying out elections—about how the registry is prepared, what documents voters must present, how voters cast their ballots, and how ballots are counted. But how polling is conducted—or cleaned up—can have important ramifications for the quality of democracy, sometimes in nonobvious or paradoxical ways. It is on the reform of this previously understudied but indispensable part of the electoral exercise that the present book focuses.

What Kinds of Damage?

The promise of clean election reform is to reduce poll fraud and error, and thereby enhance the quality of democracy, by ensuring that only valid voters are allowed to participate in the electoral exercise and that their preferences are expressed freely and registered accurately. Under certain conditions, however, clean election reforms can inflict various forms of harm to democracy.[6]

---

5. See, for instance, Kelley, Ayres, and Bowen (1967); Kim, Petrocik, and Enokson (1975); Rosenstone and Wolfinger (1978); Piven and Cloward (1988); Knack (1995); Mitchell and Wlezien (1995); and Highton (1997).

6. Additional information about the definition of "damage to democracy" can be found in the appendix.

VOTE DEPRESSION

Perhaps the most common form of damage is vote depression—a drop in the number of people who register, turn out to vote, or have their votes count. Vote depression can take three distinct forms, depending on the type of actor who causes the decline.

Legal disenfranchisement is caused by legislators who impose clean election laws that effectively put up obstacles to the electoral participation of some people but not others. While such obstacles do not make it impossible for those affected to register or vote, they do make it costly, stifling, shameful, frightening, or inconvenient to do so. In 1920s Chicago, for instance, a law that required applicants to publicly state their age kept many women from registering; they simply felt disinclined to reveal how old they were. This "legal" form of vote depression should not be confused with the kind of lawful deprivation of voting rights that applied to blacks in apartheid-era South Africa. That blanket, race-based restriction of suffrage did not have anything to do in either intent or public justification with cleaning up elections.

Administrative exclusion is caused by election officials and occurs when their implementation of clean election reforms prevents or puts up obstacles to people's registering, voting, or having their votes count. The reforms might thus remove eligible voters from the registry (as in Florida, where an overzealous purge of felons removed eligible voters from the rolls), prevent them from casting their ballots on election day (as we saw in Barangay Commonwealth High School in the Philippines), or keep valid votes from counting (as in Quebec, where instructions disseminated for the avowed purpose of improving the accuracy of vote counting during the 1995 referendum led instead to the invalidation of perfectly valid votes).

Partisan demobilization is caused by parties, candidates, and their operatives when clean election reforms motivate them to alter the strategies they use to win elections. Unlike legal disenfranchisement or administrative exclusion, which occur directly as a result of legal or administrative obstacles placed in front of the voter, demobilization is an indirect consequence of reform. The reform forces parties and candidates to alter their electoral strategies, and it is the adoption of these new strategies that depresses electoral participation. In some cases, parties and candidates find it advantageous to adopt less effective mobilization strategies. In Taiwan, turnout rates began to drop in the mid-1990s when prosecutors mounted a vigorous campaign against vote buying. Less able to mobilize supporters with personal offers of gifts and money, candidates turned increasingly to less effective mass media advertising. In other cases, parties, candidates, and their agents choose to prevent eligible votes (typically supporters of opposing candidates) from going to the polls. When the poll body in Guyana introduced voter identification cards in 1997 and required voters to present them before casting their ballots, party operatives began to buy them up, thereby purchasing the abstention of their opponents' supporters—a practice we might call "negative" vote buying.

THE PROLIFERATION OF ELECTION CHEATING

In addition to vote depression, the implementation of clean election reforms can paradoxically result in the proliferation of fraudulent electoral practices. This proliferation can take two forms. Sometimes clean election reforms beget new modes of cheating. The purchase of newly introduced voter identification cards by party operatives in Guyana not only demobilized voters but also constituted a novel form of election fraud in that country.[7] New forms of cheating may also have been unintentionally created by a 2005 voter identification law in New Mexico. In preparation for the 2006 elections, the secretary of state mistakenly mailed out at least sixty thousand new voter identification cards to the wrong addresses, raising the fear that some recipients might have used them to vote fraudulently.[8]

Clean election reforms can also facilitate or intensify already established modes of cheating. The voters' list fiasco in the 2004 Philippine elections made it easier to pad votes—an already well-entrenched mode of election fraud in that country. Since the voters' lists were prepared so late that watchdogs had little opportunity to review them for accuracy, opportunities to inflate vote totals multiplied. Among the places with high levels of vote padding were the cities of Cebu, Pasig, Taguig, Ilagan, Las Piñas, Zamboanga, and Cagayan de Oro. In Thailand, vote buying has been an enduring problem. In anticipation of the 2000 elections, civic educators organized education forums around the country to convince voters not to vote for candidates who offered them money. Post-forum evaluators found, however, that many people came away with the lesson that it was wrong to accept money and not vote for the candidate. In Venezuela, election officials tried to use a relatively new electronic election system for the unwieldy 2000 "mega-elections." Unable to manage this complex undertaking, they had to postpone the elections at the last minute. With ballots already distributed but left unsecured for two months, partisans were able to discreetly premark many ballots and thereby disqualify votes cast against the candidate that they backed. This form of cheating had been known in earlier elections, but the chaos caused by computerization created new opportunities for its spread.

7. On the twin nature of vote buying, as a strategy of both (de)mobilization and fraud, see Schaffer (2007, 4–8).

8. "60,000 New Voter Cards Go Astray; Officials See Fraud Potential," *Albuquerque Journal*, June 1, 2006.

ALIENATION

Clean election reforms can also provoke alienation, which can include feelings of disaffection toward various stakeholders in the electoral system, other citizens in the polity, or democracy itself. Alienation sometimes manifests itself passively as civic apathy. In the Philippines, for example, reforms led many poor voters to disengage from poll watching and other clean election activities during the 2001 elections. Alienation may also manifest itself actively in riots and demonstrations. In post-Soviet Georgia, for instance, the poorly executed computerization of electoral lists in 2003 sparked widespread protests. Parties and candidates can also succumb to disaffection, typically when they believe that levels of vote depression or cheating are so high that they undermine the credibility of the elections. Such was the case in Malawi, where a string of problems with a new registration process caused the 1999 elections to be postponed twice. Election losers claimed that this fiasco kept more than 160,000 people from registering and refused to accept the results.

Sometimes alienation is a direct consequence of reform. For example, the civic apathy exhibited by many poor Filipinos was produced by anti-vote-buying public education advertisements that many of them found insulting. At other times, alienation can be a byproduct of vote depression. When lawmakers or election administrators take actions that keep significant numbers of people away from the polls, such actions can provoke suspicion and animosity, not only toward those who deprived people of their opportunity to vote but also toward the whole democratic process. To recall the words of the Payatas Elementary School principal, people are "turned off." Where vote depression is widespread and publicly known, the legitimacy of election results, the electoral body, and the electoral system may thus be put into question.

At still other times, alienation can result from the real or suspected proliferation of cheating occasioned by clean election reform. In Zambia, for instance, a new system to electronically transmit election results for the 2006 elections proved too complex and unwieldy for local election workers to use. Forced to abandon it, they used instead land transportation or fax machines to communicate their tallies, which were seldom verified. This breach raised suspicions of electoral fraud and fueled rioting in Lusaka and other cities.

Depression, proliferation, and alienation are all damaging to democracy. Depression violates norms of democratic inclusiveness, generates apathy, and wears away the vibrancy of parties. Proliferation exacerbates the very problems of fraud and error that the reforms were intended to mitigate. Alienation erodes confidence in and commitment to the democratic process and may undermine stability. The irony is that clean election reforms are supposed to promote the opposite outcomes. By adopting reforms to reduce fraud and error, the promise is to make the electoral process freer, fairer, more credible, more legitimate, more robust.

A skeptic might argue that I exaggerate some of these problems in at least one respect. Even if turnout is demonstrably depressed as a result of some clean election reforms, one could contend that the impact on the quality of democratic participation is beneficial. In many cases, the reforms do not make it impossible for people to vote. They simply make it inconvenient or costly to do so; voters in South Africa, for instance, just needed to go through the trouble of acquiring new identity documents.

Following this line of reasoning, one could argue that abstainers do not vote because they do not care enough about the outcome of the election to get to the polls. And in the words of John Stuart Mill, "a man who does not care whether he votes, is not likely to care much which way he votes; and he who is in that state of mind has no moral right to vote at all" ([1861] 1975, 313). Those who make it to the polls, in contrast, are willing to suffer inconveniences or absorb costs because they take an active interest in the election. The electorate might be smaller, the argument might go, but it is of a higher caliber.

The trouble with this argument is that conceiving the decision to vote as a matter of individual preference alone shrouds the fact that those who stay away from the polls as a result of new election requirements are often not distributed evenly throughout society. In 1892 Arkansas they tended to be black; in 1920s Chicago they were mostly women; in 1999 South Africa they were disproportionately white, Indian, or mixed-race; in 2002 Georgia (the U.S. state) they were often elderly. To restrict the suffrage of such groups—especially when the number of affected people is large, as was the case in Arkansas and South Africa—is to grievously compromise the inclusiveness of the resulting democracy.

Why Do Good Reforms Sometimes Go Bad?

There are five qualities of clean election reform that make it prone, under particular conditions, to causing harm.

RESTRICTIVENESS

Many clean election reforms, especially those designed to ensure that only eligible voters cast ballots, are deliberately designed to restrict who is allowed to vote. Procedures that make it easy for eligible people to vote also make it easy for ineligible people to vote. When reforms make it harder for ineligible people to vote, they also make it harder for eligible people to vote. When government begin requiring people to produce a particular kind of identification document when seeking to register, as the government of South Africa did in preparation for the 1999 elections, they risk disenfranchising those eligible voters who do not possess that form of identification. Similarly, measures—such as those adopted in late-nineteenth-century France—that disqualify ballots with extraneous markings on them not only eliminate a mechanism of coercion or vote buying but also disqualify the votes of noncoerced and unbought people who accidentally mark a ballot or wish for whatever reason to add their own remarks.

COMPLEXITY

To attain an honest and accurate tallying of votes, reformers often turn to new technologies. On the cutting edge today are automated voting, counting, and tabulation machines and electronic systems to transmit results. These are complex systems to set up and operate. In preparation for the 2000 elections in Venezuela, for instance, separate computer programs had to be written for 1,371 different ballot configurations (Neuman and McCoy 2001, 41–45). The adoption of a new registration system and the remapping of a country's precincts are also massively complicated undertakings that require high levels of coordination and technical skill. The problem is that complex tasks are difficult for electoral bodies to manage, especially those that are underfunded, inexperienced, or lacking expertise. When election officials or poll workers are unable to meet technical challenges, voters can find themselves unable to vote, results can be manipulated, or elections can fail. In 2004, when direct-recording electronic voting machines were first used in Orange County, California, seven thousand voters were effectively stripped of their right to vote when ill-trained poll workers provided incorrect access codes to some voters, causing their votes to be recorded in the wrong legislative district. Explained one California voting expert: "[E]very system is prone to this.... Poll workers are typically amateurs—well-meaning and hard-working, but amateurs—and they mess up unless the system is absolutely foolproof. And this one wasn't foolproof."[9]

PARTISANSHIP

Clean election reform takes place within the political arena and alters the rules of electoral competition. Consequently, people who have the power to craft or

---

9. Henry Brady, quoted in "7,000 Orange County Voters Were Given Bad Ballots," *Los Angeles Times,* March 9, 2004.

implement reform seek out partisan advantage. When unfettered, partisans can turn the restrictiveness and complexity of reform to their advantage and find ways to make reform an occasion to cheat or depress turnout for their political opponents. Parties that dominate legislatures (such as the African National Congress in late 1990s South Africa or the Democratic Party in 1890s Arkansas) can pass clean election laws that help their electoral prospects. Election officials can also be partisan. In some places, they are elected on party tickets—as was Katherine Harris, the secretary of state of Florida during the 2000 elections. She both oversaw the purging of the voter rolls and cochaired the Bush presidential campaign in her state. In other places, nominally neutral election officials are beholden to the politicians who appoint them. A Philippine poll body commissioner appointed just before the 2004 elections by President Gloria Macapagal Arroyo, in a surprising moment of candor, told the press after the elections, "[I]n my region alone President Arroyo was overwhelmed and I was embarrassed."[10] He was embarrassed because Arroyo lost in the region he oversaw. If he had been truly neutral, of course, he would have had no cause for embarrassment. One can only conclude that this avowedly nonpartisan official felt that it was his obligation to help the president win. Indeed, he was later implicated in a massive effort to fraudulently alter the election results on Arroyo's behalf.

BENIGN RHETORIC

On the surface of it, little is controversial about clean election reform. What could be wrong with "cleaning up" or "safeguarding" democracy? How could reducing fraud and error be bad? The rhetoric of democratic enhancement thus provides a convenient mask for those who seek partisan gain. In Australia, the Liberal Party in 2004 advocated not allowing new voters to register once an election had been called. They argued that this measure was necessary to ensure the accuracy and validity of the electoral roll. As Liberal Party senator Nick Minchin (2004) proclaimed on the Senate floor, "[T]here is no greater safeguard to the integrity of our democracy than the security of the electoral roll." What this proponent did not say openly was that the measure was also likely to disenfranchise tens of thousands of young voters—who tend not to vote for the Liberal Party and who do tend to register only once new elections are announced. To the extent that watchdogs and citizens are lulled into believing this kind of rhetoric, the impact of exclusionary reform is likely to go unnoticed until it is too late. In Florida, the purge of felons from the voter

---

10. "Reappointed Comelec Execs Pessimistic on CA Nod," *Philippine Star,* July 7, 2004.

rolls stirred little controversy prior to the 2000 election. "It is helping to clean dead wood from the rolls," remarked one poll official a few months before the election. "And if you've got dead wood, it's a potential for fraud."[11] Indeed, civil rights watchdogs in Florida took no legal action in the summer of 2000 even though various counties reported that this purge of felons was also causing nonfelons to be removed from the voter rolls. At the time journalists described the removals as minor "glitches" or "mix-ups" of electoral housekeeping, so few members of the public realized that they resulted from a purposeful over-extension of the purge.[12]

DISCIPLINE

Clean election reform is in part a disciplinary project. To reform an electoral system—to reduce or eliminate vote buying, voter intimidation, fraudulent voting, ballot miscounting, or ballot box stuffing—is to prohibit or make unacceptable certain kinds of acts. Reforms are thus intended to check, constrict, and channel election behavior. But the people who are the target of reform—voters, local election administrators, and candidates or their agents in particular—sometimes experience and react to these disciplinary efforts in ways unanticipated by reformers. When upper-class reformers in the Philippines rolled out a civic education campaign in 2001, many poor voters experienced it as insulting and humiliating. When the Nigerian poll body computerized the voter registry in 2003, regional poll officials hoarded the new registration forms. When new voter identification cards were introduced in Guyana and Mexico in the 1990s, party agents quickly figured out that they could buy or "rent" the cards of opposition supporters and thereby purchase their abstention.

Design or Accident?

"It is undeniably true, indeed a fundamental truth of all history," observed Max Weber, "that the final result of political activity often, nay, regularly, bears very little relation to the original intention: often, indeed, it is quite the opposite of what was first intended" ([1919] 1978, 214). What Weber wrote of political action in general is acutely true of clean election reform in particular.

11. David Leahy, Supervisor of Elections, Miami-Dade County. Quoted in "State Database Reveals Felons on Voting Rolls," *Tampa Tribune,* June 14, 2000.
12. "Mix-up Tells Voters They Have a Rap Sheet," *Florida Times-Union,* June 21, 2000; "Glitch Tells Hundreds in Florida They Are Felons Who Can't Vote," *Palm Beach Post,* June 22, 2000.

Because clean election reforms are often complex and difficult to implement and because candidates, operatives, and voters often respond to reforms in unanticipated ways, well-intentioned measures can produce harm—especially when the new measures are inherently restrictive.

Not all harm, however, is an unintended by-product of benign reform (in spite of how the reforms may be presented in public). Because reform is often partisan, measures have been crafted, implemented, or responded to in ways that facilitate electoral cheating or intentionally disenfranchise, exclude, or demobilize select groups of voters. Evidence suggests that in places like Florida and South Africa, as we shall see in chapters 2 and 3, elections were "fixed" in both senses of the word—they were both repaired and manipulated. At the extreme, the commitment of reformers to cleaning up elections can be superficial, a mere public justification for a veiled attempt to manipulate electoral outcomes. Such appears to have been the case in less-than-democratic Zimbabwe, where a new law required registered voters to provide proof of residency before casting their ballots in the 2002 elections. Most observers saw in this provision only a thinly cloaked attempt to disenfranchise opposition supporters despite the insistence of the chief elections officer that it was implemented, in his words, out of a desire to hold "free and fair elections."[13]

The point is that each of the four sets of actors centrally involved in clean election reform (lawmakers; election officials and workers; parties, candidates, and their agents; and civic educators) can cause harm *either* deliberately or inadvertently—with the possible exception of civic educators (though I found no cases of educators intentionally causing harm, it is not beyond imagining). To the extent that scholars and practitioners today write about the harm sometimes caused by clean election reform, they too often focus either on intended or unintended harm without acknowledging fully that both forms exist. One goal of this book is to examine both forms of harm together and to specify the differing conditions under which each occurs.

Nevertheless, not all instances of harm can be neatly classified as either intended or unintended. At times there is an intermediate level of intentionality. For example, partisans may seek to channel participation toward one party rather than another, but this attempt at channeling may instead keep people away from the polls. This happened in late-nineteenth-century South Dakota, as we will see in the next chapter, upon the advent of the secret, state-produced ballot. When it came time to legislate how parties should be listed on the new ballot, Republicans pushed through legislation to prevent the "fusing"

13. "New Rules in Zimbabwe Likely to Aid Mugabe's Side," *New York Times,* March 7, 2002.

of Democratic and Populist tickets, a measure Republicans hoped would push Populists back into the GOP fold. To some extent, the strategy worked, but it also had the unintended effect of making large numbers of Populists stop coming to the polls altogether (Argersinger 1992).

Also complicating any neat categorization of harm as either intended or unintended is the fact that evidence is sometimes murky. On the one hand, feigned ineptitude may camouflage manipulation—which is what many supporters of Fernando Poe Jr. believed about the handling of the voters' lists in the 2004 elections in the Philippines. On the other hand, suspicious partisans perceive every instance of bungling or negligence as a deliberate design to cheat, an observation that applies equally well to the Philippines.

Still, it is useful when possible to differentiate between intended and unintended harm since they tend to occur under different conditions and are amenable to remedies that are only partially overlapping (those wishing for a preview might jump ahead to table 1 in chapter 6).

Actor-Harm Combinations

There are, to recap, four sets of actors centrally involved in clean election reform: lawmakers; election officials and workers; parties, candidates, and their agents; and civic educators. There are, in addition, three types of iatrogenic damage sometimes inflicted by these actors: vote depression, alienation, and the proliferation of election cheating. Each kind of actor can produce each type of harm. Election administrators, for instance, caused depression in the Dominican Republic (the flawed implementation of a new voter registration and identification system left around forty-five thousand people unable to vote); proliferation in Nigeria (partisan local election officials withheld voter registration forms for the new computerized voter registry in 2003 to use for their own fraudulent purposes); and alienation in Zambia (protests followed the botched electronic results transmission system put in place for the 2006 elections). Nevertheless, I do not seek to exhaustively examine all possible actor-harm combinations in this book. Evidence for depression—perhaps because it is more common or perhaps because it is more easily detected—is more ample than for alienation or proliferation. For this reason, chapters 2, 3, and 4—which I devote in turn to lawmakers, election administrators, and parties, candidates, and their agents—focus almost exclusively on legal disenfranchisement, administrative exclusion, and partisan demobilization, respectively. I take up alienation primarily in chapter 5, which examines the actions of civic educators, while I discuss proliferation in various sections of chapters 3, 4, and 5.

Methods and Evidence

It is admittedly difficult to adduce evidence of iatrogenic harm that achieves a high degree of rigor or systematization since statistics relating to vote depression, alienation, and electoral cheating are often unreliable. Take, for instance, statistics relating to vote depression. Elections are partisan contests, and numbers become partisan ammunition. In such a context, stakeholders and spin doctors have a powerful motive to inflate or deflate the totals. After the Florida 2000 election, some Republicans argued that not a single eligible voter had been unable to vote as a result of the purge of felons, while some Democrats insisted the number was in the tens of thousands. Thankfully, journalists at the *Palm Beach Post* conducted a more judicious study, which put the number at around 1,100—not a huge number but large enough to alter the outcome of the razor-close race. Statistics relating to alienation and various forms of electoral cheating are even more contested and undependable still.

To complicate matters, many instances of iatrogenic harm are difficult to quantify exactly. Often this difficulty results from how electoral bodies report statistics. In the 2000 Venezuelan presidential election, the electoral council counted double-marked ballots (which are indicative of fraud) together with other types of invalid votes, making it hard to determine the number of fraudulent votes that were cast. Making the task even harder is the fact that poll bodies often deny watchdogs access to the raw materials (often the ballots themselves) that would provide a more accurate picture of iatrogenic fraud. Venezuelan authorities in subsequent elections made it even more difficult to calculate the number of double-marked ballots by withholding the relevant electoral data. In Quebec, the poll body released only a small fraction of the questionably invalidated 1995 referendum ballots for public scrutiny. Real iatrogenic damage was done in Venezuela and Quebec, but as we shall see in chapter 3, it is possible to gauge the magnitude only roughly.

Another complicating factor is that statistics, even when accurate and complete, can be deceiving. Aggregate data on turnout, for instance, cannot speak directly to the quality of postreform electoral participation since a decline in turnout may reflect vote depression or something altogether different. Thus a decline in turnout statistics, in itself, does not bode ill for democratic participation. Such a drop may, after all, simply reflect a reduction in fraud. Vote padding and ballot-box stuffing might have been curtailed; dead people, ghost voters, and pets might have been removed from the voters' rolls, and the like. Fewer people may be recorded as coming to the polls, but those who are recorded are actually casting ballots. The implications for democracy would obviously be more serious if lowered turnout were a result of legal disenfranchisement, negative vote buying, or administrative bungling than if it were just a statistical artifact of a less fraudulent vote. This is one reason that I look carefully not only at turnout statistics, but also at the actions, strategies, and sometimes worldviews that lead (or do not lead) to lowered turnout or to other forms of apparent harm. In other words, it is important to understand specific cases and the specifics of each case. "Local knowledge" is here required (Geertz 1983).

It is nevertheless challenging to uncover good qualitative evidence for the relevant conditions that make reforms damaging in some places but not others, for information about cases is fragmentary and uneven. Country specialists and democracy practitioners, by and large, have not investigated the damaging potential of clean election reform until recently. Thus relevant data went unnoticed and unreported or were mentioned only in passing. (In all probability, the administrative exclusion of eligible voters in Florida would have remained unexposed had it not been for the intense scrutiny brought to bear on the conduct of the 2000 elections.) Consequently, at present we cannot even determine how many cases of iatrogenic harm exist.

This lack of data poses challenges for research design. It makes impossible, for instance, any study of cases that is comprehensive. It also makes impossible a sampling of cases that is truly random, thus increasing the likelihood that the cases under examination are unrepresentative of the entire universe and any conclusions drawn from this examination systematically biased.[14]

While either a comprehensive survey or random sample might have been desirable from the vantage point of research design, neither is feasible given the data available. The limits of both quantitative and qualitative data and the absence of a body of comparative literature to draw upon necessarily make the present analysis more exploratory.[15] The aim here is to identify *illustrative* cases and by comparing these cases to discern—provisionally at least—some conditions that produce harm. In this way, I hope the book will serve as a road map for future research. We will have to wait and see whether new observations allow the application of more stringent research methods or generate findings that differ significantly.

How did I discover the illustrative cases? For the nineteenth and early twentieth centuries, I surveyed the fascinating body of literature produced by students of electoral reform to identify studies that shed light on the conditions that generate iatrogenic harm. For the contemporary period, I undertook a broad

14. On the problem of selection bias in qualitative research see the contrasting views of King, Keohane, and Verba (1994, 115–49) and Collier, Mahoney, and Seawright (2004).

15. On the nature and value of exploratory comparative research see Lijphart (1971, 692), Eckstein (1975, 104–8), George (1979), and Gerring (2001, 231).

survey of newspapers and observer reports from around the world to identify at least some of the more significant clean election reforms undertaken during the sixteen-year period from 1991 to 2006.[16] This procedure produced a data set of 122 individual clean election reforms undertaken in sixty-six different countries (table 2 in the appendix lists these reforms and countries). In compiling the data set, I took special effort to ensure broad geographic coverage: it includes eleven countries from the Asia Pacific region, fifteen from the Americas, thirteen from central and eastern Europe and the former Soviet Union, four from the Middle East and North Africa, eighteen from sub-Saharan Africa, and five from western Europe. I also took care to include different kinds of clean election reform, including measures designed to safeguard the authenticity of voter eligibility (computerized voters' lists, tightened registration rules, voter identification cards, voter registry purges, etc.); ensure voter insulation (secret ballot, disqualification of candidates found guilty of vote buying, barring poll workers from assisting voters, civic education campaigns, etc.); and strengthen vote integrity (numbered ballots, electronic voting machines, transparent ballot boxes, computerized counting of votes, etc.).

Despite this broad search, the data set is not exhaustive or statistically representative of the entire universe of clean election reforms. In the United States alone, there are some ten thousand city, county, and township election administrations that share varying degrees of responsibility with state-level election officials (Fischer 2001, 1). During the sixteen-year period under study, election officials in these local and state jurisdictions implemented thousands of clean election reforms. I include in the data set only a few U.S. reforms that received major press coverage or careful expert assessment. All these reforms, except for the 2000 purge of Florida's voter rolls, are from the post-2000 period. My aim, to reiterate, was not to generate a sample that was statistically representative but one that would be rich for theorizing.

16. I used Factiva and LexisNexis online databases for the newspaper searches. My keyword searches included encompassing terms such as "electoral reform," "change [plus] elections," and "amendment [plus] electoral law," as well as more specific terms such as "electronic voting," "voting machines," "voter identification," "voter registration," and "election [plus] purge." I used a smaller number of keywords to conduct similar searches in the Spanish and French languages. I systematically reviewed election observation reports and assessments issued by the following institutions: the Commonwealth Secretariat, the European Union, the European Parliament, the Organization for Security and Co-operation in Europe, the Organization of American States, the Organization of African Unity, the Carter Center, the International Republican Institute, the National Democratic Institute for International Affairs, the International Institute for Democracy and Electoral Assistance, and the International Foundation for Election Systems. I also surveyed reports from a number of domestic, single-country observation groups—such as Red de Veedores (Venezuela), the Central Depository Unit (Kenya), and the Transition Monitoring Group (Nigeria). However, because there is no systematic way to locate domestic reports from around the world, this survey was necessarily less comprehensive.

Even so, for most of the cases included in the data set I did not find enough information to determine with certainty whether any iatrogenic harm had occurred. In 36 percent of the cases I found insufficient evidence to make any determination; in 17 percent, I found suggestive evidence that harm had been done, but that evidence was not conclusive; and in 14 percent, I saw no mention in observer or newspaper reports that harm had been done, but the quality of those reports was low or questionable (see table 2 in the appendix). For other cases, I discovered credible, concrete evidence that harm had or had not occurred, but not enough information was available to discern the conditions that led to one outcome or the other.

For a handful of cases, I was able to find quality information about both the consequences of reform and the processes by which the reforms were adopted and implemented. For some of these cases, that information came from the newspaper and observer reports that I initially surveyed. For other cases, it came from studies—produced by scholars, government agencies, research institutions, and advisory organizations—that I located during subsequent research. When there were major gaps in the documentary information I gathered, I sought out local experts to fill in the blanks. I interviewed prosecutors from Taiwan's Ministry of Justice. I worked with or interviewed a number of librarians, archivists, and experts from places like India, Canada, Venezuela, and Florida. I also thought it was important to gain deeper firsthand knowledge, especially of certain types of iatrogenic harm for which empirical evidence was intriguingly suggestive but slight. It was this desire to gather firsthand my own evidence that brought me to the Philippines (where several types of clean election reform were being implemented) for the first time in 2000 and ultimately led to my sitting in that courtyard in Barangay Commonwealth High School on election day in 2004.

From this background research I selected the particular instances of clean election reform for in-depth discussion in the book. Several criteria guided this selection of cases. Most important, since a fundamental goal of the book is simply to establish the existence and significance of iatrogenic harm, there had to be enough evidence in each case of apparent harm to plausibly demonstrate its presence. Another major goal of the book is to identify some of the conditions under which iatrogenic harm occurs. Therefore, another guiding criterion was the availability of evidence about the causal mechanisms at work.

The task of specifying conditions also required comparing, whenever evidence permitted, instances of clean election reform that caused harm with instances that did not. This mode of comparison, after all, greatly enhances our ability to identify the differing conditions that produce divergent outcomes. In the language of methodologists, this task necessitated selecting cases to provide "variation on the dependent variable." To secure this variation, I also focused on a number of reform initiatives that did not cause harm. Thus, for instance, in the book I examine not only a case in which the secret ballot led to lowered voter turnout (Arkansas) but also cases in which it did not (Michigan, Denmark, Germany, and France). I consider not only places where the introduction of new identification requirements disenfranchised or excluded voters (South Africa, Arizona) but also a place where it apparently did not (Mexico). However, for some types of iatrogenic harm—alienation in particular—the available evidence was too scant to even identify instances of nonharm, and the level of theorizing here remains more rudimentary.

In making final decisions about which cases to focus on, I was guided by two additional principles that had to be held somewhat in tension. On the one hand, I chose cases that were varied in time and space since I think the evidence shows that iatrogenic harm is not limited to a particular era or locale. On the other hand, I tried to avoid artificially isolating instances of reform and their consequences since a government might undertake multiple reforms at one time, and a single reform effort might have multiple consequences. To this end, I sometimes discuss different reform efforts undertaken more or less at the same time within a single country. I examine, for instance, civic education as well as two types of registration reform in the Philippines. I also discuss how the same reform initiative can inflict different forms of harm. In South Africa, for example, tightened registration requirements disenfranchised both nonblack voters (intentionally) and some black Pentecostal Christian voters (unintentionally). Certain countries and reform initiatives, then, appear in more than one part of the book.

A possibility exists that systematic bias in the book's findings has been introduced by the various criteria I used to select cases. The greatest potential for bias might lie in the fact that I selected for intensive study only those reforms that have attracted special attention by scholars, reporters, investigatory bodies, and research institutions. I did so because those reforms are the only ones for which adequate evidence exists. But to the extent that reforms that have attracted such attention may be systematically different from those that have not, my findings may be skewed. Still, the danger of systemic bias from this cause may be less acute than it might first appear insofar as the selected reforms have attracted attention for a range of reasons and from a variety of interested parties.

Despite its obvious limitations, there are compelling reasons to undertake this kind of exploratory research. Most important, it addresses a real-world problem that demands immediate attention. Overhauling the mechanics of democracy is today an explosively growing industry. In 2003, Election Systems & Software, a large provider of electronic registration, voting, and tabulation systems, had installations in nine countries and sales of almost $140 million. Diebold Election Systems, a leading manufacturer of electronic voting machines, posted over $100 million in sales the same year. The United States government, the United Nations, and the European Union all have well-funded electoral assistance programs that provide financial support and expertise to countries around the globe. Organizations such as the International Foundation for Election Systems, the National Democratic Institute for International Affairs, and the International Institute for Democracy and Electoral Assistance send consultants the world over to provide technical advice. In the United States, Congress, in response to the Florida debacle, passed the Help America Vote Act in 2002; it earmarked $3.6 billion to "upgrade" election systems nationwide. In the three years following the 2000 elections, state legislatures introduced 5,378 reform bills, of which 816 were passed into law (NCSL 2003, 2004). Both at home and abroad, massive resources have been devoted to clean election reform, and deep changes are under way. But these changes have received little serious attention from students of comparative politics, despite scattered evidence that all is not well. In this book alone I identify thirty-eight cases of iatrogenic harm from twenty-four different countries during a period of only sixteen years, involving, among other things, stripping millions of people of the opportunity to vote (see table 2 in the appendix). This finding is alarming and calls for a careful, critical analysis of why, and in what ways, the reforms went wrong.

A rigorous comparison of cases, given the data available today, is not possible. Yet recognizing the urgent importance of the topic and the value of informed international and historical comparison, I stipulate at the outset the illustrative nature of the evidence and the exploratory nature of the argument. This book is a heuristic study intended to shed light on an understudied problem of immediate and widespread importance. I hope it will serve as a first word, not the last, on this topic.

2

Lawmakers

Legal Disenfranchisement

Lawmakers sometimes enact clean election measures that cause vote depression. Typically, this depression occurs when legislators impose regulations upon people who differ in their ability or disposition to comply with those regulations out of fear, distrust, embarrassment, political conviction, financial constraint, or the like. These differences effectively put up obstacles to the electoral participation of some people but not others. While such obstacles do not make it impossible for those affected to vote, they do make it costly, stifling, shameful, frightening, or inconvenient to do so. The regulations themselves can range from mandatory secret balloting to restrictions on how ballots may be filled out to stiffened identification requirements. Lawmaker-induced vote depression—what I have called "legal disenfranchisement"—may be intentional or unintentional. In this chapter, I examine both forms.

Intentional Disenfranchisement

Lawmakers sometimes use the legislative reform of dirty or error-prone electoral practices as an opportunity to deliberately restrict the electoral participation of particular groups of voters. In such cases, disenfranchisement is intentional. In this section, I examine four cases of intentional legal disenfranchisement: the advent of secret balloting in 1890s Arkansas, the introduction of personal registration in late-nineteenth-century urban America (with a focus on New Jersey), the imposition of new identity document requirements for the 1999 elections in South Africa, and the enactment of new voter identification requirements in various American states after the contested 2000 elections. I then go on to identify several shared conditions that facilitated intentional disenfranchisement in these cases.

THE SECRET BALLOT IN 1890S ARKANSAS

Legal disenfranchisement in late-nineteenth-century Arkansas came with the introduction of secret balloting. Of course, in Arkansas, as in the South more generally, the secret ballot was only one of many measures adopted by Democrats to disenfranchise black voters. Poll taxes, literacy tests, and residency requirements were variously used as well (Kousser 1974). But unlike other measures, which disenfranchisers justified publicly as devices to winnow out "unfit" voters, the secret ballot was also touted, in Arkansas at least, as a mechanism to protect vulnerable voters from intimidation.

Thus the Democrat-controlled Arkansas state legislature included a secret ballot provision in a larger reform package, adopted in 1891, to calm public indignation over a series of widely publicized electoral scandals. The new law prohibited, among other things, last-minute changes in the location of polling places. Another section of the law made it illegal for friends or party members to prepare the ballot of an illiterate voter. Under the new disposition, only a precinct judge could mark the ballot, and then only after all other electors had vacated the polling place. "Defenders of this procedure," remarked one historian, "argued that it assured secrecy for the illiterates and freed timid Negroes from 'bulldozing' and coercion by arm-twisting employers and aggressive politicians" (Graves 1967, 212).

Newspaper accounts from the period reveal, however, that the new secrecy provision had less benign effects. Illiterate voters, finding the new system degrading and alienating, stayed away from the polls. As one article appearing in the *Pine Bluff Eagle Press* explained, when blacks "who could not read were told to go to the polls and vote, the majority of them declined, some being distrustful of the judges and others not caring to expose their inability to make out their tickets unassisted" (quoted in Graves 1967, 213). In a state where 27 percent of the population was illiterate, the new law had a profound impact. Twenty-one percent fewer votes were cast in 1892 than in 1890 (Heckelman 1995, 111). While the white vote dipped from 75 percent to 67 percent, the black vote plummeted from 71 percent to 38 percent (Kousser 1974, 55).

There is little doubt that the disenfranchisement of black voters was deliberately intended by Democratic lawmakers. Anticipating the new law's heavy impact, an 1892 Democratic Party campaign song openly praised the secret ballot (also called at the time the "Australian" ballot because the actual paper ballot was state-produced, as first done in Australia):

> The Australian ballot works like a charm,
> It makes them think and scratch,
> And when a negro gets a ballot
> He has certainly got his match.
> *(Quoted in Graves 1967, 212–13)*

Set to the melody of a Confederate anthem, this song could not have made the party's aims any clearer.

PERSONAL REGISTRATION IN LATE-NINETEENTH-CENTURY URBAN AMERICA

The secret ballot was not the only clean election reform that occasioned legal disenfranchisement during this period of American history. Personal registration laws adopted by most American states between the 1860s and the 1910s disenfranchised many poor, black, and immigrant voters by including provisions that made it more difficult for people who worked long hours or were naturalized citizens to register. In many of these states, only urbanites had to register in person. Such urban registration provisions were often passed by Republican legislators in hopes of suppressing turnout for Democrats, who drew much of their support from the urban lower classes.

Here is how the historian Alexander Keyssar (2000, 152) describes the politics of registration in New Jersey:

> Republicans instituted registration requirements in 1866 and 1867. All prospective voters had to register in person on the Thursday before each general election: anyone could challenge the claims of a potential registrant, and no one was permitted to vote if his name was not on the register. In 1868, the Democrats gained control of the state government and repealed the registration laws, stating that they penalized poor men who could not afford to take time off from their jobs to register. In 1870, the Republicans returned to power and reintroduced registration, this time making it applicable only to the seven cities with populations greater than 20,000. Six years later, the law was extended to all cities with more than 10,000 persons and to adjacent communities.

These partisan battles continued on and off over the next few decades, and intensified during the progressive era. At this time, Keyssar explains:

> Registration became the centerpiece of efforts, spearheaded by middle-class reformers, to limit corruption and reduce the electoral strength of immigrants, blacks,

and political machines. In 1911, a package of two bills, the Geran Act and the Corrupt Practices Act, was introduced into the state legislature by a coalition of independents, Republicans, and a few Democrats. After heated debate, during which urban Democrats succeeded in removing some of the legislation's most onerous features, the bills were passed, creating a registration system that applied to every city with a population greater than 5,000 persons. Personal registration was now required, and it had to be renewed whenever a voter moved or failed to vote in an election. Prospective voters were given only four days in which they could register, and at registration a man was obliged not only to identify himself and his occupation but to give the names of his parents, spouse, and landlord, as well as a satisfactory description of the dwelling in which he lived. To no one's surprise, these reforms sharply depressed turnout, particularly among blacks and immigrants. (152–53)

A similar pattern of partisan jockeying characterized registration politics in New York and California, among other states (Harris 1929, 72–89; Keyssar 2000, 151–59).

Assessing the magnitude of disenfranchisement nationwide caused by these new registration requirements, Keyssar writes:

> They kept large numbers (probably millions) of eligible voters from the polls. In cities such as Philadelphia, Chicago, and Boston, only 60 to 70 percent of eligible voters were registered between 1910 and 1920; in wards inhabited by the poor, the figures were significantly lower. In San Francisco between 1875 and 1905, an average of only 54 percent of adult males were registered. Electoral turnout dropped steadily during precisely the period when registration systems were being elaborated, and scholars have estimated that one third or more of that drop, nationally, can be attributed to the implementation of registration schemes. (158)

Registration, in a word, was a major cause of vote depression during this period.

There are contemporary analogues to the American electoral reforms of the late nineteenth and early twentieth centuries. A statistical study of survey data by Bratton (1999) revealed that high levels of citizen abstention in early 1990s Zambia were also attributable to burdensome registration rules. "Voter registration was," he found, "the single most important determinant... of overall participation, outweighing any other institutional, cultural, or social consideration" (570). Consider also the case of South Africa, where we can observe more closely the politics of legal disenfranchisement in the government's decision to allow only citizens with bar-coded identity documents (IDs) to register to vote.

IDENTITY DOCUMENTS IN 1999 SOUTH AFRICA

In the country's first postapartheid election in 1994, all forms of identity documentation were accepted, and voters lacking official documents were issued temporary voters' cards (IEC 1994, 10). The lack of a national voter registry and the issuance of large numbers of temporary cards in the days preceding the election gave rise to charges of fraud (Johnson 1996, 325). In early 1998, lingering concerns about forgeries, ghost voters, and double registrations led the Independent Electoral Commission (IEC) to propose a law requiring citizens to possess bar-coded identity books to qualify for inclusion on the voters' rolls. The use of these IDs, the commission argued, would make it possible to check the encoded number of each ID against the National Population Register and thus protect against fraud (Lodge 1999, 26). The IEC withdrew its support for this proposal in July, however, when a Human Sciences Research Council (HSRC) study it had commissioned reported that one out of every five eligible voters did not have a bar-coded ID (HSRC 1998a, 13).

In mid-August, the HSRC released a regional breakdown of its findings. This new survey revealed that about a third of the eligible voters without bar-coded IDs were rural blacks between the ages of seventeen and twenty-one, who tended not to possess any form of ID at all (HSRC 1998b, 2). White, mixed-race ("coloured"), and Indian eligible voters, the report suggested, also possessed bar-coded IDs at relatively low rates. This racial dimension can be explained by the fact that the government began to issue green bar-coded IDs only in 1986. Prior to that date, whites, coloureds, and Indians received blue IDs, blacks received green non-bar-coded ones, and residents of Transkei, Bophuthatswana, Venda, and Ciskei (TBVC) received homeland IDs. Only in 1994 did the government begin issuing a common green bar-coded ID to everyone. To many blacks, the old IDs were symbols of racial oppression. Consequently, as the HSRC report explained:

> Some time after the introduction of the barcoded ID (from July 1986) there was a vigorous movement for the replacement of politically "tainted" documents such as reference books, and TBVC state documents. The result of this replacement is currently reflected in the low rates of possession of these documents, and the high percentage of respondents with barcoded IDs. In effect, this makes it far more likely for Africans to have a barcoded ID if they have an ID at all. (30)

The implication was that blacks, especially those over the age of twenty-one, possessed bar-coded IDs at higher rates than did other racial groups.

A few days after the release of these findings, the African National Congress (ANC) National Executive Committee took the position that only citizens with bar-coded IDs should be allowed to register. This decision came as a surprise since leaders of the ANC had, prior to the release of the regional survey, expressed their concern about the possible disenfranchisement of a large part of the electorate. But quite suddenly after the release of the regional findings, ANC officials stopped voicing such concerns, and in September 1998 President Mandela signed into law a provision requiring bar-coded IDs for registration.

Opposition parties, especially the Democratic Party (DP) and the New National Party (NNP), had reason to worry about this development. Both drew their support mainly from nonblack voters, and a survey released in November confirmed that these voters were the least likely to possess bar-coded IDs (82 percent of blacks possessed IDs, compared with 71 percent of Indians, 67 percent of coloureds, and 65 percent of whites). These racial differences, the survey further showed, would disproportionately harm the electoral prospects of the DP and the NNP in the national legislative elections. Eighty-two percent of ANC supporters and 84 percent of Inkatha Freedom Party supporters possessed bar-coded IDs as compared with only 71 percent of NNP and 65 percent of DP supporters (Opinion '99 1998). These findings led DP leader Tony Leon to charge that "the ANC introduced this requirement of bar-coded identity not to have a corruption-free election but specifically to disenfranchise as many minority groups and opposition voters as possible."[1] In the weeks that followed, both the DP and the NNP initiated separate court cases challenging the bar-code provision. The High Court ruled against both parties, finding that the provision was "salutary" and "reasonable," while the Constitutional Court dismissed the cases on appeal.

Questions remain about the motivations of the ANC in pushing for the bar-code legislation. Was it concerned only about fraud, or did it also see an opportunity to achieve partisan advantage, as the DP and NNP charged? Those who argue that the ANC's motives could not have been partisan point out that many potentially disenfranchised citizens were young rural blacks, a group likely to support the ANC. Skeptics counter that some administration officials, most prominently the Director General of Home Affairs Albert Mokoena, believed that the HSRC had grossly overestimated the number of young people without identity documents. These political observers speculate that Mokoena was able to convince the ANC leadership that it would not disenfranchise its own supporters.

Whatever the case, internal strategy documents make clear that by April 1998 the ANC was counting on a low turnout of white voters. Survey research was showing rising voter apathy, an expanding floating vote, and the probability

---

1. "One in Five Lack Proper IDs to Vote," *Electronic Mail and Guardian,* November 10, 1998.

of lower black turnout. A combination of high white and low black turnout would endanger the ANC's chances of winning the two-thirds majority in the National Assembly that the party needed to amend the constitution unilaterally. The bar-code provision, the ANC leadership might have reasoned, would give the party a needed boost.

It also seems probable, though the evidence is again only circumstantial, that the ANC calculated that the bar-code provision would enhance its prospects in the highly symbolic and hotly contested provincial contest for the Western Cape. In 1994 the National Party, precursor of the NNP and architect of apartheid, won control of the Western Cape provincial legislature. The ANC leadership was, as one scholar noted, "keen to wipe the last vestiges of National Party government from South Africa" (Reynolds 1999, 190).

As the 1999 election approached, surveys indicated that a tight race was developing between the ANC and the NNP in the Western Cape. In this context, ANC leaders surely read the results of the August 1998 HSRC survey with great interest. They must have noted that the percentage of eligible voters without bar-coded IDs was far higher in this province than elsewhere in the country. And within the Western Cape, people without bar-coded IDs were more likely to live in regions where support for the NNP ran strong (Paarl, George, and parts of Cape Town) than in the region where it ran weak (Nyanga).[2] Requiring bar-coded IDs for voter registration was thus likely to significantly dampen turnout for the NNP within the province while only moderately affecting turnout for the ANC. One cannot say for sure that ANC leaders pushed for the bar-code provision to achieve this effect, but it could not have escaped their notice.

The ANC had cause to be moderately pleased with the results of the 1999 election. It (barely) won its two-thirds majority, and in the Western Cape provincial election, it won 42 percent of the vote against only 38 percent for the NNP, though the NNP was still able to cling to power by entering into an alliance with the DP, which took 12 percent of the vote. Analysts never determined the extent to which the bar-code provision contributed to this result. However, survey data reveal that by April 1999, one month prior to the elections, there remained uneven rates of possession. While 92 percent of blacks possessed bar-coded IDs, only 85 percent of whites and 79 percent of coloureds and Indians did. Similarly, 95 percent of eligible voters likely to support the

2. The rate of nonpossession for South Africa as a whole was 20 percent. Cape Town, George, and Paarl were the three regions in the country with the highest percentages of nonpossession, at 41 percent, 38 percent, and 38 percent, respectively. The rate of nonpossession in Nyanga was 25 percent (HSRC 1998b, 17, 25).

ANC had bar-coded IDs, against only 85 percent of likely NNP supporters and 86 percent of likely DP supporters. And of South Africa's nine provinces, Western Cape had the lowest rate of possession, at 79 percent, while the rate of possession in all other provinces fell between 86 percent and 95 percent (Opinion '99 1999).

It is not possible to quantify with any degree of precision the impact of the bar-code provision on overall participation rates. While the number of valid votes cast in the National Assembly election dropped from 19.5 million in 1994 to 15.9 million in 1999, and the number of valid votes cast in the Western Cape provincial legislature election fell from 2.1 to 1.6 million, factors other than the bar-code provision were certainly important. Nevertheless, a 1999 HSRC postelection survey found that registration issues were the most often cited reason for not voting—a full 44 percent of nonvoters stated that they did not go to the polls because they were not registered or had no ID (Lodge 2003, 110). This figure suggests that the bar-code provision was far from inconsequential: 44 percent of 3.6 million (the nationwide drop in turnout between 1994 and 1999) would put the number of people disenfranchised at 1.6 million, representing 6 percent of the voting-age population.

Whatever the magnitude of disenfranchisement, the question remains: was it intentional? While ANC politicians never admitted openly that the adoption of the bar-code provision was a deliberate strategy to keep opposition supporters away from the polls, the preponderance of evidence—from the ANC's sudden reversal of its position on the use of bar-coded IDs once the HSRC regional report was issued, to the electoral boost the party should have expected from the new requirement, to the party's unwillingness to compromise with DP and NNP critics—suggests that indeed it was.

VOTER IDENTIFICATION IN THE UNITED STATES IN THE TWENTY-FIRST CENTURY

In South Africa and late-nineteenth-century urban America, legal disenfranchisement was caused by new requirements that people needed to fulfill to register to vote. In the United States since the 2000 elections, legal disenfranchisement is being caused instead by new requirements that already registered voters need to fulfill to cast their ballots on election day.

In the name of combating electoral fraud committed by voters—"voter fraud" for short—between 2001 and 2006, lawmakers in at least thirty-seven states proposed legislation to tighten the voting identification requirements that all in-person voters would have to produce prior to casting their ballots. (In-person voters are voters who go to a polling place on election day to cast their ballots, in contrast to absentee voters.) In eleven of these states, the proposed legislation was passed into law. South Dakota and Indiana have put in place the stiffest measures, requiring voters to present government-issued photo identification, while voters lacking such identification must request a provisional ballot (Indiana) or fill out a verification affidavit (South Dakota). Seven other states have imposed less strict requirements, allowing voters to present various forms of either photo or nonphoto identification. Acceptable forms of nonphoto identification vary from state to state but typically include utility bills, bank statements, paychecks, Social Security cards, Medicare cards, birth certificates, fishing licenses, and the like. Voters in these seven states who lack identification can also vote if they fill out a verification affidavit (North Dakota), request a provisional ballot (Alabama, Colorado, Montana, Ohio, Washington), or state their date of birth and last four digits of their Social Security number (New Mexico). In another two states, Missouri and Georgia, courts blocked the implementation of the new identification laws, though a judge subsequently granted Georgia permission to implement the law in 2007. Legislation in the remaining twenty-six states either failed to make its way out of the legislature[3] or was vetoed by the governor.[4]

Proponents of tightened voter identification requirements contend that such measures are necessary to safeguard the integrity of elections. Most commonly, they argue that the requirements provide safeguards against in-person voter fraud—the fraudulent impersonation at polling stations on election day of legal voters, dead voters, or voters who have moved out of an electoral district but are still on the electoral rolls.[5] Those opposed to the new requirements, especially the more stringent photo ID-only requirement, accuse their political opponents of wanting to keep those less likely to have these forms of identification—the poor, the elderly, blacks, Native Americans—from voting. Both the arguments for and against the new identification measures require closer examination.

It is notoriously difficult to quantify rates of voter fraud (Overton 2007, 644–57). Nevertheless, regional newspapers from around the country regularly report that this type of fraud takes place. The closest we get to "hard" evidence

---

3. California, Connecticut, Illinois, Iowa, Maine, Maryland, Massachusetts, Minnesota, Mississippi, Nebraska, Nevada, New Jersey, New York, North Carolina, Oklahoma, Rhode Island, Tennessee, Texas, Utah, Virginia, West Virginia.

4. Arizona, Kansas, New Hampshire, Pennsylvania, Wisconsin. Arizona voters later passed the measure into law by referendum.

5. In-person voter fraud involves the impersonation of a voter while casting a ballot on election day in a polling station. It thus includes neither registration fraud (which takes places prior to ballot casting) nor the fraudulent use of absentee ballots (which does not involve in-person voting). Neither registration fraud nor absentee ballot fraud would be prevented by requiring voters to produce identification before voting at their precinct on election day.

relates to the impersonation of dead voters, since it is relatively easy to compare death records with voting records. Thus journalists from two news organizations matched voting records with the names, addresses, dates of birth, and Social Security numbers of everyone who had died in Georgia from 1980 to 2000 and discovered that 5,412 ballots were cast from the grave during that twenty-year period.[6] A similar review conducted in 2006 found that as many as 2,700 dead New Yorkers had voted.[7] There have also been reports of dead people voting in Philadelphia and Kings County, Washington, among other places.[8]

We should bear in mind, however, that such studies do not establish that in-person fraud actually occurred. For one, impersonators need not present themselves at the polling station to cast ballots in the names of dead voters. They can, instead, cast absentee ballots (something that in-person voter identification requirements would do nothing to prevent). Thus not all ghost voting is indicative of in-person fraud. Indeed, in Philadelphia and Kings County there was a total of only eight ghost voters, and all cast their ballots absentee.

Analyses based on matched death and voting records, furthermore, are not necessarily indicative of widespread fraud (whether in-person or absentee) since the data they rely upon are often faulty. Indeed, the journalist who reported the dead voter analysis in New York cautioned against overinterpreting the results since "typically, records of votes by the dead are the result of bookkeeping errors and do not result in the casting of extra ballots." Similarly, journalists who matched 370,000 Milwaukee voting records from 1992 to 2000 with Social Security Administration death records found twelve instances of dead people casting ballots but upon further investigation discovered that many of these resulted from clerical errors or honest mistakes (one living woman was erroneously recorded as being dead, two men had unwittingly been voting under their dead fathers' names, and the like).[9]

In fact, it may be because ghost voting, along with other types of in-person voter fraud, is so rare that criminal prosecution is exceedingly uncommon. In the 2002 and 2004 general elections, board of elections officials in Ohio's eighty-eight counties identified only four out of 9,078,728 votes cast as fraudulent and warranting legal action (Coalition 2005). In defending its new voter identification law before a court of law, the state of Indiana could not adduce any evidence of in-person voter fraud in the history of the state (Democratic Party v. Rokita, 458 F. Supp. 2d 775 [S.D. Ind. 2006]). Nor, in 2005, could

---

6. "Even Death Can't Stop some Voters," *Atlanta Journal and Constitution,* November 6, 2000.

7. "Deceased Residents on Statewide Voter List," *Poughkeepsie Journal,* October 29, 2006.

8. "Dead Men Can Vote," *Philadelphia Citypaper.net,* Oct. 12–19, 1995, www.citypaper.net/articles/101295/article009.shtml; "Dead Voted in Governor's Race," *Seattle Post-Intelligencer,* January 7, 2005.

9. "12 Votes Attributed to Dead People; Most of Them Are Explained as Honest Mix-ups over Names," *Milwaukee Journal Sentinel,* January 22, 2001.

Georgia Secretary of State Cathy Cox (2005) in her words "recall one documented case of voter fraud during my tenure as Secretary of State or Assistant Secretary of State that specifically related to the impersonation of a registered voter at voting polls" (her tenure began in 1996). A United States Department of Justice (DOJ) survey of federal election fraud prosecutions in the entire country from October 2002 through September 2005 turned up only a single conviction for in-person fraud even though the prosecution of voter fraud was a high priority of the Justice Department during this period, and U.S. attorneys who were found to be too lax in this effort were dismissed.[10] The individual convicted in this case was Leander Brooks, an East St. Louis poll worker who forged signatures on twenty ballot applications during the 2002 elections to enable his accomplices to fraudulently vote.[11] Since this scheme was made possible only by the complicity of the very election official charged with verifying the identity of voters, tighter identification requirements would have done nothing to prevent it.

Still, it has been argued that extremely low prosecution rates tell us little about how widespread in-person fraud is and reflect only how very unlikely it is that an impersonator will be apprehended. For example, appellate judge Richard Posner, who upheld the Indiana law, reasoned:

> He [the impersonator] enters the polling place, gives a name that is not his own, votes, and leaves. If later it is discovered that the name he gave is that of a dead person, no one at the polling place will remember the face of the person who gave that name, and if someone did remember it, what would he do with the information? The impersonator and the person impersonated (if living) might show up at the polls at the same time and a confrontation might ensue that might lead to a citizen arrest or a call to the police who would arrive before the impersonator had fled, and arrest him. A more likely sequence would be for the impersonated person to have voted already when the impersonator arrived and tried to vote in his name. But in either case an arrest would be most unlikely (and likewise if the impersonation were discovered or suspected by comparing signatures, when that is done), as the resulting commotion would disrupt the voting. And anyway the impersonated voter is likely to be dead or in another district or precinct or to be acting in cahoots with the impersonator, rather than to be a neighbor (precincts are small, sometimes a single apartment house).[12]

It may be, then, that in-person fraud is not rare, just rarely detected.

10. DOJ (n.d.); Toobin (2004); "In 5-Year Effort, Scant Evidence of Vote Fraud," *New York Times*, April 12, 2007; "Vote-Fraud Complaints by GOP Drove Dismissals," *Washington Post*, May 14, 2007.

11. Grand jury indictment of Leander Brooks, No. 03-CR-30201 (S.D. Ill. Oct. 24, 2003).

12. Crawford v. Marion County Election Board, Nos. 06–2218, 06–2317, slip op. at 7–8 (7th Cir. Jan. 4, 2007).

While Posner is certainly correct that collaring *impersonators* is difficult, the fact remains that discovering fraudulent *votes* is not nearly so hard. In East St. Louis, for instance, Brooks's vote fraud scheme unraveled as soon as the legitimate voters showed up at the polls only to learn that ballots had already been cast in their names.

It is telling that sweeping searches that do not require apprehending perpetrators—matching death and voting records—have turned up few cases of in-person ghost voting. Take the case of Georgia, with its 5,412 ballots apparently cast by dead voters from 1980 to 2000. We know that not all of these ballots were, in fact, cast fraudulently. The journalists who conducted the study highlighted the case of Alan J. Mandel, who cast ballots in three elections after his death. Subsequent investigation by election officials revealed, however, that poll workers had erroneously recorded the vote of another registered voter with almost the same name—Alan J. Mandell, spelled with two *l*'s—under the name of the deceased in at least one of those elections.[13] Sloppy death records, misread Social Security numbers, widows voting by accident in the names of their late husbands (e.g., Mrs. John Doe recorded as Mr. John Doe) account for other apparent cases of ghost voting. Yet even if we make the patently unrealistic assumption that each of the 5,412 votes was indeed cast in person rather than absentee, that each voter was actually dead and not incorrectly recorded as dead, and that the polling clerks accurately recorded the identity of the voter rather than making a clerical error, the percentage of fraudulent votes would still represent only a minuscule proportion of the tens of millions of votes cast in the numerous primary, local, and general elections held during that twenty-year period.

While we cannot fix the exact rate of in-person fraud—in Georgia or elsewhere—with any kind of precision, it does nevertheless appear that this type of fraud is far from commonplace. This conclusion is confirmed by experts who have comprehensively reviewed news and law databases and interviewed judges, lawyers, academicians, federal prosecutors, and election officials but have failed to turn up evidence that impersonation fraud is anything but an exceedingly rare occurrence (Minnite and Callahan 2003; Serebrov and Wang 2006).

One reason that in-person fraud is so rare is that it is among the most inefficient means for altering the outcome of an election. Votes must be picked up one at a time, and each one requires the impersonator to have prior knowledge

---

13. Records for the other two elections in which the deceased Mandel voted had been discarded and did not allow investigators to reach any conclusions. "State Plans to Update Voter Lists," *Atlanta Journal and Constitution*, February 10, 2001.

about who has died or moved or is out of town. Far more effective methods of electoral cheating are available. Registration fraud, vote buying, and absentee ballot fraud—alone or in combination—yield more votes with less effort and are thus more appealing alternatives for those inclined to cheat. It is perhaps thus not surprising that these three forms of fraud accounted for 71 percent of all federal-level election fraud convictions recorded by the DOJ (n.d.) between October 2002 and September 2005. Elections experts interviewed by United States Election Assistance Commission (EAC) consultants Job Serebrov and Tova Wang support these conclusions:

> The interviewees largely agreed that absentee balloting is subject to the greatest proportion of fraudulent acts, followed by vote buying and voter registration fraud. They similarly pointed to voter registration drives by nongovernmental groups as a source of fraud, particularly when the workers are paid per registration. Many asserted that impersonation of voters is probably the least frequent type of fraud because it is the most likely type of fraud to be discovered, there are stiff penalties associated with this type of fraud, and it is an inefficient method of influencing an election. (EAC 2006, 9)

In-person fraud is simply less attractive than other strategies of electoral cheating.

None of this, of course, is to argue that in-person fraud *never* takes place. As we saw, it took place in East St. Louis, where twenty fraudulent votes were cast in 2002. Investigative reporters also convincingly documented an instance of a dead person voting in the 2000 elections. The deceased voter was named André Alismé, and his vote was cast in Miami-Dade County, Florida. Alismé had died in May 1997, and the Elections Department canceled his registration in June of that year. On election day in November 2000, however, his name was mysteriously resurrected at a polling place a few miles away from where he had voted when alive. It appeared handwritten on the precinct roll, along with an obvious forgery of his signature, indicating that a ballot was cast in his name.[14]

It is ironic that this incident took place in Florida, which has had photo identification requirements in place since 1998. It appears that poll workers in this case failed to follow proper verification procedures (as did Leander Brooks in East St. Louis)—a hitch that, if generalizable, may raise questions about the overall effectiveness of tightening identification requirements. Be that as it may, the best available evidence suggests that in-person fraud occurs infrequently.

14. "Unregistered Voters Cast Ballots in Dade," *Miami Herald,* December 24, 2000.

What of the disenfranchising potential so feared by the opponents of more restrictive voter identification requirements? Academic research on this question is still in its infancy, and only a handful of studies have so far been completed. The largest one to date was conducted by a team of Rutgers and Ohio State University researchers under contract with the EAC (Eagleton 2006). This study analyzed aggregate and individual-level data for the 2004 elections, and found, in a nutshell, that "as voter identification requirements vary, voter turnout varies as well" (9). Unfortunately, this laudable effort was plagued with problems. An outside panel of experts expressed concern that the statistical analysis was based on unrealistic assumptions. While the researchers subsequently revised some of these assumptions, they themselves conceded that the data they had collected, from only one election cycle, were not sufficient to draw any conclusive statistical inferences. Ultimately, the EAC rejected the findings of the study. While some observers believed that partisanship lay behind this decision—an understandable suspicion given other actions taken by the EAC (more on this later)—the agency nevertheless listed a reasonable set of methodological concerns when queried by the Senate Rules and Administration Committee (Davidson 2007, 5–7).

A more modest but less contentious study was conducted by MIT political scientist Stephen Ansolabehere (2007). He analyzed a 2006 national survey that asked American voting-age respondents whether identification requirements had prevented them from voting. He found that "only 23 people in the entire 36,500 sample said they were not allowed to vote because of voter identification requirements. That figure translates into approximately one-tenth of one percent of voters" (7). Interestingly, Ansolabehere's estimate is consistent with the only existent comprehensive on-the-ground report from election administrators. Compelled by a court order, officials from fourteen of Arizona's fifteen counties tracked the number of prospective voters who lacked proper identification and chose not to cast a provisional ballot during the November 2006 elections and found that about 2,500 voters left without voting—a figure equal to about one-tenth of 1 percent of all ballots cast.[15]

Available data, then, put the level of disenfranchisement caused by voter identification requirements at around one-tenth of 1 percent—a small amount from one perspective but not so small from another. In the 2004 presidential election the race in many states was decided by less than 1 percent of the vote. Or, to think of it another way, one-tenth of 1 percent would have equaled more than 120,000 votes nationwide in that election. There is no evidence that the

---

15. "County Reports Indicate Few Tripped Up by Voter ID Laws," Associated Press, December 19, 2006.

incidence of in-person fraud has ever come remotely close to that magnitude (recall that there was only one federal prosecution for in-person voter fraud, involving only twenty votes, for the entire 2002–5 period). On balance, then, the disenfranchising potential of tightened voter identification laws, using the most concrete estimates available, would appear to be a more serious threat to democratic inclusiveness than in-person fraud is to electoral integrity.

Still, the Arizona report and Ansolabehere study leave a number of questions unanswered. Neither allows us to discern whether there were any impersonators among those turned away, or how many legitimate voters did not even bother going to the polls because they lacked proper identification. Consequently the one-tenth of 1 percent figure is a rough estimate at best. Nor do the report and study tell us how much disenfranchisement was caused by the new (more restrictive) *photo* identification requirements put in place in Indiana and South Dakota. Arizona's new law allowed voters to show either photo or nonphoto identification, and Ansolabehere's study treats the United States as a unitary whole. But twenty-six states in 2006, with a few exceptions, did not require voters to show any type of identification, and only a handful of states requested voters to show photo identification.[16] More illuminating would have been a differentiated analysis that clustered states by type of identification requirement.

Particularly worrying, in this regard, is the fact that various surveys show that minorities, the poor, and the elderly are, relative to the general population, less likely to possess driver's licenses and other forms of photo identification. One national survey of randomly selected voting-age American citizens found that about 11 percent of them did not possess government-issued photo identification, compared with 15 percent of low-income citizens, 18 percent of elderly citizens, and 25 percent of black citizens (BCJ 2006). A survey of older Indiana registered voters revealed that 9 percent of white registrants did not possess a valid Indiana driver's license or state-issued identification card, compared with 30 percent of nonwhites (Silberman 2005). Federal statistics indicate that while between 5 and 11 percent of Americans between the ages of twenty-five and sixty-nine did not possess a driver's license in 2003, the rate for older Americans was much higher: 14 percent for those aged seventy to seventy-four, 19 percent for those between seventy-five and seventy-nine, 27 percent for those aged eighty to eighty-four, and 48 percent for those eighty-five and older (Overton 2007, 658–59).

16. In two of the twenty-six states first-time voters did not need to show identification, and in the remaining twenty-four states identification was not required for first-time voters who registered by mail and did not provide ID verification with their registration.

Of added concern, photo identification can be difficult and costly for many of these groups of voters to acquire. As Wendy Noren (2006), longtime election official from Boone County, Missouri, told a congressional committee:

> Many groups of citizens do not have quick and free access to photo identification. These groups include students, women, senior citizens, disabled voters, adoptees, persons born overseas—including children of missionaries and military personnel.... In our increasingly mobile society many people are born, married, divorced and remarried in different states and the paper trail necessary to acquire photo identification becomes not only expensive but time consuming.... Many of our senior citizens also do not even have the documentation required because these documents do not exist. As keeper of historic school records in my county, I have many times certified to the Social Security administration the only record of age that exists for some seniors—an entry by a first grade teacher of a student's date of birth.

Not only are some voters less likely than others to possess photo identification, but it is not always easy for those voters without identification to obtain it.

It might be argued that Noren and I are making too much of the photo identification requirements. Voters in Indiana and South Dakota who do not possess photo identification can, after all, still vote—as long as they sign a verification affidavit (in South Dakota) or request a provisional ballot and later execute a verification affidavit claiming indigence or religious objection to being photographed as the reason for not possessing identification(in Indiana). Yet some voters may lack identification for reasons other than indigence or religious objection. Others may be unaware that affidavit or provisional balloting options exist. We should also keep in mind that many voters are apparently put off by having to go through that extra hassle or having to experience the embarrassment of being singled out for different treatment. Recall that 2,500 Arizonians left their polling places without voting in 2006 rather than fill out provisional ballots. Consider, too, that in 2004 many members of the Lakota tribe in South Dakota, particularly the elderly, found the new photo identification requirement in that state to be so embarrassing that they refused to vote.[17] As the Lakota example suggests, some voters are more likely to be affected by photo identification requirements than others. Indeed, Ansolabehere found, in the survey data he analyzed, that blacks were four times more likely to have been turned away from the polls than were whites for lack of identification, and Democrats were two times more likely to be kept from voting than

---

17. "Proposal to Relax Voter ID Law Stalls," Associated Press, December 7, 2004.

Republicans (2007, table 1). Though the sample size was too small for these findings to be statistically significant, and the data did not distinguish between types of identification requirements, the differences he detected are nonetheless roughly in line with what we know about the demographics of photo identification possession. Plainly, there are many unknowns about the impact of photo (and nonphoto) voter identification requirements on turnout. But what we do know should give us pause.

Whatever the actual impact of tightened voter identification requirements on turnout, what can we say about the intent of the legislators who passed them into law? On this question, there are grounds for believing that behind their imposition in many states lay a Republican desire to reduce the turnout of voters—poor and minority voters in particular—who tend to vote Democratic. In this context, it is important to note the partisan breakdown of support for tighter identification laws. Between 2001 and 2006, legislatures in Georgia, Indiana, Missouri, New Hampshire, Pennsylvania, South Dakota, and Wisconsin passed bills requiring voters to present photo identification. In each of these cases, Republican-dominated legislatures pushed the measures through over the opposition of Democrats, though Democratic governors in New Hampshire, Pennsylvania, and Wisconsin were able to veto the bills, and courts struck down Missouri's law and temporarily blocked Georgia's. Republicans also passed into law less restrictive requirements (allowing voters to also present nonphoto identification) over the objection of almost all Democratic legislators in Colorado, Montana, and Ohio and opponents among a split Democratic Party in North Dakota. In Alabama, Republicans favored stricter legislation but had to reach a compromise with Democrats. In New Mexico and Washington, Republicans also fought for stiff requirements but were unable to block the passage of less strict legislation favored by Democrats. In Arizona, Republican legislation was vetoed by the Democratic governor but later enacted into law when the measure was approved by voters in a referendum. Republican legislators around the country, in sum, supported tight identification requirements, while Democrats either opposed them or favored requirements that were less restrictive.

Of course, a tendency for Republicans to support restrictive legislation does not, on its own, substantiate an intent to disenfranchise. But circumstantial evidence of such an intent can be found in the details of the legislation crafted by Republican lawmakers. In Georgia, for instance, the Republican-passed legislation that required voters to show photo identification did not extend in any way to absentee balloting. If the intent of the photo identification measure were genuinely to curb voter fraud, this omission would have been glaring insofar as most experts agree that absentee ballot fraud is far more pervasive than in-person voter fraud (EAC 2006, 9). But in Georgia, absentee balloting is common (20 percent of all votes cast in the 2004 presidential election), and absentee voters tend to tilt Republican (in 2004, 60 percent of absentee voters cast their ballots for George W. Bush versus 57 percent of in-person voters).[18] Subjecting absentee balloting to photo ID verification would thus have cut into a vote block that leans Republican. Imposing the requirements on in-person voters only, in contrast, disproportionately affects voters that lean Democratic. In 2007, 6 percent of registered Georgian voters did not possess a valid driver's license or state identification card, and minority voters were significantly less likely than other registered voters to possess these forms of identification. Black registrants, for instance, were twice as likely not to possess a license as were white registrants (Hood and Bullock 2007).

Some Republican politicians around the country no doubt believe sincerely that voter fraud is a real and sizable danger and also find the possible disenfranchisement of citizens, even Democrat-leaning citizens, objectionable. For instance, South Dakota state representative Stan Adelstein, a Republican who supported the original photo identification law in 2003, sought to loosen identification restrictions after learning that the new requirements kept elderly members of Lakota tribe (who tend to vote Democratic) from voting. Indeed, he proposed amending the law to allow voters to forgo showing identification or signing an affidavit if two poll workers know the voter's identity. This proposal, however, did not generate enthusiasm among his fellow Republicans, and the more restrictive rules still stand.[19]

Surprisingly, a few Republican operatives around the country admit that they support stiffened identification requirements only because they might depress turnout for Democratic candidates. Most candid has been Royal Masset, former political director of the Republican Party of Texas. In 2007, as the voter identification issue heated up in that state, he told a *Houston Chronicle* reporter that he did not believe voter fraud was causing Republicans to lose elections but that in his opinion (as the reporter paraphrased it), "requiring photo IDs could cause enough of a drop-off in legitimate Democratic voting to add 3 percent to the Republican vote."[20]

This kind of reasoning may help make sense of the intense interest of national Republican leaders in issues of voter fraud and voter identification following the 2000 elections. Top Republican officials worked hard to ensure that states—especially battleground states—passed photo identification laws. Missouri was

18. Calculated from county-level data reported by the Georgia Secretary of State, www.sos.state.ga.us/elections/election_results/2004_1102/precincts.htm.

19. "Proposal to Relax Voter ID Law Stalls"; "Legislator Wants Voter ID Law Eased," *Argus Leader,* January 8, 2005.

20. "In Trying to Win, Has Dewhurst Lost a Friend?" *Houston Chronicle,* May 17, 2007.

one such swing state, and according to the Missouri Republican floor leader, the White House was "heavily involved" in efforts to pass that state's 2006 photo identification law (which was later thrown out by the courts for being an unconstitutional infringement on voting rights).[21]

Consider, too, the unprecedented and exhaustive effort of the DOJ to uncover cases of possible voter fraud after Bush's victory in 2000. Some observers believe this campaign was an attempt to trump up voter fraud as a political issue. Proof that voter fraud is rampant, after all, would justify stringent identification laws, such as the one passed in Missouri, and the partisan advantage they would yield. So serious was the campaign that the administration fired federal attorneys it perceived to be ineffective in prosecuting voter fraud. Among those who were apparently removed for this reason was Todd Graves, U.S. attorney for western Missouri, who was replaced just weeks before the photo identification bill came up for a vote in the state legislature.[22]

And then there was the EAC-commissioned report on voter fraud, which EAC officials edited, many believe, to obscure the fact that this type of fraud is quite rare. Whereas the original report submitted by a bipartisan pair of election experts concluded that "there is widespread but not unanimous agreement that there is little polling place fraud" (Serebrov and Wang 2006, 7), the version released to the public stated that "there is a great deal of debate on the pervasiveness of fraud" (EAC 2006, 1). In fact, the original report identified only one person who believed that polling place fraud is widespread: Jason Torchinsky of the American Center for Voting Rights (ACVR). This organization was headed by Mark "Thor" Hearne, the national election counsel of Bush-Cheney '04, and staffed by Republican operatives; Torchinsky himself was the deputy general counsel to Bush-Cheney '04. After the federal prosecutor firings scandal broke in 2007, the ACVR suddenly and silently disbanded. Hearne thereafter refused to speak publicly about the organization and even expunged reference to it from his resume (Hasen 2007). Many of the ACVR's inflated claims about voter fraud have since been debunked by the Brennan Center for Justice at the New York University School of Law, which has posted its various reports on its website, truthaboutfraud.org.

All of this lends plausibility to the sobering assessment of Joseph Rich, former chief of the DOJ Voting Rights Section:

> As more information becomes available about the administration's priority on combating alleged, but not well substantiated, voter fraud, the more apparent it is

21. "Campaign against Alleged Voter Fraud Fuels Political Tempest," *McClatchy Newspapers,* April 19, 2007.

22. "Missouri Attorney a Focus of Firing," *Boston Globe,* May 6, 2007.

that its actions concerning voter ID laws are part of a partisan strategy to suppress the votes of poor and minority citizens.[23]

The accumulated evidence, in short, suggests that there is indeed validity in the accusation that at least some Republican lawmakers have supported new voter identification laws as a means to depress the turnout of Democratic-leaning voters, though we have only a rudimentary understanding of how much of an impact those measures are actually having.

As a coda to this discussion, it bears noting that in addition to enacting tighter voter identification laws, another partisan strategy of legal disenfranchisement may be taking shape in the United States today: putting up legal obstacles to nonpartisan voter registration drives. Republicans have long been suspicious that various nonpartisan organizations such as the nonprofit Association of Community Organizations for Reform Now (ACORN) have engaged in fraudulent practices in their drives to register low-income and minority citizens—people, not incidentally, likely to vote Democratic. Most recently, ACORN employees from various locales around the country were accused of submitting fraudulent registration forms in the run-up to the 2006 elections. At least a few of these allegations have proven to be true: two ACORN workers from Minnesota and Missouri pled guilty to election fraud in 2006 and 2007, respectively.

In the name of electoral integrity, states such as Florida and Ohio have enacted strict laws to regulate voter registration drives, laws that impose hefty fines and criminal penalties for a variety of infractions (BCJ 2007). Some skeptics see in these laws not only an effort to curb registration fraud but also a strategy to deter poor and minority citizens from voting. A *New York Times* editorial, for instance, warily declared:

> Florida recently reached a new low when it actually bullied the League of Women Voters into stopping its voter registration efforts in the state. The Legislature did this by adopting a law that seems intended to scare away anyone who wants to run a voter registration drive. Since registration drives are particularly important for bringing poor people, minority groups and less educated voters into the process, the law appears to be designed to keep such people from voting. It imposes fines of $250 for every voter registration form that a group files more than 10 days after it is collected, and $5,000 for every form that is not submitted—even if it is because of events beyond anyone's control, like a hurricane. The Florida League of Women Voters, which is suing to block the new rules, has decided it cannot afford to keep

23. Quoted in "Campaign against Alleged Voter Fraud."

registering new voters in the state as it has done for 67 years. If a volunteer lost just 16 forms in a flood, or handed in a stack of forms a day late, the group's entire annual budget could be put at risk.[24]

Ohio's law, made more restrictive still by rules promulgated by Secretary of State J. Kenneth Blackwell, caused a precipitous drop in the number of new registration cards collected by grassroots organizations in that state. The number gathered by Ohio ACORN, for instance, fell from seven thousand a month before the law went into effect to less than two hundred after.[25]

Despite the ominous implications of these observations, it is too soon to gauge the impact of such laws. Many are so new—both the Ohio and Florida laws only went into effect in 2006—that we do not yet know what long-term impact they will have on registration rates, or even if they will survive legal challenge. Indeed, a few months prior to the 2006 elections, judges blocked the continued enforcement of both the Ohio and the Florida laws. We will have to wait and see what develops in other states around the country.

Conditions for Intentional Legal Disenfranchisement

The South African and post-Florida American stories are by no means universal around the world today: few complaints about disenfranchisement were heard in Mexico, for example, when the government introduced new photo voter identification cards in the early 1990s to combat election fraud (Carter Center 1993, 17–22). Nor did all American states impose depressive registration measures on their urban centers in the late nineteenth century: Indiana did not enact a registration law until 1911, and its scope was statewide (Harris 1929, 85–89, 93, 97–99). Disenfranchisement was not a universal consequence of the secret ballot in the late nineteenth and early twentieth centuries either. In Michigan, turnout in the first secret ballot election rose by 14.2 percent (Heckelman 1995, 111). When the secret ballot was introduced in Denmark in 1901, turnout rates in the town of Fredericia jumped by eight percentage points (Elklit 1983, 260). Participation in Germany rose in the decade following the passage of secret ballot legislation in 1903, as it did in France following the strengthening of secrecy laws in 1913, with the exception of the 1919 election (Suval 1985, 21–36; Lancelot 1968, 14–15).

Under what conditions, then, are politicians likely to impose rules that selectively depress the participation of voters who might vote against them? For

---

24. "Block the Vote," *New York Times,* May 30, 2006.
25. "New Regulation Rules Stir Voter Debate in Ohio," *New York Times,* August 6, 2006.

one thing, strategies of selective disenfranchisement that rest upon the application of rules would seem most likely to be deployed only in places where laws guaranteeing political equality are actually enforced. Where such laws are not enforced, parties inclined to restrict the suffrage of particular groups have extralegal methods at their disposal, which are often more direct and reliable. In Cambodia, for instance, prospective voters in 1998 were turned away from registration centers if not accompanied by officials from Second Prime Minister Hun Sen's Cambodian's People's Party. Bar-code legislation in South Africa, in contrast, had to survive High and Constitutional Court challenges, the outcomes of which were far from certain. Even the heavy-handed disenfranchisement laws devised by Southern Democrats in the United States were framed in color-blind terms to keep within the limits of the newly enacted Fifteenth Amendment (Key 1949, 536–39).

Yet at the same time, for a strategy of legal disenfranchisement to work, laws guaranteeing political equality cannot be interpreted and enforced too strictly. If courts demand stringently that all people be treated equally, measures that have a differential impact on prospective voters might be struck down. Indiana legislators passed restrictive registration laws for the state's urban centers in 1867, 1889, and 1891, only to watch the courts declare them unconstitutional one after another on grounds that they did not apply uniformly to all parts of the state (Harris 1929, 85–87). Courts also blocked in 2006 the implementation of photo voter identification requirements in both Georgia and Missouri though a federal judge cleared the way for the Georgia law to take effect in 2007. In a case that will have national repercussions, the Supreme Court will decide in 2008 whether the Indiana photo identification law is constitutional.

Legal disenfranchisement is also facilitated when a single bloc or party has a free hand to shape new electoral legislation. It was an overwhelmingly Democratic state legislature in late-nineteenth-century Arkansas that passed the secret ballot measure despite opposition by every Republican and labor union member.[26] In New Jersey, New York, and California, late-nineteenth and early-twentieth-century Republican lawmakers imposed burdensome registration laws on their cities over the protests of urban Democrats. It was, in addition, a National Assembly dominated by the ANC that passed the bar-coded ID provision in South Africa in spite of objections and legal challenges from the DP and NNP (Lodge 1999, 28). After the 2000 elections in the United States, the strictest voter identification laws were passed exclusively in states where Republicans controlled both the legislature and the governorship.

---

26. "Opposed to Fair Elections," *Arkansas Gazette,* March 14, 1891.

Consider, too, Australia, where the governing coalition of parties had to wait until it took control of both chambers of parliament to push through its plan of legal disenfranchisement. It proposed in 2004 a law closing the electoral roll to first-time voters as soon as an election is called. It argued that this measure was necessary to give the Australian Electoral Commission adequate time to prepare the electoral roll and thus to safeguard its integrity. Against the measure were the opposition Labor, Democratic, and Green parties, which attract a large proportion of the youth vote. Since the measure threatened to disenfranchise the eighty thousand or so new voters who tend to register only after an election has been called, these parties saw in this measure a deliberate effort to keep their young supporters from voting. When the proposal came up for consideration in the Senate, they had enough votes to defeat it. But after the ruling coalition gained a majority in both chambers in 2005, it passed the measure into law. The new, more restrictive enrollment rule is scheduled to be implemented in late 2007 or early 2008.[27]

Now contrast Mexico, where the Partido Revolucionario Institucional (PRI) in 1990 needed to build a legislative coalition with other parties to secure passage of its proposed reform of the registration process. That proposal, part of a larger package of electoral reforms, necessitated constitutional change. By law, constitutional amendments require a two-thirds majority in both chambers of Congress, which the PRI after 1988 no longer maintained in the lower chamber. Consequently, the PRI had to negotiate with opposition parties over the content of the reforms to win their support (Lujambio 1998, 171). In the end, the reform package passed only when 63 of 122 Partido Acción Nacional legislators joined the PRI in voting for it.

Similarly, in Denmark at the turn of the century the Conservatives held a safe majority in the upper house (Landsting), while the Liberals held a secure majority in the lower house (Folketing). The secrecy issue was debated from 1887 until 1900 and was settled only when all parties in parliament came to an agreement, which was necessary to get it through both houses (Elklit 2000). In Germany, too, secret ballot legislation had long been debated. It passed only when the National Liberals joined the Center Party, Left Liberal Party, and the Social Democrats in supporting the reform (M. L. Anderson 2000, 242–44). A similar process of debate and coalition building unfolded in France (Garrigou 1988), as well as in Michigan (Fredman 1968, 35).

Of course, if a dominant party were secure in its majority, it would have no compelling incentive to bend clean election reforms to its advantage. For this

27. "Young Voters Face Lockout," *Courier Mail,* May 24, 2004; *Senate Hansard,* June 24, 2004, pp. 24584–606; Sawer (2006).

reason, intentional disenfranchisement is most likely to occur when a legislatively dominant party is uncertain about its electoral future—something that was true in the nineteenth century of Democrats in Arkansas and Republicans in New Jersey, New York, and California. It was also true of the ANC in South Africa, particularly in the Western Cape, and of Republicans after the 2000 elections in states such as Missouri, Georgia, Indiana, and South Dakota.

Legal disenfranchisement would also seem to be facilitated when opposition supporters can be singled out easily (because they are poor, young, mobile, illiterate, work inflexible hours, possess certain kinds of identity documents, etc.) under the guise of clean election legislation. Where such markers are difficult to identify or, perhaps more to the point, where it is difficult to craft legislation to exclude people based on those markers, exclusionary provisions are less obvious choices for parties seeking an electoral edge. It is in part for this reason that the PRI in Mexico never even appeared to consider new exclusionary provisions in the series of electoral reforms it implemented. It may have been simply too hard for the party to figure out how to disenfranchise, through the application of clean election law, the educated urbanites who were most likely to vote against it. That the PRI had nothing in principle against keeping its opponents away from the polls can be seen in its stance on voting rights for Mexican citizens residing outside the country. The party had long resisted extending the franchise to these expatriates, who numbered more than 6 million in the late 1990s, because it was widely believed that many Mexicans abroad would throw their support to the opposition (Escobar 2006, 513). As late as 1999, when Mexico was already deep into the reform process, the PRI-dominated Senate voted down a proposal approved by the opposition-controlled lower chamber to grant the vote to Mexican expatriates.

In sum, intentional legal disenfranchisement requires a rather special set of circumstances: an electorally vulnerable party that is constrained by the rule of law but unfettered to craft election legislation, as well as a citizenry whose demographic profile permits that party to put up special obstacles to the electoral participation of opposition supporters.

Unintentional Disenfranchisement

Not all instances of legal disenfranchisement are intentional. Sometimes clean election provisions collide unexpectedly with the beliefs, sensibilities, or commitments of prospective voters. In this section I examine first how unintentional disenfranchisement resulted from new document requirements in South Africa and Malawi, identification regulations in 1920s Chicago, and ballot-marking restrictions in nineteenth-century France. I then identify several conditions that facilitated this unintentional disenfranchisement.

RELIGIOUS ANXIETIES AND POLITICAL DISTRUST
IN 1990S SOUTH AFRICA AND MALAWI

Returning to the case of South Africa, the 1999 bar-coded identity document requirement occasioned a surprising reaction in one locale, as described in the following news item:

> Villagers in Mpumalanga's rural hinterland have refused to register for the coming elections and have instead accused the Independent Electoral Commission (IEC) of paving the way for the Anti-Christ. People in villages such as Daggakraal chased IEC registration officers out of their villages last week, insisting the campaign to issue bar-coded ID books smacks of biblical prophecies predicting the end of the world. "Villagers are terrified of bar-coded IDs because of the belief that the Anti-Christ will force people to have numbers tattooed on their foreheads," said provincial IEC spokesman Leon Mbangwa. "It's all part of some strange form of rural millennium fever and clearly illustrates the kind of obstacles we have to fight just to get people registered." Some rural residents also insist election officials are collecting names and addresses to assist debt collectors.[28]

The new bar-coded ID requirement apparently clashed with the religious beliefs of Mpumalanga villagers, resulting in their refusal to register. These beliefs most likely drew upon millennialist African Zionist and Pentecostal Christian teachings about the return of the Antichrist at the end of time foretold in Revelations 9–13 (Thompson 1997, 89–90; A. Anderson 2000).

But there is more to the story. Fear of Satan's tattoo, we learn from the news item, went hand in hand with a fear of debt collectors. It may not be coincidental that the rural municipality in which Daggakraal is located had been the site of bitter land clashes between wealthy white farmers and impoverished black rural laborers. President Thabo Mbeki, when he toured the region, went so far as to describe it as the home of modern slavery.[29] It may well be that the religious qua electoral anxieties of poor laborers overlay a deeper conflict with landowners. If so, this form of unintended legal disenfranchisement resulted not only from a clash of millennialist and secular worldviews but also from a conflict between the state's desire to reduce electoral malfeasance on the one hand

---

28. "Press Clippings," *Mail and Guardian*, February 26, 1999.
29. "Mpumalanga Spends R32m Uplifting Rural 'Slaves,'" African Eye News Service, April 11, 2000.

and suspicion among voters of collusion between state agents and landlords on the other.

Interestingly, similar misgivings were voiced by voters in Malawi when the government contemplated tightening registration procedures following the 1994 transitional elections. Research consultants hired by the government asked rural voters who participated in focus group discussions how they felt about the possible use of photo identity cards for either voting or registration. After interviewing over 180 people in eighteen focus groups, the researchers discovered that "suspicions over the intended use of the photos [were] widespread." Many villagers, they found, "question[ed] why authorities would need the photos. There were also concerns that the photos would be turned over to the police" (NDI 1996, 5, 10).

After decades of oppressive rule under former president Hastings Kamuzu Banda, distrust of the Malawian government ran high, even after Banda was no longer in power. Indeed, at one point a few years after the focus group study rumors began to circulate that the government was conspiring with vampires to collect human blood, rumors that became so widespread that newly elected president Bakili Muluzi felt compelled to go public with a response. "No government," he told the press, "can go about sucking the blood of its own people."[30] This announcement did not allay fears. Weeks later, hundreds of angry Malawians stormed the house of a governor whom they accused of harboring vampires and nearly stoned him to death.

Given the specific fears voiced by villagers about having their photos taken and the general climate of distrust out of which these fears grew, the researchers who conducted the focus group study recommended that any attempt to introduce photo identity documents be accompanied by an aggressive civic education campaign. In preparation for the 1999 elections, the government conducted a new general registration and decided to require each registrant to acquire a photo voter identity card. Ignoring the recommendations of the focus group study, however, the cash-strapped and time-pressed Electoral Commission mounted an education campaign that was, at best, meager (Afronet 1999, 18; MEC 1999a, 13–14; Kadzamira 2000, 56).

In the end, low registration rates—caused in part by logistical problems, in part by partisan manipulation, and perhaps also in part by voter suspicion in certain areas of the country—forced the elections to be postponed twice. Election losers, decrying the registration fiasco as being responsible for keeping some 168,000 people from voting, contested the victory of the incumbent president in

---

30. "A Fear of Vampires Can Mask a Fear of Something Much Worse," *New York Times,* December 29, 2002.

court. Rioting broke out in various parts of the country. Opposition supporters, believing the president's party to be dominated by Muslims, burned down seventeen mosques. Retaliations followed (Wiseman 2000, 640, 645).

While the claim of 168,000 disenfranchised voters appears to be inflated, international observers did nonetheless conclude that "potential voters were denied the opportunity to register" (MEC 1999b, 5). Whatever the actual level of vote depression, registration reforms intended to build confidence in the electoral system instead spawned skepticism, controversy, and violence. The lesson: when people are leery of state motives, they may respond warily to state efforts to gather their personal information for any purpose, including the project of cleaning up elections; and when such projects go awry, crises of legitimacy ensue.

Fear of Embarrassment in 1920s Chicago

Unintentional legal disenfranchisement can be caused not only by religious anxieties or political distrust but by more prosaic fears of embarrassment as well. Consider the case of women in Chicago. In the early 1920s, Charles Merriam and Harold Gosnell conducted a study of the causes of nonvoting in that city. As in the urban centers of New Jersey, New York, and California, selectively disenfranchising registration procedures were put in place in Chicago (Harris 1929, 81–85).[31] Keyssar (2000, 154) describes how the procedures worked in that city:

> To register, a prospective voter had to appear in person before the election judges, on the Tuesday of either the third or fourth week prior to an election. If an applicant's qualifications were challenged (by a judge or any other voter), he was required to file an affidavit of eligibility, which then would be verified by the judges. . . . Three details of the Illinois law revealed its restrictionist thrust. The first was the small size of the precincts: although justified as a means of insuring that election judges would be familiar with their constituents, the creation of tiny precincts [containing a maximum of 450 voters] meant that anyone who moved even a few blocks was likely to have to register again and meet a new thirty-day residency requirement. The second telling feature was more obvious: there were only two days on which a person could register, a small window by anyone's reckoning. Finally, the burden of

---

31. The politics of registration was, however, somewhat different in Illinois than in these other states. The main battle in Illinois was not between upstate Republicans and urban Democrats but between the Chicago business elite and Democratic machine politicians. A registration bill drafted by members of the elite was passed by the state legislature in 1885. That law then had to be adopted by each town or city though a local referendum, which Chicago voters quickly did (Grant 1955, 67–80; Keyssar 2000, 153–55).

proof, for a person who was challenged or whose name showed up on the remarkably labeled suspect list, was placed on the prospective voter himself.

Merriam and Gosnell (1924, 103–6) discovered that these rules, beyond putting up barriers to the electoral participation of immigrants and the working poor, also kept many women away from the polls. Women, they found to their surprise, feared disclosing their ages in public to election board judges.

This fear was most commonly voiced by middle-aged and elderly women, including women of English decent and of the upper classes:

> Mrs. Lane, living in a fine house in the Hyde Park neighborhood, told the interviewer frankly that she did not want to tell her age. She thought it was nobody's business just so she was twenty-one. Therefore she refused to register. Mrs. Miller lived in a good apartment on the North Side. She did not like to tell her age, nor did she like to lie about it. Consequently she was not interested in politics. (105)

There were also a few men who were sensitive about revealing their ages. One, for instance, "appeared to be much younger than he actually was. He did not wish to give his age because he feared that if it were known he would lose his job as a laborer in a cooper shop. His boss had been in the habit of discriminating in favor of younger men" (104). Still, the disclosure of age was mostly of concern to women.

The authors were unable to determine how important this concern was, relative to other factors, in keeping people away from the polls. As they remarked:

> The method employed in this investigation makes it difficult to estimate how many people balk at registering because of the age requirement. The precinct committeemen and the persons prominent in political life both regarded fear of disclosure of age as an important reason why some people did not register. On the other hand, the interviewers found only 14 people out of 5,000 or more approached who frankly admitted that they did not register because they did not want to tell their age to the election officials before their neighbors. Persons who were sensitive about their age were likely to avoid the subject altogether and to give general indifference or disbelief in woman's voting as the verbal explanation of their abstention. In fact, one of these two reasons was quite commonly linked with fear of disclosure of age as a secondary explanation. (103)

Whatever the magnitude of the problem in Chicago, kindred problems in other locales were significant enough for lawmakers outside Illinois to modify their registration laws. California and Oregon removed the registrant's age from his or her record. New York allowed voters to say "over twenty-one." In Maryland female applicants were exempted from stating their exact age (Harris 1929, 171). Illinois lawmakers finally removed the requirement in 1936.

RESTRICTIONS ON VALID ELECTORAL BEHAVIOR IN NINETEENTH-CENTURY FRANCE

Unintentional legal disenfranchisement can result not only from anxiety, distrust, or embarrassment. It can also come about when new regulations narrow the boundaries of valid electoral behavior. French lawmakers in 1852, for example, imposed strict rules to disqualify ballots with extraneous writing or markings on them to prevent landlords, employers, and other local notables from monitoring how their underlings voted, an important safeguard after the extension of universal male suffrage in 1848 (Ferté 1909, 43).[32] Ballots with extra writing or distinctive marks, after all, could be used by people in positions of power to identify who had voted for whom, especially if they told each voter beforehand what to add. Archival research by two French scholars revealed, however, that some ordinary people felt a need to express their opinions about candidates, politicians, and issues while voting in ways that the 1852 voting regulations did not sanction.

The researchers studied voided ballots cast during the 1881 legislative elections, focusing their attention on thirty electoral districts (*circonscriptions*) where relatively complete sets of invalidated ballots have been preserved. In those elections, dominated by competition between republicans and monarchists, some voters penned their own messages:

> Wishing that the son of the lowest peasant might rise to the highest rungs of society by means of education I vote for the citizen ACHILLE AUGER, a proponent of free, obligatory, secular education, and leave aside Mr. PAUL LE ROUX who—by being a partisan of the Ignorantine friars and beggarly monks, vermin feeding on the blood of workers—keeps the people in ignorance. LONG LIVE THE PROGRESSIVE REPUBLIC. (Déloye and Ihl 1991a, 167–68, my translation)

More poetically, another voter added to his ballot (I reproduce here only the first two stanzas):

> Oh powerful and holy republic
> Rush and deliver your children

---

32. This new form of protection was premised on vote secrecy, which was established by law in 1831. This law mandated that each voter receive a blank ballot on which he was to write, in secret, the name of his preferred candidate. The voter was then to fold the ballot and hand it to the polling place president, who would put it into the ballot box (Ferté 1909, 3).

> From the heavy yoke of these monarchists
> Who dream only of debasing you
>
> Hear from the bottom of the ballot box
> The voice of justice
> Rising from the people
> Spreading light and banishing vice
>
> *(163, my translation)*

Other messages were more earthy but equally memorable. "*Merde* to all the deputies" scribbled another voter, "none of them are worth one good pig, however dirty it is. It would do a better job than those damn animals" (165, my translation).[33]

Around 3 percent of all votes nationwide were voided during the 1881 elections, though in some areas of the country the rate of invalidation was over 20 percent (Déloye and Ihl 1991a, 152). In the circonscriptions under study, around 10 percent of all invalidated ballots were voided because of the inclusion of annotations (while others were voided because they were blank, had distinctive tears or markings, or listed more than one choice of candidate) (156). If the same annotation rate held throughout the country, the number of annotated ballots voided nationwide would have been around twenty-two thousand.

We do not know how many voters were aware that they were invalidating their ballots by including their own messages. Circumstantial evidence suggests, however, that some may well have known but cast them as a form of protest. For one, the regulation invalidating extraneous writing had been around for about a generation at the time of the 1881 elections, so voters had had long exposure to the rules. Judging by their messages, furthermore, many of these people were not political neophytes. It is also worth noting that while bureau presidents were forbidden from reading the messages out loud during ballot counting, spectators were allowed to circulate freely and could read them on their own (147). Hence, some voters may have anticipated that their opinions would be made public, if not counted. Whatever the case, a measure designed in the 1850s to protect anonymity unexpectedly caused vote depression in the 1880s.

Conditions for Unintentional Legal Disenfranchisement

Clean election regulations can inadvertently keep people away from the polls in a variety of ways. I have singled out for discussion the triggering of

---

33. Additional ballot notes can be found in Bercé (1969), Déloye and Ihl (1991b), and Garrigou (1992, 42–44).

political distrust, the stirring up of religious anxiety, the infliction of social embarrassment, and the constriction of valid forms of electoral expression, but other means surely exist as well. Like the intentional variants of legal disenfranchisement, these unintentional forms occur when a legal requirement is imposed upon people who differ in their ability or disposition to comply with it. When intentional, legal disenfranchisement is typically a partisan strategy to depress turnout for one's opponents and presupposes accurate information about targeted voters. Unintentional disenfranchisement, in contrast, appears to be occasioned by the absence of such information or (possibly in the case of Malawi) by the failure to act upon it. Under what conditions might we expect to find this absence or failure?

Transformed Electorates. An information deficit can be an artifact of timing. Sometimes an electorate changes in some significant, unanticipated way after regulations are put into effect. In Chicago, the law requiring registrants to state their age dated to 1885, but women did not win the right to vote until 1913.[34] Lawmakers in 1885 thus had no reason to consider issues of gender, age disclosure, and privacy. The law was drafted for a different kind of electorate.

In France, the electorate in 1852, the year provisions invalidating marked ballots were put into effect, was very different from the electorate in 1881 in its level of political awareness and engagement. As the eminent historian Eugen Weber (1982, 359) noted of this earlier period:

> Very roughly, political rivalries among the notables left the populace unengaged (except for local aspects) at least into the 1860s. Even so, one may well ask how much ideology and what Alexis de Tocqueville called "politics properly speaking" entered into the electoral activities of the enfranchised. "Very little, infinitely little," the deputy of Valognes assured his friend, Gustave de Beaumont, in 1842.

Tocqueville himself ([1893] 1987, 95) captured the nature of this disengagement when he described election day, 1848, in his "poor, dear" village of Tocqueville:

> We had to go in a body to vote at the town of Saint-Pierre, a league away from our village. On the morning of election day all the electors, that is to say the whole male population over twenty years old, assembled in front of the church. They formed themselves into a double column in alphabetical order; I preferred to take

---

34. In 1913, Illinois state legislators passed a law giving women the right to vote in presidential and municipal elections only. Unrestricted suffrage did not come until the ratification of the Nineteenth Amendment to the U.S. Constitution in 1920.

the place my name warranted, for I knew that in democratic times and countries one must allow oneself to be put at the head of the people, but must not put oneself there. The crippled and sick who wished to follow us came on pack horses or in carts at the end of this long procession. Only the women and children were left behind. We were in all a hundred and seventy persons. When we got to the top of the hill overlooking Tocqueville, there was a momentary halt; I realized that I was required to speak. I climbed to the other side of a ditch. A circle formed around me, and I said a few words appropriate to the occasion. I reminded these good people of the seriousness and importance of the act they were going to perform; I advised them not to let themselves be accosted or diverted by people who might, when we arrived at the town, seek to deceive them, but rather to march as a united body with each man in his place and to stay that way until they had voted. "Let no one," I said, "go into a house to take food or to dry himself (it was raining that day), before he has performed his duty." They shouted that they would do this, and so they did. All the votes were given at the same time, and I have reason to think that almost all were for the same candidate.

The candidate, to represent the department of La Manche in the newly formed Constituent Assembly, was Tocqueville himself, and he won with 92 percent of the department vote, suggesting that nearly unanimous voting was not confined to his village. With the advent of universal male suffrage, the electorate nation-wide in 1848 mushroomed from less than 250,000 to 8 million. This was, then, the first election for most voters, and the scene of villagers, led by local notables, marching together to the polls as a community was a common one (Guion-net 1996, 570). This was an electorate over which notables, such as Tocqueville himself, wielded enormous influence, whether as a result of deference ("I realized that I was required to speak") or susceptibility to pressure and enticement ("I advised them not to let themselves be accosted or diverted by people who might...seek to deceive them").

The individualization of political opinion began to emerge, according to Weber, only in the 1860s "as factional conflicts were nationalized by a growing awareness of national politics (war, military service, tariff measures) impinging on local life. Beginning in the later 1860s and culminating in 1877, freer (or at least livelier) elections and a greater variety of candidates introduced real competition for the popular vote" (1982, 359). The electorate of 1852 was thus very different from the electorate of 1881. As a result, concern about freedom of the vote in 1852 was largely in the context of liberating the voter from external pressure. Issues of individual expression—so apparent in the voided ballots of 1881—were not yet salient in 1852.

The cases of Chicago and France are historical, but they have contemporary relevance, for they teach us that the danger of inadvertent disenfranchisement increases when the pool of prospective voters changes in some significant way without concomitant procedural adjustments. Today this change might come about in a variety of ways. Economic development might alter the electoral sensibilities of new middle classes, something that occurred in Taiwan and Thailand (Chu 1996; Ockey 1999). The pool can also expand suddenly if the voting age is lowered, as happened in Morocco in 2002. It can also grow rapidly if out-of-country citizens are granted the right to vote, as they were in the Philippines in preparation for elections in 2004.

In the Philippine case, disenfranchisement did in fact take place, largely because of in-person voting and registration requirements imposed by lawmakers. In-person voting and registration were not, to be sure, innovations in the administration of Philippine elections; they were foundational procedures established by the first electoral code promulgated in 1907 after the American conquest of the islands (Villamor 1909, 190–207, 229). The extension of these procedures to overseas voting was not, consequently, an instance of clean election *reform* since no *new* clean election protections were adopted. Nevertheless, this case does add to our understanding of the hidden pitfalls of imposing novel or established clean election measures on newly enfranchised classes of voters and thus warrants brief examination.

When lawmakers extended the vote to overseas Filipinos for the 2004 elections, only 4 percent of an estimated 4.7 million overseas Filipinos went through the trouble of registering. A major inconvenience was the requirement that individuals abroad register and vote in person at designated registration and polling centers. Overseas centers were set up in Philippine embassies, consulates, or other foreign service establishments, often located far from where prospective voters live. Thus a Filipino residing in Lisbon needed to travel twice to the Philippine embassy in Paris (the designated registration and polling site for Filipinos living in France, Monaco, and Portugal)—once to register and then again to cast a ballot. The only exception was for Filipinos living in Japan, Canada, and the United Kingdom, who were allowed to register and vote by mail. In these countries, the mail system and ballot-handling capacity of the Department of Foreign Affairs staff were deemed secure enough to prevent fraud.

Given the highly restrictive nature of registration procedures for most overseas voters, one might ask whether their effective disenfranchisement was, in fact, deliberate. This question is all the more pertinent to the extent that pundits and politicians believe that overseas Filipinos are, as many journalists and politicians put it, "quality voters" likely to support candidates who stand for clean, accountable, transparent government. Senate Majority Leader Loren Legarda expressed this idea, somewhat obliquely, when she told reporters that overseas voters "are the missing middle-class vote in Philippine politics that can change the face of our democracy."[35] One newspaper editorialist laid out the logic of such an expectation:

> The OFWs [overseas foreign workers] and other overseas Flips [Filipinos] are among the most patriotic, upright and well informed. They will vote guided by the high measures of good governance and meritocracy they have seen abroad. They will not choose candidates solely on parochial, tayo-tayo [clannish], kumparehan [crony] considerations. And their votes are not for sale.[36]

Did dirty politicians, then, deliberately sabotage the new law for fear of being voted out of office by upright overseas voters?

Available evidence indicates that they did not. In the first place, reformist politicians popular among the domestic middle classes, who presumably had the most to gain from the enfranchisement of overseas voters, were leading critics of registration and balloting by mail. These advocates of transparency and accountability feared that the law would become, in the words of one senator, "an instrument for cheating."[37] In addition, the law allowed overseas voters to cast ballots only for national candidates (president, vice president, senators, and party-list members of the House of Representatives), while most votes are bought by candidates for local office (mayors, city councilors, governors, district members of the House of Representatives).[38] In other words, those politicians most engaged in clientelist politics were not affected by the overseas vote. In this context it is interesting to note that the Senate version of the bill was much laxer than the House version. While the original Senate bill authorized registration and voting by mail in all countries and allowed immigrants the right to vote, the House bill prohibited both. Thus senators, for whom overseas Filipinos would have the right to vote, wanted an expansive franchise. This alignment of support suggests that the restrictions placed on overseas voters were not part of a deliberate strategy of disenfranchisement cooked up by nervous politicians.

Slow transformations of the electorate (as in France) are harder to detect and respond to than sudden changes brought about by discrete acts of legislation (as

---

35. "Senate Passes Bill on Absentee Voting," *Philippine Daily Inquirer,* October 9, 2002.

36. Rene Q. Bas, "Who's Afraid of the OFW Vote?" *Manila Times,* March 6, 2001.

37. This statement was made by Joker Arroyo, who voted against the bill, "Senate Passes Bill on Absentee Voting." The Senate passed the bill by a vote of 17 to 2, while the House passed it by a vote of 132 to 9.

38. This observation is based on data collected in a survey module I commissioned in 2001. The survey was conducted by Pulse Asia (2001). Data were gathered through face-to-face interviews with 1,200 adult respondents nationwide, using multistage probability sampling for an error margin of +/- 3 percent.

in Chicago and the Philippines). In the former, the information deficit really was an artifact of timing. In the latter, disenfranchisement occurred because lawmakers who enacted the electorate-changing legislation *missed an opportunity* to revise electoral rules accordingly. Why did Illinois and Filipino lawmakers fail to anticipate how the newly enfranchised would respond to the registration requirements already in place? In Illinois, it may have had something to do with novelty. Illinois was, after all, the first state east of the Mississippi to grant women at least partial voting rights. In several western states (California, Kansas, Oregon, and Arizona) women had been voting for only a year or two when Illinois extended the franchise. With only few and distant precedents to observe, perhaps Illinois lawmakers had, at that point, little reason to anticipate such a problem.

The Philippines, in this regard, was different. During legislative debates, there were many concerns raised in and out of Congress about the potential for disenfranchisement if personal appearance were required for registration and voting. Indeed, as already noted, the Senate version of the bill allowed both to be accomplished by mail in all countries.

Nonetheless, members of Congress feared massive cheating by spurious voters and partisan foreign service officials, anticipating that elections abroad would be conducted like elections at home. At the same time, these lawmakers misjudged the lengths to which overseas citizens would go to register and vote. Exalted nationwide as "heroes" for keeping both national economy and individual families afloat with their remittances,[39] overseas Filipinos were expected to make giant efforts to have their opinions counted. This expectation was articulated by the Philippine ambassador to the United States, Albert del Rosario, who told the press: "No matter how distant the voting registration centers may be from their place of work or residence, they should exercise their right to vote and to shape their country's future as a matter of patriotic duty."[40] The very same (myth of?) patriotic devotion that made overseas Filipinos "quality voters," it appears, also led to their disenfranchisement. Legislators simply overestimated the depths of their heroism, patriotism, and pockets. Unlike the information deficit in Chicago, which was seemingly caused by novelty, the one in the Philippines appears to have been a consequence of wishful thinking.

Localized Beliefs or Sensibilities. A transformed electorate is not the only cause of information shortfalls. Lawmakers may also lack adequate knowledge when

39. According the Central Bank of the Philippines, in 2002 overseas Filipinos sent home $7.19 billion (through official channels alone), an amount equaling almost 10 percent of the country's Gross Domestic Product for that year. See www.bsp.gov.ph/statistics/sefi/ofw.htm.

40. "Pinoys in US Ho-hum on Absentee Voting," *Philippine Star,* September 19, 2003.

the beliefs or sensibilities of voters are highly localized. In South Africa, a fear of satanic identity documents appears to have been restricted to a relatively small number of communities. Of course, a belief that bar codes carry the mark of the beast is not unique to Mpumalanga villagers or black South African Pentecostals. White South African urbanites discussed the satanic use of bar codes when their use spread throughout the country in the 1990s (Steyn 2002). Indeed, this belief appears to be but a local manifestation of an urban myth gone global (Mikkelson 2007). What does seem peculiar to Mpumalanga is how villagers acted upon this belief in the realm of elections. In fact, these beliefs were so localized that they were not detected at all by the prereform survey conducted by the HSRC in 1998 to figure out who was likely to possess (or not possess) different forms of identification and why (1998a, 1998b).

Salient sensibilities, it should be noted, can be specific not only to cultural groups but to age cohorts as well. Researchers found that the turnout of elderly voters in the U.S. state of Georgia dropped after the advent of computerized voting in 2002. Comparing turnout immediately before and after the change in equipment, they found that for every 1 percent of a county's population that was elderly, turnout dropped by 0.3 to 0.4 percent. Elderly voters, the researchers hypothesize, were habituated to older technologies of voting and feared computerized voting enough to stay away from the polls (Roseman and Stephenson 2005).

Political and Material Constraints. In South Africa, the HSRC survey did not detect the beliefs that led to the disenfranchisement of Mpumalanga villagers. Malawi, in this respect, differs from South Africa insofar as a prereform study *did* detect voter leeriness in Malawi—indeed, widespread leeriness. Lawmakers and election officials, as a result, presumably knew how voters felt about the innovations they were contemplating. These decision makers were nevertheless unable to act upon these findings, given severe budget constraints. Registration reform and the use of photo identification were pushed strongly by Western donors, whom observers from the Organization of African Unity (1999, 18) described as "dictatorial, patronizing and obtrusive." Since almost half of the cost of the elections was to be covered by these donors, Malawian officials were not in a position to reject those recommendations, which various local political leaders, fearful of fraud, welcomed as well (Butler and Baxter 1998, 25–29; MEC 1999a, 4–8, 24). Compounding these problems was the fact that the European Union and the United Nations Development Fund—which both took responsibility for funding voter identification, registration, and voter education—were slow to disburse the funds because of what they perceived to be managerial incompetence in the Malawi Electoral Commission. The lesson here is that even if lawmakers or election officials know about potential disenfranchisement problems and wish to avoid them, they may lack the political freedom, material means, or administrative capacity to do so.

Other Cases of Legal Disenfranchisement

In this chapter, I have examined cases of legal disenfranchisement for which evidence was most robust and detailed and thus most fruitful for comparison and theorizing. My survey of clean electoral reform during the 1991 to 2006 period uncovered, in addition, two other cases for which evidence was thinner. Even so, they merit brief mention.

In Bolivia, lawmakers tightened identification requirements for voter registration in preparation for the 1993 elections. They removed birth certificates from the list of acceptable forms of identification because this type of document is easily forged and had been used frequently in the past to commit registration fraud. But because birth certificates were (according to news reports at least) the most commonly possessed form of identification, many citizens were apparently disenfranchised as a result. According to the National Electoral Tribunal, roughly 1 million people—around one-third of the voting-age population—were unable to register because they lacked one of the prescribed forms of identification.[41] But this figure is less informative than it might first appear since we do not know how many potential registrants did, in fact, possess birth certificates but not one of the other forms of identification. Furthermore, those analysts who have studied most closely the causes of low participation in Bolivian elections—such as Lazarte (2003), Romero Ballivián (2003), and Madrid (2007, 4–6)—have little to say about the politics behind the new law's adoption. Consequently, I could not draw any firm conclusions about legislative intent.

In Zimbabwe, lawmakers put in place for the 2002 presidential election a requirement that voters present proof, on election day, that they were in fact residents of the particular constituency in which they were registered. Acceptable forms of proof included land title deeds, utility bills, official residency documents, and the like. While this requirement was touted by the government as an effort to enhance election integrity, most observers believed that the real intent was to disenfranchise urban voters. City folk, these observers noted, were less likely than rural dwellers to possess any of the acceptable forms of proof. As

41. "Bolivia: One-Third of Electorate Unable to Vote," Global Information Network, May 3, 1993.

one newspaper report explained, "the great majority of urban people are poor, living in 'illegal structures,' and renting their accommodations. Bills are not in their name."[42] Urban voters, too, were widely expected to turn out heavily for the main opposition candidate, Morgan Tsvangirai. This expectation was confirmed by official election results. Rural voters turned out overwhelmingly for incumbent Robert Mugabe, while a majority of urban voters supported Tsvangirai (SADCPF 2002, 23). On election day there were indeed scattered reports of voters being turned away at the polls because they lacked proof of residency. Still, none of the major observation missions (the Commonwealth Observer Group, the Southern African Development Community Parliamentary Forum, the Norwegian Election Observation Mission, the South Africa Observer Mission, and the Zimbabwean Election Support Network) ventured any estimates about the number of people who were in fact unable to vote. Consequently, we know little about the actual magnitude (or geographic distribution) of disenfranchisement.

Even including Bolivia and Zimbabwe, the incidence of legal disenfranchisement in the 1991 to 2006 data set was relatively uncommon compared with that of administrative exclusion, the subject of the next chapter. (There were seven instances of legal disenfranchisement and twenty-six of administrative exclusion—see table 2 of the appendix.) Still, we cannot make too much of this finding. Because the data set does not constitute a representative sample, the relative infrequency of legal disenfranchisement is not significant in a statistical sense. We thus do not know whether legal disenfranchisement occurs less frequently or is just less frequently brought to light.

Ambiguities of Intentionality

Intentional and unintentional disenfranchisement have different sets of causes. The former is a partisan strategy that targets particular groups of voters and is facilitated when a bloc or party enjoys legislative dominance and can identify segments of the electorate to be kept away from the polls. The latter is an unplanned consequence of clean election legislation and tends to occur when lawmakers lack information to anticipate disenfranchisement or the means to prevent it.

Yet sometimes it is difficult to distinguish clearly intentional from unintentional disenfranchisement. For one thing, unintentional disenfranchisement can result in partisan-looking patterns of vote depression, as we saw in the

42. "Focus on Forced Disenfranchisement," *All Africa,* March 5, 2002.

Philippines, where high obstacles to the electoral participation of most overseas voters were erected. Conversely, lawmakers who craft a legislative strategy of disenfranchisement are not likely to admit it, as we saw in South Africa, and instead typically insist steadfastly that the measures are desperately needed to combat fraud.[43]

Adding to the difficulty of distinguishing intentional from unintentional forms of disenfranchisement is the reality that there are differing degrees of intentionality. A deliberate attempt to channel electoral participation may, for instance, inadvertently result in disenfranchisement. Such was the case in South Dakota more than a century ago, after the secret ballot was adopted in 1891. The legislation providing vote secrecy also mandated that ballots be printed and distributed by the state. In adding that provision, as historian Peter Argersinger (1992, 173) tells it:

> Lawmakers necessarily had to consider other subjects, such as the structure of the ballot, the question of who could be listed on the ballot, and the rules for register-ing nominees, printing ballots, and so forth—all of which heretofore had been left up to the parties. In establishing these procedures, politicians responded to political conditions and manipulated the rules to achieve partisan ends.

In 1893, for instance, the Republican-controlled legislature passed a law re-quiring that "the name of no candidate shall appear more than once on the ballot for the same office." This law was designed to prevent "fusion." Fusion, writes Argersinger, was

> the term applied to the common nineteenth-century practice by which two or more political parties attempted to combine the votes of their followers by naming the same candidates to their tickets. Fusion typically involved a third party cooper-ating with the weaker of the two major parties, in opposition to the stronger major party, in the hope of sharing political influence that would otherwise be denied to both when acting separately. . . . In the Dakotas of the 1890s, fusion usually in-volved the Democratic party and the radical Populist or People's party. (176)

The antifusion law of 1893 thus sought to protect the hegemony of the Repub-licans by making cooperation between Democrats and Populists more difficult.

---

43. Circumstantial evidence, of course, can provide important clues about intentions. When disen-franchisement is intentional, votes for the new law tend to be lopsided and partisan. All or most members of the beneficiary bloc or party vote for it, while all or most of those most likely to suffer vote against it, arguing that it will make it more difficult for their supporters to vote. This occurred in South Africa but not in the Philippines.

Although repealed after the Populists, with support from a subsumed Democratic Party, eked out a victory in the 1896 elections, the antifusion law was reenacted, permanently this time, by the Republicans in 1901 after they swept the 1900 elections. As a result of the new law, Argersinger explains:

> Some Populists returned to the GOP rather than vote under the Democratic name, as Republicans had predicted. Other Populists, especially former Democrats, did move into the Democratic party, but large numbers simply dropped out of politics altogether. Unwilling either to vote as a member of the "corrupt" old parties or to cast a futile vote for a symbolic third party, they were citizens legislated out of the effective electorate. (185)

By enacting and reenacting the antifusion law, Republicans had hoped to force Populists back into Republican fold, something to which they publicly admitted (184). To some extent this came to pass. But the law also had the unintended effect of making other people stop voting altogether. Republicans were probably not displeased that some former Populists no longer went to the polls, but it does appear that this was an outcome that Republicans foresaw. We find in the actions of Republican lawmakers, then, an intermediate degree of deliberateness. They lie somewhere between the poles of intentional and unintentional disenfranchisement. Consequently, "intentional" and "unintentional" might best been seen as two endpoints on a continuum.

Gray zones notwithstanding, many instances of legal disenfranchisement fall at the outer points of the continuum and can be categorized as either intended or unintended. These two forms have distinct sets of causes. Intentional disenfranchisement is a strategy adopted by parties that find themselves in a precarious position of present strength and future vulnerability; unintentional disenfranchisement, in contrast, is an unintended outcome resulting from the unexpected collision of voter sensibilities with new electoral regulations. If intentional disenfranchisement is premised on sound and detailed knowledge of the dispositions of the electorate, unintentional disenfranchisement results instead from the lack of such knowledge, or the inability to act upon it. These differences will be important to bear in mind when, in chapter 6, we consider various safeguards or strategies that might be deployed to prevent vote depression and other forms of iatrogenic harm.

3

Election Officials and Poll Workers

Administrative Exclusion

Clean election laws, as we have seen, sometimes become vehicles of disenfranchisement. But the depressive effect of new clean election measures can crystallize not only at the moment of formulation but also at the stage of implementation. In an effort to clean up elections, lawmakers often legislate new rules with no obvious disenfranchising import. Nevertheless, election officials and poll workers might enforce them unevenly, apply them falteringly, or subvert them altogether in ways that result in vote depression. I have called these various modes of depressive implementation "administrative exclusion" for short.

Administrative exclusion can result from either manipulation (the deliberate bending or subversion of clean election rules) or mismanagement (their inept implementation). In this chapter, I examine each of these two modes. As we shall see, administrative exclusion often occurs when reforms impact voter registration or ballot counting—parts of the electoral process over which election officials typically enjoy discretion and that greatly affect who gets to vote or whose votes get to count.

Manipulation

At the extreme, manipulation entails the deliberate subversion of new clean election procedures in a partisan attempt to keep a select group of voters away from the polls or to keep their votes from counting. This most blatant form of manipulation involves the outright contravention of lawful procedures. It is, as a result, unlikely to have a wide impact in countries where the rule of law prevails, since open contravention of the law usually attracts public attention and demands swift remedy.

When South African government agents attempted to subvert new registration procedures in 1998, for instance, the scheme was quickly quashed. The agents in question were Department of Home Affairs employees. They operated mobile units deployed to process new identification document applications in preparation for the upcoming 1999 elections.[1] While many units performed their duties with a high level of professionalism, one unit servicing Queenstown in the Eastern Cape province began to separate the applications of government supporters from those of opposition supporters and to process them differently. Opposition applicants reportedly did not receive receipts, and without receipts they would not be able to register. New National Party leaders soon caught wind of what was taking place. When they went public, the Department of Home Affairs took fast action to put an end to the practice.[2] Open transgression, as this example shows, runs a high risk of exposure. Consequently, manipulation usually assumes more subtle forms that are more difficult to detect or remedy at election time and are thus more likely to have an impact on electoral outcomes. I turn now to two such cases: the overzealous purge of the voter rolls in Florida and the hyperstrict invalidation of ballots in Quebec. Afterward, I explore the shared conditions that gave rise to administrative exclusion in these two places.

THE PURGING OF THE VOTER ROLLS IN FLORIDA

One instructive case of deliberate but subtle manipulation occurred in Florida, where overzealous election officials removed eligible voters from the voter rolls prior to the 2000 elections. It all began when incumbent Miami mayor Joe Carollo was forced into a runoff with former mayor Xavier Suarez in the 1997 mayoral election.

Between the general election and the runoff, news broke of a Florida Department of Law Enforcement sting operation: a Suarez campaign worker was arrested for buying from undercover agents the absentee ballots of three dead voters. The probe widened. Days before the runoff agents found in the house of one campaign volunteer one hundred absentee ballots, twenty-one voter

---

1. As discussed in chapter 2, the South African government in 1998 began requiring every citizen to present a bar-coded ID when registering to vote, a form of identification that many people did not possess.

2. "Nash waarsku oor kieserregistrasie," *Die Burger,* November 4, 1998.

registration cards, and fifty blank applications for absentee ballots. Details emerged of a well-orchestrated absentee ballot fraud scheme in District 3, a part of Little Havana. At the center were campaign workers and volunteers for Commissioner Humberto Hernandez, a backer of Suarez. These "vote brokers" bought absentee ballots for about ten dollars each, procured and voted with the absentee ballots of deceased voters, and induced a number of out-of-city residents to fraudulently register to vote in the district.

Carollo contested the general election results in court, arguing that he should have been declared the outright winner since he had won a majority if the absentee ballots were excluded from the count. During hearings, a documents expert testified that there were at least 225 illegal absentee ballots cast. An FBI agent found that 113 absentee voters had used false addresses. Another expert produced evidence that more than 480 ballots had been procured or witnessed by only 29 vote brokers. In March 1998, the judge voided the election results, and ordered a new election. An appeals court later amended this decision and installed Carollo as mayor.

As the legal drama played out, journalists from the *Miami Herald* conducted their own investigation. In February 1998, the paper published an article, which would later win it a Pulitzer Prize, on illegal voting by felons. Felons, under Florida law at that time, did not have the right to vote until they completed their prison term, as well as their parole or probation, and then successfully petitioned the clemency board to restore their civil rights. Among the findings of the investigative report: 105 ineligible felons voted in the 1997 Miami mayoral election, while 2,800 ineligible felons were on the voter rolls of Miami-Dade County.[3]

In the first months of 1998, the Republican-controlled Florida state legislature began work on a package of anti-vote-fraud measures to prevent a Miami-like scandal from happening again. Among the provisions were tightened absentee ballot rules and mechanisms to eliminate from the voter rolls dead people and felons who had not had their civil rights restored.

Opposition to the bill came mostly from lawmakers (and the State Association of Supervisors of Elections) who thought that loopholes in the absentee ballot regulations would allow vote brokers to continue to operate. Black legislators were also disproportionately against the bill. Three of five black senators declined to support it, as did fourteen of fifteen members of the House Black Caucus. The main concern they voiced in floor debates was that tightened absentee ballot rules would make it more difficult for elderly (presumably

---

3. "Felons Vote, Too—But It's a Crime," *Miami Herald,* February 15, 1998.

minority) Floridians to vote. Nobody, in either committee or floor debates, raised questions about the cleansing of the voter rolls.

In April 1998, both houses of the Republican-controlled Florida state legislature voted in favor of the bill. It received strong bipartisan support in the senate, garnering the votes of nineteen out of twenty-four Republicans, and eleven of the sixteen Democrats. In the house, almost all Republicans voted for it (fifty-eight of sixty-six), along with almost a third of the Democrats (fifteen of fifty-four). The antifraud package became law in May 1998.

A few months later, the U.S. Justice Department blocked Florida from implementing the new absentee ballot rules (but not the purge of ineligible voters). Minorities, the department pointed out, make disproportionate use of absentee ballots since they are more likely to have trouble getting time off from work to vote or finding transportation to get to the polling place. The new restrictions would thus prevent more blacks and Hispanics than whites from voting.

In Florida, the secretary of state, an elected official, is charged with overseeing the administration of elections. In 1994, Republican Sandra Mortham had been elected to that post and had come out strongly in favor of tightened voting rules. "It's a sad state of affairs," she said, "when it's easier to get a voter's card than it is to get a card from Blockbuster's."[4] Indeed, her office had helped craft the election reform package passed by the legislature. After the law's adoption, she was bitterly disappointed when the federal government put the absentee ballot restrictions on hold. "When the next dead man votes here in the State of Florida," she told reporters, "it's at the courtesy of the U.S. Department of Justice."[5]

With the absentee ballots rules in limbo, Mortham implemented the part of the law that she could—namely, the purging of the voter rolls. The new law authorized the Florida Department of State's Division of Elections to create a central voter file and to contract with a private company to cross-check the names in this file against names in databases containing criminal records, records of deceased persons, and other information. The Division of Elections was required to distribute the resulting list of names to county election supervisors, who were charged with verifying the information and using it to purge the voter rolls. By August 1998, a Tallahassee firm ran the first cross-check and found that more than fifty thousand felons were illegally registered to vote, or so it appeared. The list contained so many errors that Division of Elections

---

4. "Voter Registration Crackdown Proposed," *Florida Times-Union*, April 3, 1998.
5. "U.S. Justice Department Delays Florida Vote-Fraud Laws," *Tallahassee Democrat*, August 11, 1998.

director Ethel Baxter issued a series of memoranda to all county supervisors instructing them to allow a listed person to vote if there was "reasonable doubt" about the accuracy of the information (CCR 2001, 68). The list was soon scrapped, and in November Baxter hired a different contractor, Database Technologies (DBT), to prepare a new one.

In January 1999, Republican Jeb Bush assumed the post of governor, and Republican Katherine Harris took over as secretary of state, both having won the November election. Soon after, DBT produced a new list of 42,322 names. While DBT executives voiced concerns about the high number of false positives likely contained in the list, Division of Election officials in the new administration pressed for looser search parameters in future checks. Thus while the company recommended that first and middle names match in the right order, state officials decided that the two names could occur in either order so that, say, a Floridian named Betty Sue would match a felon named Sue Betty. The company also recommended that last names match exactly, but state officials decided instead to require only a 90 percent match. As a Division of Elections official wrote at that time in a memo to DBT, "obviously, we want to capture more names that possibly aren't matches and let the supervisors make a final determination rather than exclude certain matches altogether" (quoted in CCR 2001, 62).

When state officials discovered in the spring of 1999 that DBT had databases of felony convictions in other states, they requested the company to expand the search to include out-of-state felons as well. In dealing with felons from states that automatically restore civil rights, the Division of Elections instructed DBT to verify the person's status with the other state's executive board of clemency. Felons from states with no executive board of clemency, Division of Elections officials decided, should be required to apply for clemency in Florida to have their voting rights restored (CCR 2001, 64–66).[6]

This policy led to the exclusion of felons from Ohio, Texas, Illinois, and other states (Stuart 2004, 471–72). The policy also ran counter to Florida law. An ex post facto investigation by the United States Commission on Civil Rights (CCR 2001, 65) concluded that Division of Election officials failed to

---

6. Not incidentally, the clemency process in Florida at that time was expensive and difficult. The state had the largest backlog of cases in the nation: some 50,000 people were put on waiting lists for two to three years. To be successful, applicants often had to request hearings, which could cost up to $10,000. Thus in 2000, Florida granted clemency to only 1,832 felons, about 1 out of every 300 in the state (Thompson 2001; CCR 2001, 66–67; CCR 2002). In 2003, a court ordered the state to help with the clemency applications of nearly 125,000 felons who did not receive proper guidance when released from incarceration. In 2006, newly elected governor Charlie Crist ushered in new rules that automatically restored the civil rights of nonviolent offenders who owed no restitution payments and had no pending criminal charges, a category into which roughly 80 percent of felons fell.

[a]ssess the interpretation of comparable statutes that require Florida's acceptance of a sister state's restoration of civil rights conferred upon a convicted felon. Although the issue of voting rights was not specifically addressed, two Florida courts of appeal have ruled that if an individual enters Florida with his or her civil rights, then through the full faith and credit clause of the U.S. Constitution, he or she need not apply for clemency upon arriving in Florida.

The Division of the Elections had, in other words, no right to require that citizens request the restoration of rights they already possessed. There were, however, compelling partisan motives for the Republican-controlled Florida Department of State to keep out-of-state (and Floridian) felons off the voter rolls. Nationwide, felons are disproportionately black (the felony conviction rate for black men is seven times higher than that of white men), and blacks are likely to vote overwhelmingly Democratic. Indeed, in 2000, nine out of ten black voters in both Florida and the country as a whole turned out for the Democratic presidential candidate, Al Gore (Bositis 2000).[7]

While no Florida officials ever admitted publicly that the overextension of the purge was motivated by partisanship, the evidence points strongly in that direction. Perhaps most revealing is the fact that DBT employees had discussed with state officials in late 1997 or early 1998 a specific flaw in the matching procedures, a flaw that caused Hispanics—who tend to vote Republican in Florida—to be systematically omitted from the purge lists. This flaw resulted from an incongruity between the voter registration database and the database of Florida felons. Because the felon database contained no Hispanic category while the voter registration database did (voter registration forms asked for such information), the records of people who had identified themselves as Hispanic when registering to vote did not match any felon database records. Thus anyone who self-identified as Hispanic when registering was not included on the purge lists. DBT and state officials became aware of this problem and analyzed one of the resulting lists together. In the words of a company spokesperson, "we determined jointly that it was not reliable."[8] But state officials took no action to correct the flaw. Despite their eagerness to expand other match parameters, they chose not to loosen this one. It is worth noting, in this context, that according to the Division of Elections official most directly involved in the management

---

7. It was perhaps for this reason that the Republican-controlled legislature was averse to granting voting rights to felons. In 1997, a member of the Black Caucus introduced a bill in the Florida House of Representatives to automatically restore the voting rights of felons once they complete their sentences. It died in committee three days after the House voted in favor of the anti-vote-fraud package.

8. "State Knew of Felon-list Flaw," *Sarasota Herald-Tribune,* July 20, 2004.

of the purge lists, it was Secretary of State Katherine Harris—who was also a high-ranking Republican Party official and cochair of the state Bush for President campaign—who approved the selective loosening of those search parameters (Lantigua 2001). Because the purge was extended with such deliberate selectiveness despite the concerns raised by DBT contractors, and because it was a partisan official who approved the match parameters, I am led to conclude that the purge was intentionally molded to maximize impact on likely (black) Democratic voters but leave likely (Hispanic) Republican voters untouched.

Not surprisingly, pinpointing the number of wrongly purged voters has become a contentious partisan issue. On one extreme, some liberals put the number in the tens of thousands (see, for instance, Raskin 2005, 15). On the other extreme, a conservative journalist maintained that "no one has yet identified a single eligible voter who was actually and finally kept from voting by the purge" (Carney 2001). Perhaps the most judicious analysis to date was conducted by the *Palm Beach Post.* It put the number at a little over 1,100: 108 wrongly identified nonfelons, plus 996 out-of-state felons who should have been allowed to vote.[9] It is also noteworthy that the purge left an even greater number of ineligible felons on the voter rolls, largely because some twenty of sixty-seven county election supervisors refused to use the error-plagued purge lists. About 5,600 of these ineligible felons voted in 2000.[10] The raw numbers may not appear large, but they were enough to potentially alter the outcome of an ever-so-tight presidential race, won in the state by a margin of only 537 votes.

While much of the responsibility for the exclusion of eligible voters lies squarely on the shoulders of election officials who implemented the new anti-vote-fraud law, that exclusion was facilitated by lawmakers. The law, after all, placed the burden on county supervisors to determine whether any eligible voters were incorrectly included on the list:

> If the supervisor *does not* determine that the information provided by the division is *incorrect,* the supervisor must remove from the registration books by the next subsequent election the name of any person who is deceased, convicted of a felony, or adjudicated mentally incapacitated with respect to voting. (Fla. Stat. ch. 98.0975{4}[1999], emphasis added)

Underfunded county supervisors simply did not have the capacity to do what the law required, especially given the large number or names and false positives contained in the list. For this reason, supervisors in some twenty counties ended

---

9. "Felon Purge Sacrificed Innocent Voters," *Palm Beach Post,* May 27, 2001.

10. "Thousands of Felons Voted Despite the Purge," *Palm Beach Post,* May 28, 2001; Stuart (2004, 461–62).

up ignoring the list, but supervisors in more than forty other counties did not. Eligible voters who were wrongfully placed on the list in one of these forty or so counties and failed to appeal were removed.[11]

Whatever latent defects the law contained, the secretary of state and the director of the Division of Elections still had broad authority under Florida law to anticipate or redress problems of electoral administration. Katherine Harris and Clay Roberts (who succeeded Ethel Baxter in October 1999 as Division of Elections director) could have, among other things, not circumvented Florida law regarding the voting rights of out-of-state felons. They could also have given narrower search criteria to DBT or at a minimum disseminated the purposively overinclusive purge lists in a more cautious manner. As the CCR (2001, 40) noted:

> An example of what could have been done to attempt to ensure that all legal voters would be permitted to vote is illustrated by the actions of the previous secretary of state [Sandra Mortham] and director of the Division of Elections [Ethel Baxter]. When confronted with inaccuracies in the voter purge lists being prepared by a private contractor that were used by some county supervisors of elections to remove voters, the then director of the Division of Elections in a memorandum to all supervisors of elections said, "In short, if there is a reasonable doubt as to the accuracy of the information, you should allow a person to vote...." Despite continuing problems with the accuracy of these lists, there is no evidence of any comparable attempt made by the secretary of state or the director of the Division of Elections during the 2000 presidential election to ensure that supervisors of elections were aware of continuing problems with these lists and to permit individuals to vote if there were reasonable doubts as to the accuracy of the information on the lists.

Election officials, not lawmakers, were most heavily and directly responsible for the wrongful purging of eligible voters.

Within a year of the 2000 election, state lawmakers passed legislation to reform the purge process. The new law mandated that the state no longer contract out the task of matching names to private companies and placed the burden instead on county election supervisors. Supervisors, under the new law, were also required to verify that a voter was ineligible before removing his or her name form the voter rolls (whereas before they were required to remove anyone whose *eligibility* they could not verify). The CCR was left unimpressed by these changes. In its assessment, "the same sweeping efforts to identify former

---

11. CCR (2001, 43); "Thousands of Felons Voted"; Stuart (2004, 461–62).

felons that wrongfully purged eligible voters from the central voter file can be repeated" (2002). After the NAACP and other civil rights groups filed a federal voting rights lawsuit, the state made additional changes. As part of a settlement reached in 2002 it agreed to restore the names of people who had been improperly purged and to apply more stringent search criteria for the purge lists.

THE INVALIDATION OF BALLOTS IN QUEBEC

Manipulation does not always require the knowing participation of election administrators, as odd as that may sound. During the counting of ballots in the 1995 Quebec sovereignty referendum, poll workers unwittingly participated in a strategy of manipulation devised by partisan operatives.

The referendum was to decide the constitutional future of Quebec. Support for separation from Canada came largely from portions of the Francophone community, while support for the federal union was strongest among ethnic minorities (i.e., English speakers and other non-Francophones). In the end, the federalists won, though by a slim margin of 54,288 votes, only 1 percent of the vote total.

Election returns showed an unusually high number of rejected ballots in three electoral districts (called "ridings" in Canada). In the riding of Chomedey, 11.6 percent of the ballots were rejected, in Marguerite-Bourgeoys 5.5 percent, and in Laurier-Dorion 3.6 percent. Excluding these three ridings, the average rate of rejection for the rest of Quebec was less than 1.7 percent. In 1992, when a similar sovereignty question was voted upon, the rejection rate for Chomedey was only 1.5 percent, and for Marguerite-Bourgeoys it was merely 1.4 percent (Laurier-Dorion did not yet exist).

Suspicion of foul play was aroused since support for continued union with Canada was most concentrated in ethnic minority communities, and the ridings of Chomedey (located in the city of Laval), Marguerite-Bourgeoys (in the city of LaSalle), and Laurier-Dorion (in the city of Montreal) all had high concentrations of non-French speakers. A disproportionate share of rejected ballots, furthermore, came from ethnic minority enclaves within these ridings. In Laurier-Dorion, for instance, 49 percent of the rejected ballots came from just 56 polling stations in Park Extension, a strongly federalist ethnic enclave (the riding had a total of 197 polling stations). Ballot rejection rates in certain polling stations within the three ridings were stunningly high, reaching more than 50 percent.[12]

---

12. "Yes-Side Organizer Known for Hard Line," *Gazette* (Montreal), November 25, 1995; DGEQ (1996, 29–38).

In Quebec, ballots are counted (or determined to be invalid and thus rejected) by the deputy returning officer presiding in each polling station. There is also a poll clerk whose duty it is to "assist" the deputy returning officer. For regular elections, the deputy returning officer is appointed on the recommendation of the leading party in each riding, while the poll clerk is appointed on the recommendation of the second-placed party. In the case of a referendum, the deputy returning officer is appointed on the recommendation of the official delegate of the national committee that has the greatest number of members in the provincial assembly (called the National Assembly of Quebec, or NAQ for short). The poll clerk, in turn, is appointed on the recommendation of the official delegate of the national committee that has the second greatest number of members in the NAQ. Thus in the 1995 referendum it was the prosovereignty Yes National Committee, dominated by the governing Parti Québécois, that recommended individuals for appointment as deputy returning officers, while the federalist Committee of Quebecers for the NO, led by the Quebec Liberal Party, recommended individuals for appointment as poll clerks.

This party-based method of appointing polling station officials dates to 1936 (Bernard and Laforte 1969, 148). It was among the first pieces of legislation passed into law by the new administration of Quebec Prime Minister Maurice Duplessis. Duplessis was head of a newly formed party, the Union Nationale, which won the election of 1936 and put an end to thirty-nine years of Liberal Party rule.

Prior to 1936, poll workers often manipulated electoral procedures to favor the party in power. They would give voters known to be opposition supporters quill pens with slow-drying ink. When the voter folded the ballot, the still wet ink would make a second "x" on the ballot, thereby annulling it. Other forms of fraud, from voter impersonation to intimidation to ballot box theft, were also committed with the complicity of poll workers (Hamelin and Hamelin 1962, 96–97; Quinn 1979, 64).

The motive for the 1936 reform was, in the words of Duplessis himself, to assure "the impartiality of election officials" (Debates of the Legislative Assembly, October 22, 1936). While certain provisions of the new election bill were debated fiercely, the section on appointing polling station officials was passed without comment by either Union Nationale or Liberal Party legislators. At a time when neither party could predict its electoral future (indeed the Union Nationale would lose the next election, in 1939, only to regain power again in 1944), deputies from both parties may have found bipartisanship at the polling station, and the impartiality it promised, to be reassuring and uncontroversial.

By the 1950s, as the Union Nationale consolidated its hold on power, expectations of impartiality eroded. Deputy returning officers presiding in strongly

Liberal ridings would intentionally invalidate ballots by initialing them improperly, while in ridings supportive of the Union Nationale, ballot boxes were stuffed with ballots properly initialed (Quinn 1979, 149–50). The presence of poll clerks named by the Liberal Party did little to prevent these abuses. As one historian explained:

> Many of these [Liberal] representatives were housewives and other political amateurs whose main concern was making a few extra dollars for the day. They had no knowledge of the detailed procedures and technical aspects of an election and were easily hoodwinked and intimidated by the deputy returning officer in charge of the poll. Some of these representatives, for instance, were easily lured away on the pretext that they were needed immediately at Liberal headquarters. (Quinn 1979, 150)

Given these types of abuses, reform-minded election specialists called for changes in how polling station officials were appointed (see, for instance, Boily 1970, 86–87).

In later decades, and after the demise of the Union Nationale, the overt partisanship of poll workers seems to have declined. But well into the 1990s, many deputy returning officers were, like the Liberal poll clerks of the 1950s, political amateurs. Take the example of Mathieu Lefebvre, the deputy returning officer for a Chomedey polling district who rejected 53 percent of the ballots cast in the 1995 referendum. Lefebvre, eighteen years old, had no prior experience as a poll official, did not belong to any political party, and took the job only to earn some extra cash.[13]

This inexperience proved key to the manipulation strategy devised by local Yes National Committee officials for the 1995 referendum. In preparation for the referendum vote, deputy returning officers received training from local representatives of both the Yes National Committee and the chief electoral officer. While chief electoral officer trainers directed all deputy returning officers to exercise good judgment in accepting ballots with any markings accepted by law (x, cross, check, or dash), Yes National Committee trainers in Chomedey, Marguerite-Bourgeoys, and Laurier-Dorion (and in a few other ethnic enclaves, but not elsewhere) gave new and more detailed instructions about various markings that, they said, "had" to be rejected.

Detailed ballot rejection rules are, in themselves, necessary for vote integrity. A fair and accurate tallying of votes is premised, after all, on correctly discerning voter intent and applying consistent rules in ambiguous cases. Such rules

---

13. "First 1995 Vote Fraud Case Ends in Acquittal," *Gazette* (Montreal), November 5, 1997.

are also needed to thwart voter intimidation and vote buying. Idiosyncratically marked ballots, after all, can be used to identify the voters who cast them. And the new rejection instructions disseminated by the local Yes officials were, if anything, detailed. Included with them were some one to two hundred photocopied examples of ballots that, the trainers asserted, had been rejected by a Quebec judge named Roland Robillard during a judicial recount requested by a losing candidate in the electoral division of Vimont following the 1994 provincial election.

There were, however, two problems with the actions of the Yes National Committee trainers. First, they gave these new, stricter instructions only to deputy returning officers serving in non-Francophone ridings. Second, their representation of what had happened in the Vimont case was false. Robillard had never rejected any ballots or rendered any legal decision, since the losing candidate had dropped his challenge. Furthermore, when, after the referendum vote, Robillard was shown the photocopied markings distributed by the Yes National Committee, he stated that in his judgment many were in fact perfectly valid.[14]

As a result of a subsequent investigation conducted by the chief electoral officer, prosecutors filed charges of fraud against twenty-eight deputy returning officers and charges of aiding and abetting against two Yes National Committee trainers. Only two deputy returning officers actually stood trial, and both were acquitted on the grounds that they were only following in good faith the instructions given to them by Yes National Committee trainers and thus did not intend to commit fraud. Ultimately, the chief electoral officer withdrew all charges against the remaining defendants since it was impossible to demonstrate that the deputy returning officers had fraudulent intentions, and since nobody was found guilty of fraud, there was no foundation in law to charge the trainers with aiding and abetting.

The high ballot rejection rate in ethnic, profederalist enclaves did not alter the outcome of the 1995 referendum, since the separatist option was rejected. Nevertheless, the narrow victory of the federalists and the shady circumstances surrounding the vote count left the issue of sovereignty unsettled and the legitimacy of the electoral system tarnished. Years after the referendum vote, federalist lawyers were still pressing in court to have all 86,501 rejected ballots released for public inspection. They suspected fraud was more widespread and had higher level authorization than revealed by the limited investigation of the chief electoral officer.[15]

14. "Scrutineers Say They Were Misled by Yes-Side," *Gazette* (Montreal), November 11, 1995; "Yes-Side Organizer Known for Hard Line"; DGEQ (1996, 31).

15. "Our Right to Transparent Democracy," *Gazette* (Montreal), August 5, 2000.

CONDITIONS FOR MANIPULATION

There were several factors that combined to make manipulation an appealing and feasible strategy in both Florida and Quebec. First, a close and high-stakes vote in both places provided a motive for partisans to use aggressive tactics. There were surely partisan motives to vigorously seek out and remove ineligible Democratic voters from the voter rolls in Florida with the prospects of a tight election in this battleground state. In Quebec, the hot-button issue of sovereignty made the 1995 referendum a defining moment for the province.

In addition, partisans in both places held positions that allowed them to influence who could vote or whose vote would count. It was Republican control of the Florida Department of State that made an excessively enthusiastic purge possible, and it was Katherine Harris—cochair of the state Bush for President campaign—who approved the selective loosening of the search parameters.

In Quebec, parties played a central role in appointing and training poll workers. The fact that it was a *referendum* vote further increased the opportunity for partisan meddling, since the Referendum Act gave the Yes National Committee the authority to recommend deputy returning officers for each polling station in the whole province. In elections (as opposed to referenda), the winning candidate in each riding recommends a deputy returning officer for that riding only. Thus in both the 1994 and 1998 elections, members of the Liberal Party recommended deputy returning officers in Chomedey and Marguerite-Bourgeoys. This difference between provincewide referendum appointments and ridingwide election appointments helps to explain why the administrative exclusion of Anglophone and allophone voters in these ridings appeared during a referendum vote and not during a regular election. Only during a referendum vote could the Parti Québécois recommend deputy returning officers to serve in ridings where the Liberal Party prevailed. It also helps explain why significant reports of administrative manipulation have not surfaced at the federal level, in Ontario or in Prince Edward Island, where similar riding-level methods of partisan appointment are employed.

Finally, partisans in both Quebec and Florida were able to single out opposition voters for differential treatment. In Florida, it was easy to identify a group of voters likely to turn out against Republican candidates: felons, who are disproportionately black and Democratic. In Quebec it was simple for prosovereignty partisans to pick out federalist ridings for hyperstrict ballot invalidation. Not only were the locations of ethnic enclaves well known, but a sovereignty referendum had been held only three years earlier, in 1992. Yes National Committee members could figure out precisely how people in each polling subdivision were likely to vote again. Chomedey, Marguerite-Bourgeoys, and Laurier (a part of which would be incorporated into the new riding of Laurier-Dorion for the 1995 vote) were among only 17 of 125 ridings that had a 60 percent or more federalist vote. Polls leading up to the 1995 referendum confirmed these preferences. Eighty-five to 90 percent of Anglophone and allophone voters reported that they would vote against sovereignty.

There were, then, at least three factors that made manipulation a desirable and viable strategy: a close and high-stakes election, partisan involvement in the administration of elections, and the ability of partisans to identify opposition supporters for differential treatment.

Mismanagement

Sometimes administrative exclusion is the result of deliberate manipulation. At other times, however, it can be a simple consequence of mismanagement. I examine two instructive cases of mismanagement in this section: the faulty implementation of new voter registration procedures in the Philippines and the botched automation of vote counting, tabulation, and results transmission in Venezuela. I then investigate the shared conditions that gave rise to mismanagement in these two countries.

REGISTRATION REFORM IN THE PHILIPPINES

The Philippines adopted new procedures for voter registration in 1996. Unfortunately, the failure of the Commission on Elections (COMELEC) to inform voters of the new procedures and corresponding deadlines resulted, in the run-up to the 2001 elections, in the unintended administrative exclusion of up to an estimated 3 to 6 million people.

From 1984 until the 1996 reform, registration was done on a "periodic" basis. Under this system, a nationwide general registration was held (in 1984 and then again in 1986) to establish a permanent voters' list. Thereafter, one or two Saturdays were set aside, several weeks before each regular election, to register newly qualified voters or anyone else who had not yet registered. This type of registration proved vulnerable to fraud. Election officials did not have the time or resources to weed out spurious registrants given the large volume of people who showed up during the one or two days set aside for each periodic registration. The magnitude of this fraud became apparent in 1995, when investigations following a vote padding scandal revealed that there were an estimated 2 million invalid entries in the voter registry (CSER 1995, 17). Alarmed legislators soon went to work devising a new, more fraudproof, system of registration.

The product of that work was the Continuous Voter Registration Act of 1996. Among its main provisions was the cancellation of the existent voters' list, the authorization of COMELEC to conduct a new general registration in June 1997, and the establishment of a continuing system of registration based upon the 1997 voters' list. Under this system, newly qualified voters and others who had not yet registered would submit their applications during any regular business day, though no registration would be conducted during the period starting 120 days before each regular election. A board of registration officials would hold quarterly hearings to review the applications.

The promise of continuous registration was, foremost, to enhance the ability of COMELEC officials to detect and deter fraudulent registration. As Ernesto Maceda, sponsor of the Senate bill, explained during the floor debate:

> Under the [periodic] system... usually we only have the one-day registration. As they would put it in ordinary language, in the *gulo-gulo* [tumult] of the seven hours election process when jeepney loads and truck-loads of voters descend on the precincts to register, it is harder to monitor and manage the registration. While if we have it year-round and people do not have to rush, then it is more manageable. (Record of the Senate, October 23, 1995, p. 296)

Not only would continuous registration make it easier to assess the validity of individual applications, it would also make it possible to analyze registration growth rates to spot unusual spikes or drops that might indicate large-scale fraud (Borra 2001).

Another antifraud measure built into the new system of continuous registration was precinct mapping. The old system assigned registered voters to precincts alphabetically by last name. This assignment method facilitated fraud since, among other things, it grouped together voters from a wide geographic area. Voters were, as a result, often unknown to one another and to poll watchers. Grouping voters together in precincts defined by compact territory and mapping out the boundaries of each precinct would make it possible on election day, as one advocate explained, "to detect easily who is not a resident of the specific precinct" (Tancangco n.d., 18).

Continuous registration also promised to make it more convenient to register, especially for people who might have otherwise missed the opportunity because they were out of town during the one or two designated days. Sponsors of the legislation believed that provincial students studying in Manila or other urban centers would benefit in particular from the new system. For this reason, the principal sponsor of the House bill, Representative Emigdio Tanjuatco, Jr., argued that the new legislation would "minimiz[e] the disenfranchisement of qualified voters" (House of Representatives, Transcript of Session Proceedings, March 19, 1996).

The bill passed unanimously in the Senate and received only one vote against it in the House, and it was quickly signed into law by President Ramos in June 1996. The new general registration was held, as planned, a year later. The 1998 election followed soon after.

The first real test of the new continuous system came in the run-up to the next election in 2001. COMELEC set December 27, 2000 as the last day of registration prior to the May 14, 2001 elections. Yet despite having a budget of 8 million pesos, the Education and Information Department of COMELEC failed to mount a campaign to inform the public of this deadline or about the new system of registration. There were no posters, no press releases, no print, radio, or television ads. As one columnist fumed: "[T]he Comelec slept on the job. The media should have been flooded with Comelec announcements and advisories that such dates or periods were for the youth to register.... Ample time should have been given. But none came."[16]

Estimates vary of the exact number of people who might have registered had they known of the deadline.[17] COMELEC officials used past registration rates to determine that 3 million eligible voters—2.4 million people aged eighteen to twenty-one plus six hundred thousand people from other age groups—failed to register before the December 27, 2000 deadline. Statisticians at the National Statistics Office (NSO) used census data to peg the number of eighteen- to twenty-one-year-old Filipinos at up to 6 million, of whom only 282,482 reportedly registered. To the 5.7 million eighteen- to twenty-one-year-olds who did not register must be added those older people who also did not register, a number the NSO did not try to calculate. Thus somewhere between 3 million and 6 million people were eligible to register and did not—a substantial proportion of the potential electorate, considering that the total number of registered voters for the 2001 elections was only around 37 million.[18]

---

16. Teodoro C. Benigno, "The Youth Must Vote," *Philippine Star,* March 9, 2001.

17. It is even difficult to get a fix on the number of voters who did register. For the 2001 elections, the Election and Barangay Affairs Division of COMELEC recorded 36,611,362 registered voters, the Records and Statistics Division of COMELEC listed 36,605,346, while the National Board of Canvassers initially reported 37,142,294 and then revised it down to 36,491,794.

18. "Youth Groups to Rally Today for Right to Vote," *Philippine Daily Inquirer,* March 7, 2001; "Comelec Assures Congress: Special Registration Possible," *Philippine Daily Inquirer,* March 20, 2001; "Senate Debate on New Voter Registration Stalled," *Philippine Daily Inquirer,* March 21, 2001.

The failure of COMELEC to mount a public education campaign was due largely to a lack of foresight. The person most heavily responsible for this failure was a new COMELEC commissioner named Luzviminda Tancangco. COMELEC is an independent constitutional body directed by seven commissioners appointed by the president of the Philippines. A few months after being elected president in 1998, Joseph Estrada chose Tancangco to take the place of a commissioner whose term had just expired. Tancangco was a University of the Philippines professor of public administration already well known in government and academic circles as the author of a dubious study on electoral fraud. Her most widely publicized, and questionable, finding was that the National Citizens' Movement for Free Elections (NAMFREL)—a nongovernmental poll-watching group lauded for its roll in exposing electoral cheating by the Marcos regime— was complicit in electoral fraud in the post-Marcos era. So much controversy was stirred by this assertion that the president of the University of the Philippines took the unusual step of organizing a public symposium to evaluate the quality of her scholarship. During peer review, colleagues and outside experts alike made biting critiques of her methods and assumptions ("Tancangco Report" 1991).

However unimpressive her academic achievements, Tancangco was nevertheless well connected. Her mentor was Raul de Guzman, the dean of the University of the Philippines College of Public Administration, who also happened to be the brother-in-law of President Estrada. On de Guzman's recommendation, the president appointed her.

Tancangco brought to her new job a deeply held conviction that the 1997 general registration had not been conducted properly. Congress had not released enough money for COMELEC to conduct any precinct mapping, which was to her the bedrock of meaningful registration reform.[19] She thus believed that the existent voters' list was, in all likelihood, still bloated with fraudulent registrants (Tancangco n.d.; COMELEC 1999).

With the behind-the-scenes backing of President Estrada, the neophyte Tancangco wielded considerable influence within COMELEC (Demetriou 2001). Soon after taking office, she launched a project to verify the new voters' list through a nationwide house-to-house enumeration and to reassign voters to territorially based precincts delineated on newly drawn-up maps as the Continuous Voter Registration Act mandated. The goal was to conduct the house visits in April and May 2000 so that a new, verified list of registered voters, along with a list of prospective applicants, could be prepared for the 2001 elections (COMELEC 2000).

---

19. Indeed, Tancangco was the author of these provisions as a legislative aide to Senator Miriam Santiago, who introduced the precinct mapping provisions into the voter registration bill as amendments.

To the extent that Tancangco and her allies anticipated that house-to-house visits would be conducted nationwide, mounting a mass media education campaign on the continuous registration deadlines seemed to them a low priority and perhaps even undesirable. People who were truly qualified to register, after all, would be identified and informed during house-to-house enumeration or by local field officers. Sending out mass appeals to register over the airwaves might be an open invitation to fraud. For the top decision makers at COMELEC, then, registration education was something best done at the grassroots level (Borra 2001; Rosello 2001).

In the end, house-to-house verification and mapping proved to be a far more daunting task than Tancangco had anticipated. By the end of 2000, only 24 percent of the precinct maps had been drawn up. By early March 2001, only ten weeks before the elections, verification and mapping had been completed in only two of the country's fourteen regions, and only a small fraction of these maps were judged to be in order when later reviewed by the COMELEC Election and Barangay Affairs Division.[20] As Tancangco herself explained after the fact: "[M]apping is a long and tedious process, not to mention its technical nature. Most of our election officers do not have the technical skills in drafting maps."[21] With the project bogged down, the COMELEC chairman decided, without consulting Tancangco, to use the 1998 voters' list (along with the additions made during the continuous registration) as the basis for the May 2001 elections. By that time, of course, the deadline for new registrants had already long passed.

As election day approached, President Gloria Macapagal Arroyo convened Congress to authorize a special youth registration. This was not a disinterested move on her part since middle-class youth played a key role in bringing her to power. She had assumed office when President Joseph Estrada was forced to step down in January 2001. At the time, he was being impeached on charges of corruption. When, during his Senate trial, it became clear that there were not enough votes to remove him from office, hundreds of thousands of people—many of them young—took to the streets to protest. Within days, the military and his cabinet withdrew their support for him, and Vice President Arroyo was sworn in to replace him.

Arroyo and her People Power Coalition (PPC) allies in Congress were well aware that many demonstrators and sympathizers were young and constituted a big block of pro-PPC votes. As an Arroyo associate explained, "[F]our million new voters mostly coming from the youth sector are a definite plus for the

20. CA (2001a, 2001b); "Precinct Mapping Had Irregularities," *Philippine Star,* June 25, 2001.
21. Letter from Tancangco to the Commission on Audit, quoted in Bernas Law Offices (2002, 59).

People Power Coalition."[22] The only problem for the PPC was that many of these youngsters were not yet registered. Arroyo thus called the special session of Congress to enfranchise her young supporters in time for the May elections. But when COMELEC chairman Alfredo Benipayo, a new Arroyo appointee, testified before Congress that the poll body would be unable to conduct the registration without postponing the elections, the idea was dropped.

At that point several youth organizations and civil society groups filed a petition before the Supreme Court to force COMELEC to conduct the special registration. But in a vote of eight to six, the court denied the petition on the grounds that "the law does not require that the impossible be done" (Akbayan v. COMELEC, G.R. No. 147066 [Mar. 26, 2001]). With that ruling, the last chance for a special registration passed.

AUTOMATED VOTE COUNTING, TABULATION, AND RESULTS TRANSMISSION IN VENEZUELA

Mismanagement also occurred during the Venezuelan elections of 2000. The presidential election was originally scheduled for the month of May, but technical difficulties caused by the automation of vote counting, tabulation, and results transmission forced it to be postponed until July. With ballots stored in unsecured areas, partisan election workers or perhaps political operatives (the culprits have never been identified) obtained and premarked ballots in an effort to void votes cast against incumbent president Hugo Chávez.

The decision to automate the electoral process was made in the wake of two fraud-ridden national elections in which the results of one-quarter of the states were declared void because of alleged vote rigging. The new election system, put in place in 1998, was one piece of a larger bundle of clean election reforms passed into law in 1997. Other provisions included an updating of the voter registry and the establishment of a nonpartisan body to administer elections, the Consejo Nacional Electoral (National Electoral Council, or CNE).

There were dramatic changes taking place in the political arena as well. Support for the two traditional political parties that had dominated Venezuelan politics for many years began to collapse in the early 1990s, culminating in the election to the presidency of outsider Hugo Chávez, a former lieutenant colonel in the Venezuelan army who had led a failed coup attempt in 1992. Chávez vowed to rewrite the constitution if elected. Soon after assuming power in 1998 he put the question to the electorate, which approved of the plan

---

22. "Lakas, LDP Call for a Special Voter List-up," *Philippine Star,* March 12, 2001.

overwhelmingly in a referendum vote. In July 1999, voters chose members of the Constituent Assembly. Voters ratified the new constitution in another referendum held in November 1999. With the inauguration of the Fifth Republic, new elections were to be held for all elected positions, including the presidency.

On the day of the presidential election in July 2000, the attorney general's office received 161 complaints about premarked ballots, while domestic and international observers reported their circulation at polling places around the country (OAS 2000, 29; Neuman and McCoy 2001, 70; Red de Veedores 2001, 8). Premarking—filling in an oval on an optical scan ballot before giving it to a voter—proved to be an effective way to commit large-scale fraud.

The fraud was made possible by a peculiarity of the Venezuelan ballot. A candidate may appear on it multiple times, depending on the number of parties that back the candidacy. Chávez, for instance, appeared ten times on the 2000 ballot, under the banner of ten different parties, while his main opponent, Francisco Arias Cárdenas, appeared six times. A voter thus needs to specify a nominating party when choosing a candidate. Filling in multiple ovals (i.e., choosing multiple nominating parties) for the same candidate does not invalidate the ballot. A ballot filled out in this way—what might be called a valid multiple vote (VMV) ballot for short—is counted as a valid ballot. Filling in the ovals of two or more different candidates, however, does invalidate the ballot, and that provided the opportunity to commit fraud in the 2000 election. In many locales, unwary voters received ballots with an oval for one presidential candidate already filled in. If the voter then filled in another oval for the same candidate, the counting machine tallied it as a valid vote for that candidate. If, instead, the voter filled in an oval for a different candidate, the ballot was recorded by the machine as a null vote. In short, premarking a ballot in favor of one candidate had the effect of voiding the vote of anyone who intended to cast a ballot for a different candidate.

It is impossible to determine with any precision the number of premarked ballots that might have been used by voters in July 2000 or the number of votes that might have been declared invalid as the result of premarking. Nevertheless, the number of "null votes" in the presidential election—a category that included blank ballots, ballots with an oval incompletely filled out, and ballots with two or more candidates selected—was 348,465, or 5.3 percent of the total number of votes cast. Tests after the elections showed that hardware malfunctioning did not generate these null votes (as had happened during the July 1999 Constituent Assembly election). An analysis of the null votes by sociology professor and former CNE member Miriam Kornblith (2001, 139) showed, furthermore, that their geographic distribution did not fit the random pattern one would expect if their prime cause was simple voter confusion. The percentage of null votes was particularly high, for instance, in the states of Amazonas (14.0 percent), Guárico (10.4 percent), and Yaracuy (8.5 percent), while in eleven other states and the Federal District of Caracas it was under 5 percent. At most voting tables (*mesas electorales*)—where the ballots are actually cast and counted at each voting center—the number of null votes did not exceed 5 percent, but in 161 tables it exceeded 10 percent, and in 40 tables it exceeded 15 percent (145). There was, in addition, a clear partisan distribution of VMV ballots in favor of incumbent president Chávez. VMV ballots accounted for 6.9 percent of the valid votes for him but only 3.7 percent for his main challenger, Arias (155).[23] While these numbers do not indicate that the use of premarked ballots altered the outcome of the race, their distribution did nevertheless distort, as Kornblith phrased it, "the genuine expression of the voter's will" (159, my translation) and thus tarnished the credibility of the election.

It was not, as one might suspect, ballot design alone that precipitated this fraud. The new scannable ballot retained the same layout as ballots used before automation, and similar rules for determining null votes were in place. While isolated reports of premarking had surfaced in earlier elections, the scale of premarking in July 2000 had never before been seen. The ability to commit fraud on such a large scale resulted, rather, from the inability of the CNE to manage the technical challenges of readying the new electronic system for elections originally scheduled to be held in May. In the end, the presidential poll had to be delayed, leaving thousands and thousands of blank ballots unsecured for a period of two months—the very ballots, most observers believe, that had been premarked and distributed during the July 2000 election.

The presidential election was originally scheduled to take place on May 28, 2000, on the same day as polls for every other elected position in the country. Preparations for these "mega-elections," as they came to be called, followed the approval of a new constitution by national referendum in December 1999. In charge of administering these elections was an all-new CNE appointed by the Constituent Assembly.

The CNE quickly contracted out the main tasks to four private companies. Continental Web printed up the ballots; Unisys compiled the database of candidates; Indra took charge of the electronic transmission and tabulation system; and Election Systems & Software (ES&S), the company that manufactured the counting machines, programmed the electronic memory "flash" card on each machine with the information it needed to record and tally votes.

---

23. The other challenger, Claudio Fermín, was nominated by only one party, so there could be no VMV ballots for him.

Coordinating the work of these companies proved to be a daunting challenge. Just readying the machines for such a massive set of elections proved to be a huge task. With more than thirty-three thousand candidates competing for more than six thousand positions, programs had to be written for 1,371 different ballot configurations (Neuman and McCoy 2001, 41–45). The whole system broke down because errors in the candidate database system made it impossible to coordinate the candidates' database fields with the parameters established for ballots, voting machine flash cards, and counting software. The Organization of American States (OAS) electoral observation mission found that these database errors had three causes:

> 1) the candidates' database was fragmented and compiled with different parameters in various parts of the country, so that there was no nationwide consistency; 2) the contract operators introduced a significant number of errors in transcribing candidacies, basically because of the complexity of the alliances among parties and candidates; and 3) most candidacies were presented within the last three days before the deadline, producing great paperwork congestion that led to errors in transcription. (OAS 2000, 22)

Until the very end the CNE tried to correct these problems. It was however unsuccessful because, as the OAS mission found:

> It did not have a systematic correction procedure. In effect, corrections were made in a parallel but isolated manner, without any mechanism of coordination among the various components of the system, which were in the hands of four different companies. (22–23)

Many of these problems related to shifting electoral alliances and changes in nominating parties—the normal stuff of Venezuelan politics, but a nightmare for those who needed to program the flash cards. ES&S scurried to process the over 11,200 changes submitted by election authorities. To compound the company's difficulties, less than a week before the scheduled election day a software glitch prevented technicians from opening the program that ran the balloting system, causing the Venezuelan government to frantically dispatch a military jet to the ES&S headquarters in Omaha, Nebraska, to fetch more experts and equipment.

All these problems came to a head only three days before the scheduled date of the elections, after civil society groups filed a petition with the Supreme Court to postpone the elections. When the head of the CNE automation department testified that his department could not ensure the proper functioning of the technology, the justices ruled to suspend the elections. The mega-elections, as the joke went, became a mega-failure.

Within days all members of the CNE resigned under intense pressure, and the transitional National Legislative Council named a new set of directors perceived to be more experienced in electoral administration. The revamped CNE set July 30, 2000, as the new date of the presidential election.[24] Despite concerns voiced by civil society groups about the possibility of fraud, the CNE decided to use in July the presidential ballots already printed for the May mega-elections as a way to reduce its already high expenditures. Control over the ballots in June and July was, however, loose. Stacks of ballots were found in people's homes. Security and accountability were lax. These unsecured ballots, many observers suspect, were the ones that had been misappropriated and pre-marked for the presidential vote (Neuman and McCoy 2001, 55, 60).

It has never been determined who, exactly, conspired to premark ballots. Political operatives working for Chávez surely had a hand. But, as Kornblith notes, "the massive introduction of premarked ballots requires the complicity of a multiplicity of agents" (2001, 160, my translation). Hence in all likelihood officials handling the production, storage, or transport of the ballots were involved as well.

The attempt to automate the election process, in sum, precipitated the administrative exclusion of voters in the July 2000 election. Specifically, technical difficulties caused the postponement of the mega-elections, allowing the misappropriation and premarking of ballots in the run-up to the July presidential election. As a result, the votes of up to 5 percent of the electorate were voided.

CONDITIONS FOR MISMANAGEMENT

Administrative exclusion in both Venezuela and the Philippines was caused, at least in part, by the inept implementation of new clean elections procedures. In Venezuela, the inability of election officials to prepare the automated system for the 2000 mega-elections led to their postponement. Once the elections were postponed, officials proved unable to secure the ballots. These failures created an opportunity for partisan operatives and/or election workers to pull off the premarked-ballot scheme. In the Philippines, a newly implemented verification and mapping project, and the promise of grassroots outreach it held, led election officials to forgo a public education campaign about new registration procedures. When the project bogged down, first-time voters were left unaware

24. Elections for governors, National Assembly, mayors, and Andean and Latin American parliamentary representatives were held on that day too. Elections for state legislatures and local councils took place on December 3, 2000.

of the new registration deadline, making it impossible for them to register for the 2001 elections.

The mishandling of clean election reform in these two countries had several shared causes. For one thing, electoral bodies in both places suffered from a lack of technical expertise in areas crucial to the implementation of reform. In the Philippines, COMELEC field workers did not possess adequate mapmaking skills, slowing down their house-to-house enumeration. The automation of vote counting, tabulation, and results transmission in Venezuela was such a complicated undertaking that the CNE had to outsource to private contractors many vital tasks—from preparing the ballots to programming the counting and tabulation machines. It was the complexity of coordinating so many activities that caused the 2000 mega-elections to be delayed.

The lack of technical expertise was made more acute by the fact that the implementation of new clean election procedures, in both countries, was directed by neophyte election officers. Tancangco was a newly appointed academic with no significant administrative experience. Directors of the CNE in Venezuela had taken office only five months before the scheduled mega-elections. The new CNE directors who took their place, though more qualified, had been on the job for less than two months before the presidential poll. Inexperience, we can only suppose, played a part in leading election officials to either make bad decisions (i.e., to reuse ballots) or hold unrealistic expectations about their ability to meet inflexible election deadlines.

Another, related, cause of mismanagement was inadequate funding. In Venezuela, it was pressure to save money that led CNE officials to recycle presidential ballots from the aborted mega-elections. As international observers noted, "the failed election cost more than $80 million U.S. dollars, and the CNE was loath to expend more than absolutely necessary" (Neuman and McCoy 2001, 55). In the Philippines it was the failure of Congress to provide sufficient funding that prevented COMELEC from conducting precinct mapping in 1997 as mandated by law, setting the stage for the 2000-2001 verification and mapping project and the administrative exclusion of many first-time voters that resulted.

Not all budgetary problems, though, result from inadequate funding. In the Philippines, Congress allocated a substantial 1.8 billion pesos between 1998 and 2000 for the modernization of the electoral system. Of that amount, COMELEC decided to allocate 502 million pesos for the verification and mapping project. By the end of 2000, it had spent 56 percent of this budget to complete the project in a mere 24 percent of the total number of precincts in the country. An external audit found that several months after the suspension of the project some 60 million pesos—about 20 percent of the total amount disbursed—remained unaccounted for and presumably lost to corrupt project supervisors and workers (CA 2001a, 2001b). This misappropriation of funds surely impeded progress on the project as well.

Some combination of inadequate funding and bureaucratic venality has been a root cause of exclusionary mismanagement in other countries as well. In Senegal, for instance, lawmakers overhauled the electoral code in preparation for elections in 1993. One of the new provisions tightened rules for voter registration. Prior to the reform, a prospective voter living in a rural area could register even if he or she did not possess a valid form of identification as long as the applicant could present to the registration commission two registered voters bearing witness to his or her identity (NDI 1991, 12). The reform eliminated this form of testimonial registration, thus requiring all prospective voters to produce a valid identity document. Unfortunately, this new requirement placed a prohibitive financial burden on rural registrants, since government agents asked them to pay high fees to process national identity cards that were supposed to be provided free of charge. As a team of international assessors found:

> Although the Ministry of the Interior officials insist that the cards are absolutely free to voters, virtually no one outside government received a card without some cost since the cards were first available. Normally, the greatest cost is little more than the cost of a photo and an official stamp. The photo cost should therefore be standardized at 300 francs CFA. Instead, the leaders of rural villages indicate that their people are often required to pay 1000 francs CFA for the photograph, plus 100 francs for official stamps on birth certificates and another 100 francs for related public functions. In all, they have to pay 2400 francs or approximately eighteen dollars per two heads of household plus two days' lost work. This amount becomes formidable when one considers that the estimated medium income of the peasants, who make up 70 percent of Senegalese voters, is only about 35,000 francs or $145 a year. (Guerin, Morris, and Tessier 1992, 18)

It is unclear to what extent the charges were predatory or reflected instead the real cost of producing the cards. Whatever the case, the high expense appears to have dissuaded an undetermined number of rural dwellers from registering. The larger point is that budget constraints and administrative corruption can pervert even the best-intentioned reforms.

Mismanagement has, then, a multiplicity of underlying causes that range from inadequate funding to bureaucratic corruption to administrative inexperience to a lack of technical expertise. In this context, it is interesting to contrast Lesotho, which established a new computerized voter registration system in advance of general elections in 2002. The project received ample funding, registration officials were well trained, and safeguards were adopted to prevent corruption and malpractice. Not coincidentally, international observers and most political parties judged the implementation of the system to be highly successful, and no instances of administrative exclusion were reported (SADCPF n.d., 14–15; CS 2006, 11–13, 29).

The Lesotho success notwithstanding, many syndromes of mismanagement are commonplace in poorer parts of the world. In this regard, Senegal, Venezuela, and the Philippines are hardly exceptional. Some of these problems afflict richer countries as well. Consider a recent example from Marion County, Indiana, home of Indianapolis. After Republicans held the county clerk post for almost thirty years, a Democrat was elected in November 2006. The inexperienced new clerk proved to be so inept that during her first election day, in May 2007, 5 of the county's 917 precincts never opened, and 45 more opened late; 150 poll workers went missing; ballots and voting lists were sent to the wrong precincts; and some poll workers who did show up were given the wrong keys and thus could not turn on the voting machines. As a result, officials estimate that around three thousand voters were unable to vote.[25] In other parts of the country, the lack of technical expertise is being felt especially hard at the precinct level. In the post–Help America Vote Act world of electronic voting, many local jurisdictions are struggling to adequately train poll workers—many of whom are retirees habituated to old ways of voting—to operate newly purchased voting machines.[26] In both poor and rich countries, it seems, the mismanagement of reform, and the possibility of exclusion it occasions, is likely to remain a widespread and recurrent possibility.

Blurred Boundaries

In this chapter I have distinguished cases of administrative exclusion that are deliberate (manipulation) from those that are not (mismanagement). Sometimes, of course, it is difficult to distinguish between them. On the one hand, a strategy of manipulation, deftly executed, may look to the outside observer like mere mismanagement. On the other hand, what appears to the leery or aggrieved as manipulation may be a simple instance of mismanagement. In countries with a history of electoral malpractice, people often assume that any technical problem—from flawed voter registration to the slow distribution

25. "Voters Shut Out of Marion County," *Indianapolis Star,* May 9, 2007; "City Council to Probe Election Trouble," *Indianapolis Star,* May 11, 2007.

26. "More Poll Workers Recruited, but Training Proves Daunting; Some Frustrated by Electronic Devices, Remedial Learning," *Washington Post,* November 2, 2006.

of election materials to anomalous ballot counting—is politically driven. But in many poorer countries, as Robert Pastor notes, "the officials charged with administering and conducting elections are generally unskilled, and technical irregularities are the rule" (1999, 78).

The implementation of registration reform in Venezuela is one such ambiguous case. A sweeping set of clean election reforms was adopted there after the fraud-ridden, contested elections of 1993 and 1995. Part of the 1997 reform package called for an updating of the voter registry by the newly created CNE. One scholar explained how foot dragging on the part of the Immigration and Naturalization Service led to the administrative exclusion of up to 2 million people during the 1998 elections:

> The process of registering voters proved difficult for the CNE. When registration opened in April 1998 only 2,500 of the 8,500 registration centres opened on time. When registration closed in July 1998, an estimated two million people had missed the deadline. This was largely the result of major delays in the issuing of *cedulas* [identity cards] by the Immigration and Naturalisation Service, which meant that people who could not produce a *cedula* were not entitled to register. (Buxton 2001, 193)

Populist presidential candidate Hugo Chávez, among others, contended that many of those whose identity cards had not arrived were supporters of his electoral alliance, the Polo Patriótico, and that the foot dragging was intentional. Despite Chávez's certainty, it is hard to say whether the delays were part of a deliberate strategy of exclusion or a product of mere inefficiency, for which the Immigration and Naturalization Service is well known. Whichever the case, a slow delivery of identity documents prevented a large number of Venezuelans from registering, especially young people newly eligible to vote.[27] Without inside knowledge, however, we cannot say for certain whether this sluggishness was deliberate.

To complicate matters further, mismanagement sometimes provides an opening for manipulation since administrative incapacity can be exploited by opportunistic operatives and election workers. In Venezuela, it was poor preparation for the mega-elections that pushed back the election date and gave pro-Chávez partisans—among them, it appears, election workers—a chance to obtain and premark ballots. Administrative incapacity, in this case, probably extended to the inability of the CNE leadership to effectively police and discipline its own personnel. Nigeria provides a more clear-cut example of this type of disciplinary

27. "Operativo de cedulación exigen a la Onidex," *Notitarde,* June 28, 1998.

incapacity. After the fraud-ridden elections of 1998–99, the Independent National Electoral Commission (INEC) decided to computerize the voter registry. Even though INEC produced 72 million registration forms for an estimated voting population of 60 million, many people could not register for the 2003 elections because of a shortage of forms. Partisan local election officials, in cahoots with politicians, had hoarded them (NDI 2002, 4). Clean election reforms undertaken by low-capacity electoral bodies, in a word, invite manipulation.

Despite these areas of ambiguity and overlap, it is still important to treat manipulation and mismanagement separately, for each has a distinct set of facilitating conditions. Mismanagement tends to occur when there is a low level of bureaucratic integrity and effectiveness and results from inadequate funding, administrative corruption, managerial inexperience, and a lack of technical expertise. Manipulation, in contrast, tends to occur during high-stakes elections in places where partisan involvement in the administration of elections is deep and where it is easy to identify opposition supporters for exclusionary treatment. It can also occur when partisans find ways to exploit the disarray produced by mismanagement.

Failed Safeguards

Virtually all democracies have safeguards in place to hold abusive or incompetent election officials accountable. Why, in the cases of manipulation and mismanagement discussed in this chapter, did those safeguards fail? Effective safeguards, students of institutions tell us, require both vigilant monitoring and vigorous enforcement. When either or both monitoring and enforcement are ineffective, abuses go unchecked.

Monitoring

To effectively monitor misconduct on the part of election officials and bodies, agents of accountability (courts, legislatures, civic associations, political parties, international observers) require information (Schedler 1999, 16, 22–25). To prevent or remedy abuses, timing is key. When information reaches agents of accountability too close to an election or after an election, the options available for redress are few.

The CNE in Venezuela, for instance, made repeated public pronouncements in the months and weeks leading up to the May mega-elections that preparations were progressing smoothly and that the elections would be held successfully even as technicians and contractors began talking behind the scenes of the possibility of a failed election (Neuman and McCoy 2001, 49). When it became apparent to civil society organizations that the CNE was not, in fact, prepared to carry out the elections, they filed a brief before the Supreme Court. It was not until three days before the election, however, that CNE technicians disclosed to the court and to the public the electoral body's dismal state of preparedness. With only hours until the scheduled elections, the court had few options but to postpone them.

Similarly, when youth groups, civic organizations, and political parties in the Philippines finally turned their attention to the May elections after the tumult of Estrada's ouster and noticed that youth registration rates were woefully low, it was already too late for them to mobilize their allies in Congress to legislate a special youth registration. COMELEC chairman Benipayo testified that only by delaying the elections could a new registration be held. "We had to scrap it in light of the admission of the Comelec that it just couldn't do it within the time limit set out in the bill," Senate President Aquilino Pimentel Jr. told reporters, "and the alternative of postponing the elections is to our mind a worse cure than the disease."[28] When youth groups then filed a brief before the Supreme Court, the judges ruled that COMELEC could not be compelled to do the "impossible." In both Venezuela and the Philippines, then, the lack of an early warning system left agents of accountability with little room for maneuver.

Even when such agents are able to intervene successfully to prevent administrative exclusion, their options are often limited if they act too late. In Ghana, new identification requirements put in place for the 2000 elections threatened to exclude up to 2.5 million voters because the distribution of new photo identity cards was delayed. The Supreme Court ruled, just three days before the election, that people without cards could vote if they were registered (Smith 2002, 625). A shortage of time left the court with only the bluntest of tools. While this action laudably prevented massive exclusion, it vitiated efforts to clean up the elections.

In Venezuela, the Philippines, and Ghana, election officials were guilty mostly of mismanagement. When abuse instead results from manipulation, which usually involves fewer individuals and the discreet bending of select procedures, it is even harder to detect beforehand. In the cases of Florida and Quebec, the abuses did not come to light until after the proclamation of the election results. In both cases, redress was still being sought in the courts years later.

Effective monitoring, in short, requires agents of accountability to be vigilant and electoral preparations to be transparent. Where electoral bodies are shielded

---

28. "Senate Kills Bill for New Voters Listing," *Philippine Daily Inquirer,* March 22, 2001.

from public scrutiny by a veil of constitutional independence (as in Venezuela and the Philippines) or where political parties are positioned to quietly manipulate electoral procedures (as in Florida and Quebec), the dangers of opacity and abuse increase.

ENFORCEMENT

Vigorous enforcement requires strict rules to punish wrongdoers, both to stop their abuses and to deter others who might emulate them. Administrative abuses tend to occur and reoccur when sanctions are weak or the threat of sanctions is low.

Sanctions can sometimes be made hollow by the partisan penetration of electoral bodies. In Nigeria, INEC suspended around 250 election officers for their role in hoarding registration materials prior to the 2003 elections. This disciplinary action was, however, limited. At least thirteen higher-level officials involved in misconduct were simply reshuffled to other regions. Since INEC commissioners are appointed by the executive, without any oversight mechanism, the body lacks independence. Sensitive to political pressure, it appears that commissioners were unwilling to conduct a more thoroughgoing purge (NDI 2003a, 2; 2003b, 3).

Partisan interference with the enforcement of sanctions was also high in Florida (where the secretary of state was a partisan elected official) and Quebec (where the chief electoral officer was appointed by the NAQ, which has long been dominated by the Parti Québécois). In neither place were the individuals involved in perpetrating abuses sanctioned. In Florida, none of the election officials involved in the overzealous purge were fired or reprimanded. In Quebec, successive chief electoral officers were reluctant to investigate thoroughly or prosecute energetically those involved in the ballot rejection scheme. After election officials flubbed the legal case against two deputy returning officers, interim chief electoral officer Francine Barry decided to drop all charges against the remaining defendants. Barry, not incidentally, had been appointed by the Parti Québécois cabinet.

In Venezuela, the CNE is nominally independent, as mapped out in the 1997 reform that created the body. But it increasingly lost its independence under the heavy hand of Chávez. There was never an official investigation into the source of premarked ballots in the 2000 elections. Moreover, the CNE refused to release data that would allow outsiders to track the number of multiple vote ballots cast in subsequent elections.[29]

---

29. "CNE guarda un CD y no da información," *El Universal,* June 17, 2002.

If excessive partisan influence is a problem, so is excessive independence. Former Philippine COMELEC chairman Christian Monsod (1997, 36) wrote of the body he once directed: "Because of the constitutional wall around the Comelec as an independent commission, a chairman or commissioner can be vindictive, arbitrary and incompetent, and maybe even crooked, without too much risk of disciplinary sanction or removal. This is the downside of independent constitutional bodies." The fate of commissioner Tancangco confirms this observation. After the 2001 elections, NAMFREL and other civil society groups submitted to the House of Representatives an impeachment complaint against her. These groups believed that Tancangco's verification and mapping project violated the intent of the 1996 Continuous Voter Registration Act, which did not authorize what appeared to be another general registration. These groups were, in addition, outraged that Tancangco, as head of the Modernization Committee of COMELEC, refused to implement another law that mandated the computerized counting of ballots. Because of her "gross inexcusable negligence" they sought her removal (Bernas Law Offices 2002, 5).

Members of the House, however, did not oblige. They voted sixty-nine to fifty-seven to throw out the complaint for lack of substance. Insiders report that new COMELEC chairman Benjamin Abalos lobbied hard in defense of Tancangco. Many representatives were apparently reluctant to support the complaint out of fear that COMELEC might rule against them in future electoral disputes. Given the power of COMELEC over the fortunes of candidates for reelection, the ability of Congress to act as an agent of accountability is severely hampered.

To conclude, administrative exclusion in places like Quebec, Florida, Nigeria, Venezuela, and the Philippines was allowed to occur because effective safeguards were not in place to guard against the abuses of inept or manipulative election officials. In some cases, agents of accountability did a lackluster job. In other cases they were blocked. Often, sanctions against abusive officials were weak or nonexistent. To the extent that these conditions remain unchanged, there is a strong possibility that future offenses may go unnoticed or unchecked.

Other Cases of Administrative Exclusion

In this chapter, I have focused on a handful of well-documented cases of administrative exclusion that provide a rich body of material from which to generate comparative insights about the circumstances that gave rise to the exclusion. But I discovered other instances of administrative exclusion during the 1991 to 2006 period that deserve at least brief mention. I found many of these cases, not surprisingly, in low- or middle-income countries with quasi or emerging democratic systems:

- In post-Soviet Georgia, the flubbed computerization of the electoral lists in 2003 led to the exclusion of between 10 and 15 percent of the electorate.[30]
- In preparation for the 1999 parliamentary elections, Armenia adopted a new electoral code with various provisions to prevent illegal voting; however, "inadequate enforcement of election code requirements regarding voter lists resulted in near chaos at numerous polling stations and in the apparent disenfranchisement of large numbers of voters" which media sources put in the hundred to two hundred thousand range (NDI 1999a).
- In Macedonia, voter identification cards were produced for the first time for the 1998 elections, but because the distribution system was faulty, thousands were left undistributed, leaving their owners unable to vote (IRI n.d.).
- In Sierra Leone, by the electoral commission's own projections, administrative problems implementing a new voter registration system and a lack of voter education led to the exclusion of between five hundred thousand and a million citizens during the 2002 elections (Monitor Project 2001).
- In Cameroon, a system of continuous registration was established in 1997 prior to elections held that same year. But of 6,020,000 eligible voters, only 3,719,202 registered. Not only was the number of registrants low, but it was 300,000 less than in 1992, despite an annual population increase of 2.9 percent. Two International Foundation for Election Systems (IFES) election assessors explained what happened:

> Widespread shortcomings in the registration process seem mostly to blame for the low registration figures for the 1997 elections. IFES heard many complaints about discriminatory registration practices which may have resulted in the disenfranchisement of a number of citizens.... Concern was expressed that those authorities belonging to one ethnic group or political affiliation would not accept the proof of citizenship submitted by members of other ethnic groups, particularly if they were perceived to support a rival political party. Many Cameroonians also alleged that the registration process was disorganized and that little information concerning the period

30. "Georgia Braces for Elections," BBC News, October 3, 2003.

of registration was disseminated to the public (Bakary and Palmer 1997, 27; see also 25–26).

- In Zambia, the voter registry was computerized in preparation for the 1996 elections. As a result, "fewer voters registered in the 1996 voting exercise than in 1991—a reduction from 2.9 million in the 1991 exercise to 2.3 million registered in 1996—from an estimated population of 4.4 million eligible voters. The registration process was irregular; numerous incidents of omission of voters, incorrect coding and blank voter cards in circulation were reported" (Rakner and Svåsand 2005, 91).
- In Mali, new voter cards were produced for the 2002 elections in response to concerns voiced by opposition parties about election integrity. Local government offices, however, mismanaged their distribution. As a result, 40 percent of the cards had not been distributed by election day of the first round of the presidential vote in April. While some voters were allowed to vote without producing their cards, voter turnout for that round still sank to a record low of 23 percent. International observers, furthermore, heard "many stories of voter card theft, indicating inadequate controls over the security of the supply of voter cards and raising the possibility of vote fraud on election day" (Carter Center 2002, 15–16, 30–31, 35). Indeed, 55,799 cards intended for Bamako voters simply disappeared prior to the first round of the legislative elections in July (35).
- In Guyana, logistical problems with new registration procedures involving the issuance of new photo identification cards led to the exclusion in 2001 of 5 percent of the electorate by the electoral commission's own estimate.[31]
- In Antigua and Barbuda, new photograph and fingerprint identity cards were produced for the 2004 elections. However, international observers reported that "many" eligible voters were not able to retrieve their cards prior to election day, thus preventing them from voting. The observers also received allegations from many voters that "opposition supporters were the ones whose cards were delayed" (CS 2004, 13).
- In the Dominican Republic, around forty-five thousand people—mostly opposition supporters—were stripped of the opportunity to vote in the 1994 presidential election after the manipulated implementation of a new voter registration and identification system. Since the margin of victory

---

31. IDEA (n.d., 19); "Courts Mull Guyana Polls," *Financial Times,* March 29, 2001.

was only 22,281 votes, international observers concluded that the "legitimacy of the.... elections must be called into question" (NDI 1994, 1).

I also found cases of administrative exclusion in very wealthy and established democracies. In Belgium, the expanded use of electronic voting machines in 2003 was attended by computer failures and organizational problems that led to long delays for voters waiting to cast their ballots. As a result an estimated 10 percent of the electorate in certain locations did not vote despite Belgium's well-enforced compulsory voting laws (Benoit 2004, 317).

Quebec again had problems with high rates of ballot rejection in the 2005 municipal elections, though in these elections the problem lay with the use of new voting technologies and not with manipulated poll workers. The province, which began small-scale use of electronic voting in 1996, expanded the deployment of various types of electronic voting machines for the 2005 municipal elections to cover 10 percent of the province's municipalities. Five different types of machines were used for the elections. Because of a combination of mismanagement, machine limitations, and inadequate voter education, the eighty-one municipalities that used three of the machine types experienced rates of ballot rejection that were on average two to four times higher than those in municipalities that used traditional voting methods. In effect, the expanded use of electronic voting voided thousands of votes that would have counted had the new technologies not been used (DGEQ 2006, 125–47).

Turning our attention to the United States, we see quickly that the Florida purge was not the only case of administrative exclusion in recent history. Aggressive ballot security operations undertaken by the New York City Board of Elections reportedly led to the exclusion of thousands of eligible voters during the 1993 mayoral election, most of whom were apparently poor or people of color (Hayduk 2005, 145–73). A faulty purge of Kentucky's voter rolls prior to the 2006 elections improperly removed some eight thousand people,[32] while post-Help America Vote Act voter registration database policies adopted in Iowa, Maryland, Pennsylvania, South Dakota, Texas, Virginia, and Washington have inadequate safeguards to protect eligible voters from being wrongly purged because of data entry errors such as typos or the transposition of names (Levitt, Weiser, and Muñoz 2006, ii). More than fifteen hundred registration forms submitted in Los Angeles County, California, in 2006 were rejected because of glitches in its new database system.[33] The restrictive interpretation of

32. "Judge: Purged Voters Should Be Reinstated, Put on Inactive List," *Associated Press*, October 2, 2006.
33. "New ID System May Block Voters," *Los Angeles Times*, March 29, 2006.

a new voter registration law by Ohio's secretary of state dramatically lowered for five months before the 2006 elections the number of new registration cards collected by grassroots organizations (the law was later thrown out by a federal judge).[34] The improper or unlawful implementation of voter identification requirements in South Dakota (2004), Washington (2005), Ohio (2006), Missouri (2006), and Georgia (2006) caused an unknown number of legitimate voters to be turned away from the polls.[35]

Also worth noting are new dangers of manipulation that attend the rollout of electronic voting machines in the United States. Computer experts have demonstrated that many of these new machines are easy to hack and that their vote totals can be manipulated without leaving any electronic traces (Compuware 2003; Kohno et al., 2003; BCTF 2006; Feldman, Halderman, and Felten 2006; Hursti 2006). The integrity of the vote count thus depends heavily on the physical security of the machines—keeping them under lock and key to ensure that nobody will tamper with their software. Diebold Election Systems, the largest supplier of electronic voting systems in the country, acknowledged this fact while trying to downplay its significance. Remarked David Bear, company spokesman, "For there to be a problem here, you're basically assuming a premise where you have some evil and nefarious election officials who would sneak in and introduce a piece of software. I don't believe these evil elections people exist."[36] It is difficult to share Bear's optimistic belief in the unfailing morality of every precinct worker in the country. In Ohio, two Cuyahoga County election workers were convicted of rigging the ballot recount that followed the contested 2004 presidential election.[37] Recall, too, Leander Brooks, the East St. Louis poll worker who was convicted of forging signatures on twenty ballot applications in the 2002 elections (see chapter 2). In this context, it is especially troubling that election officials around the country do not always guarantee the secure storage of electronic voting machines. In San Diego County, for instance, precinct workers were

34. "New Regulation Rules Stir Voter Debate in Ohio," *New York Times,* August 6, 2006.

35. "Legislators Endorse New Rule Requiring Signs at Polling Places," Associated Press, September 3, 2004; "2 Groups Object to Ad about Bringing ID to Vote," *Seattle Times,* August 26, 2005; "IDs, Balky Machines Trip Up Some Voters," *Columbus Dispatch,* November 6, 2006; "Secretary of State Blasts County on IDs," *St. Louis Post-Dispatch,* November 9, 2006; Carnahan (2007, 15–17); "Not All Bibb Workers Knew That Photo ID Not Required," *Macon Telegraph,* July 19, 2006; "Letters on Voter ID under Fire; 200,000 Mailed Out after Law Struck Down," *Atlanta-Journal Constitution,* October 13, 2006.

36. Quoted in "New Fears of Security Risks in Electronic Voting Systems," *New York Times,* May 12, 2006.

37. "2 Election Workers Convicted in '04 Tally," *Plain Dealer,* January 25, 2007.

allowed to keep touch screen machines in their homes for as along as three weeks before the 2006 elections.[38]

Without a representative sample of reforms, it is imprudent to hazard guesses about the relative frequency of different forms of iatrogenic harm. It is, nevertheless, clear that administrative exclusion is hardly uncommon around the world, no doubt because the basic conditions that give rise to both its intentional and unintentional forms are fairly widespread: high-stakes electoral races administered by partisan administrators who can identify opposition supporters for differential treatment on the one hand, and election administrators who lack technical expertise, experience, adequate funding, or sometimes probity, on the other.

Administrative Exclusion and Legal Disenfranchisement Compared

Administrative exclusion is a distinct mode of vote depression occasioned by clean election reform. To be sure, some forms of administrative exclusion, especially those precipitated by inadequate budget allocations of legislatures, look similar to legal disenfranchisement, which, as pointed out in chapter 2, results directly from the actions of lawmakers. As we have seen, when lawmakers inadequately fund the implementation of new reforms—as they did in Senegal, the Philippines, and Florida—they facilitate vote depression as well. At that point, little seems to separate legal disenfranchisement from administrative exclusion. There is, however, an important distinction. Legal disenfranchisement follows from the varying abilities or dispositions of potential voters to comply with new requirements. It does not presuppose any inept or manipulative behavior on the part of election officials, as does administrative exclusion. In South Africa, legal disenfranchisement occurred because blacks and nonblacks had different attitudes toward a newly required form of identification. Election officials did not evidence the kind of gross ineptitude witnessed in the Philippines or Venezuela, nor did they take discriminatory actions against particular groups of voters as they did in Florida or Quebec, with the exception of the Queenstown mobile unit discussed at the beginning of this chapter.

Not surprisingly, some conditions that make manipulation feasible also make the intentional form of legal disenfranchisement feasible. Both, after all, involve partisan efforts to lower turnout for opposition candidates, and both are premised on the ability of partisans to identify and single out opposition

38. "Touch-screen Voting's Steep Learning Curve: Rollout in 21 Counties Brings Glitches," *San Francisco Chronicle,* June 19, 2006.

supporters for exclusion. But where intentional legal disenfranchisement requires partisan control of the legislature, manipulation requires instead partisan intervention in the administration of elections. Still, not all instances of administrative exclusion or legal disenfranchisement are intentional, and it is important to recognize that exclusion can result as well from simple ignorance, mismanagement, or incapacity. In these cases, vote depression follows from a different set of causes and points to a somewhat different set of remedies, which I will take up in chapter 6.

4

Parties, Candidates, and Their Agents

Partisan Demobilization

S ometimes clean election reforms damage the quality of democracy directly. When lawmakers enact restrictive voter registration procedures, participation rates decline as a direct result. When election administrators remove eligible voters from the registry, people are immediately excluded. Sometimes, however, the damage to democracy is indirect. Lawmakers and election officials put in place clean election reforms that cause parties, candidates, and their agents to alter their campaign strategies, and it is the adoption of these new strategies that keeps people away from the polls.

In this chapter, I focus on the reaction of political parties, candidates, and agents to clean election reforms and the adverse effects that these reactions can have on voter turnout. Specifically, I examine the effect of reforms on the strategies that parties, candidates, and agents use to convince eligible voters to get to the polls—what might be called partisan strategies of "mobilization." In this context, it is helpful to distinguish two kinds of mobilization. "Personal" mobilization relies on face-to-face contact with friends, neighbors, coworkers, party workers, or candidates and takes place anywhere—in the home or workplace or at a club, rally, or parade. "Impersonal" mobilization relies instead on mass media exposure and advertising or on things like campaign mailings and commercial phone banks.

Partisan "demobilization" occurs when parties, candidates, and their operatives, reacting to clean election reforms, alter their campaign strategies in ways that keep people away from the polls. This form of demobilization typically occurs in one of two ways. On the one hand, candidates may adopt relatively less effective get-out-the-vote strategies such as mass media advertising where once they relied on relatively more effective face-to-face canvassing. We might characterize this shift as one from personal to impersonal forms of election campaigning, and the reduction in turnout that results is typically unplanned. On the other hand, parties, candidates, and their agents may deliberately choose to pursue strategies of demobilization: instead of focusing only on inducing their supporters to vote, they may also deliberately keep supporters of their opponents away from the polls. We might characterize this shift as a calculated move from mobilization to a mixed strategy of mobilization and demobilization. In the following sections, I look at each variant in turn.

From Personal to Impersonal Mobilization: Cutting Out the Go-Between

Over the past century, political parties in Europe and the United States have come to rely less and less on personal modes of mobilization and more and more on impersonal ones. This shift has brought about changes in how voters participate in elections. Wattenberg (2000, 66) explains:

> As voters have come to experience campaigns through television rather than through personal contact with members of party organizations, voting has become less of a social act and more of a civic duty. No longer do voters go to the polls because they have been urged to do so by their friends, relatives, and neighbours. Rather, those who decide to vote do so largely to express their opinions.

It is, in part, to this decline in personal mobilization that Wattenberg attributes the "nearly universal" decline in turnout in the industrialized West (71).

The importance of face-to-face contact for turnout has been demonstrated empirically by a series of field experiments conducted by Yale University political scientists Alan Gerber, Donald Green, and their associates. In one experiment, they conveyed nonpartisan get-out-the-vote messages to a random sample of some thirty thousand registered voters in New Haven, Connecticut, through either personal canvassing, direct mail, or telephone calls. Their findings: door-to-door canvassing increased voter turnout by almost ten percentage points and direct mail by less than one percentage point, and telephone calls had no effect on turnout at all.[1] Field experiments conducted in the cities of Bridgeport, Columbus, Detroit, Minneapolis, and St. Paul similarly found that

---

1. Gerber and Green (2000, 660). An independent statistical analysis of the same data by Imai (2005) suggests that telephone calls are more effective than Gerber and Green first estimated but still not as effective as door-to-door canvassing, a finding that Gerber and Green (2005) contest.

door-to-door canvassing raised turnout an average of almost eleven percentage points (Green, Gerber, and Nickerson 2002).[2] The bottom line, as Green, McMillion, and Smith put it, is that "voters, like prospective guests at a social function, are more likely to attend if personally invited" (2002, 18).

However important face-to-face contact is for mobilization, clean election reformers in many parts of the world today are adopting measures that discourage it. Some reforms place limits on the number of party workers a candidate may hire. Other reforms restrict the kinds of activities that these workers can engage in. In South Korea, we find both. A law first implemented in 1995 aimed to reduce vote buying by decreasing from two hundred to twenty the number of paid workers each candidate was allowed and by prohibiting door-to-door campaigning (Shim 1994; Leuthold 1997, 19). To what extent these measures affected turnout is unknown, though perhaps not coincidentally, the 1996 parliamentary elections were marked by unprecedented rates of abstention (Shin 1999, 208).

The vigorous enforcement of other types of electioneering rules or the introduction of new voting technologies can also dampen grassroots campaigning. In India, the formerly pliant Election Commission took the lead in electoral reform with the appointment of T. N. Seshan as its chief in 1990. He banned graffiti and megaphones, enforced strict spending limits, and ordered investigations into electoral corruption. Many credit Seshan with administering elections that were "the cleanest for years" (Economist 1994). But during his tenure elections also became "subdued," as one journalist put it:

> One hardly witnessed the usual accompanying din and cacophony. The walls of both public and private places were not defaced with the customary party slogans and publicity posters. There were no cut-outs, buntings and banners. The media persons, who toured various constituencies to assess the mood of voters and to know the broad trends, were surprised to find the total absence of any exuberant or visual electioneering in both urban and rural centres. They felt as if it was not the election time.[3]

The clean election crusade of Seshan not only worked but perhaps worked too well, to the extent that it flattened the excitement and boisterousness of past election campaigns.

More recently the Election Commission has expanded the use of electronic voting machines (EVMs) to reduce the incidence of "booth capturing"—the

---

2. In another field experiment, conducted in Raleigh, North Carolina, turnout decreased by 2.8 percent, an anomalous finding that Green, Gerber, and Nickerson attribute to the unusual logistical and racial problems encountered by canvassers in that city.

3. "Malpractices Despite Seshan's Writ," *Hindu,* May 4, 1996.

seizure of polling stations by hired thugs who then stuff the ballot boxes.[4] Journalists have noted the enthusiastic response of voters in several parts of the country to the new technology. Local election officials, moreover, have observed that inquisitiveness about the new machines lured some people to the polls who would not have bothered to go otherwise. As one voter explained, "I was feeling lazy about walking out of the house on a Sunday. But we heard so much about the EVM, and I was curious."[5]

Piqued curiosity may boost turnout, at least temporarily, but the new technology is also transforming a previously shared experience into a private one. In the city of Ahmedabad, for instance, one journalist attributed to the EVMs a "lack of festive atmosphere":

> Just after noon, crows were in full cry outside the Gujarat College which has seen fisticuffs and vijay sarghas' [victory rallies] after midnight in the past. But with the introduction of Electronic Voting Machine (EVM) this time the job was done quickly and clinically. One could almost feel that the mounted police, ambling down the Alliance Francaise road, would doze off and fall flat on the face as he had no job on hand, no crowd to control, no one but the bunch of crows for company.[6]

People turned instead to their televisions, "making the party workers in particular and the common man in general a sort of couch-potato poll addict." The bustle and unruliness of the election-day crowd was replaced by a seemingly clinical silence as campaign workers and voters alike withdrew into their private spaces. It is too early to discern whether EVMs will have any impact on mobilization and turnout and if so, what kind.[7] Nevertheless, this anecdotal evidence suggests that these issues deserve study.

Let us focus now on two cases for which the data are richer. The first case is nineteenth-century New Jersey, where the shift from personal to impersonal

---

4. Two features of the EVM make booth capturing difficult. First, the control unit has a close button that freezes the machine. It can be pressed by the presiding officer in the event of an attempted booth capture. Second, even if the presiding officer is incapacitated or co-opted, only one vote can be entered every twelve seconds, for a maximum of three hundred votes in one hour, a major disincentive to those who might contemplate booth capturing, which typically must be accomplished quickly before the police arrive.

5. "Voting Machines Steal the Show," *Statesman,* October 3, 1999.

6. "Usual Scenes on Counting Day Missing This Time," *Times of India,* October 7, 1999.

7. The EVMs were first used (aside from pilot testing in the 1980s) in the 1998 state elections of Delhi, Rajasthan, and Madhya Pradesh but only in a handful of constituencies. They were used in about 8 percent of all constituencies nationwide for the 1999 general elections and in all constituencies for the 2004 general elections. Because the boundaries of these constituencies have changed over time (there were many changes made prior to the 1998 elections in particular), comparing turnout levels in specific constituencies over time does not yield useful data. Nationwide turnout in the (mostly non-EVM) 1998 general elections was 62 percent; in the (partial EVM) 1999 general elections it was 60 percent, and in the (all-EVM) 2004 general elections it was less than 58 percent.

campaign strategies was occasioned by the adoption of the state-printed ballot. The second case is Taiwan after 1994, where prosecutors cracked down on vote buying and the vote brokers who engaged in it. In both cases, shifts in campaign strategy led to a decline in voter turnout.

THE STATE-PRINTED BALLOT IN 1890S NEW JERSEY

Clean election reforms are often designed to achieve goals that depart from their avowed purpose of reducing election fraud and error. In Arkansas, as we saw in chapter 2, secret ballot legislation was crafted to disenfranchise illiterate voters. In other states, leaders of incumbent parties used ballot reform to achieve different goals. Party leaders in late-nineteenth-century New Jersey, for instance, saw the printing and distribution of ballots by the state (often called the "Australian" ballot because it was first adopted in that country) as an innovative way to shore up their position relative to their own local workers.[8] If ballot reform in Arkansas had a directly partisan intent, reform in New Jersey was fashioned to tighten intraparty discipline, with similarly negative consequences for voter turnout.

By the late nineteenth century, New Jersey had become one of the most urban and ethnically diverse states in the country. According to the 1880 census, over half of the state's population lived in towns and cities, and over one-third was foreign-born (Reynolds 1988, 8). Prereform politics were dominated, as a result, by ethnic city machines that sought aggressively to bring out the vote, which they did with great success. Political clubs, parades, and meetings flourished, while voting itself was for many people an all-day event. Many businesses closed on election day as crowds gathered to gossip, drink, and follow the returns (15–49).

Local party workers played a crucial role on election day, for it was their job to distribute ballots—which had the party ticket already printed on them—to voters as they approached the polling place. These workers were, as a result, well positioned to alter the outcome of contests, something they did repeatedly. Factionalism within both the Republican and Democratic parties spurred them to distribute modified party tickets that substituted the names of maverick candidates for those supported by the party leaderships, a practice known then as "knifing" (Reynolds and McCormick 1986).

Leaders of both major parties, consequently, tended to view local operatives as "treacherous." To these leaders, the Australian ballot championed

8. It is helpful here to distinguish between two types of ballot reform. The establishment of ballot secrecy (the secret ballot) is distinct from the state's taking on responsibility for printing and distributing ballots (the Australian ballot). New Jersey introduced both at the same time. For the present discussion, the introduction of the Australian ballot is most salient, so I focus only on that reform.

by outside reformers offered a convenient means to wrest control of elections from the hands of unreliable go-betweens. To the extent that ballots would henceforth be produced and distributed by the state, the role of local party operatives would be diminished. When the Australian ballot measure came up for a vote in 1890, it won unanimous, bipartisan approval in the Senate and all but one vote in the Assembly (Reynolds and McCormick 1986; Reynolds 1988, 64).

Once implemented, the Australian ballot did indeed have its intended effect. Grassroots party workers began to disappear from the scene, and authority within the two major parties became more centralized at the state level. But the disappearance of local party workers also made face-to-face campaigning more difficult, and candidates found themselves having to rely more and more on newspapers instead (Reynolds 1988, 116). Local political clubs faded in importance, attendance at partisan rallies waned, and the number of political parades and events declined (71–73, 108–17). People also began coming to the polls in smaller numbers year after year. Between 1888 and 1900, turnout in presidential elections declined by seven percentage points (McCormick 1953, 185). The *Jersey Journal* captured the changed mood when it reported that the 1906 election was "about as dull as the back side of an ox." The article described the new climate of apathy:

> Generally speaking, there is less enthusiasm over an election now than in bygone times, and each year seems to reduce the party feeling and the exuberance. Torch-light processions are now a rarity, and are confined to relatively small bodies. There is no such involvement as characterized the elections of twenty years ago, and it is not a move for the better. The old plan made thousands take an interest, if only to get the best company in line, old and young shared in the interest. The street pageants were interesting and the sidewalks were lined with partisans and critics, all more or less interested. Everybody had a part in the proceedings and party lines were more tightly drawn. (October 25, 1906, quoted in Reynolds 1988, 114–15)

The introduction of the Australian ballot, in short, had consequences beyond reducing incidences of corruption or even centralizing power within the major parties. It also resulted in the decline of both local political activity and levels of voter turnout.[9]

---

9. Still, over the long haul it is unclear to what extent the demobilizing effect of the Australian ballot depressed turnout relative to other factors such as ballot secrecy, direct primaries, poll taxes, industrialization, diminishing ethnocultural conflict, and, as we saw in chapter 2, personal registration. There is continuing debate about the relative importance of these other factors nationwide among students of American politics such as Key (1949), Burnham (1970), Converse (1972), Rosenstone and Wolfinger (1978), and Rusk and Stucker (1978).

THE CRACKDOWN ON VOTE BUYING IN TAIWAN

Since the mid-1990s, go-betweens in Taiwan have also been the object of reformist attention, and a crackdown on their election activities has led to a decline in turnout. The go-betweens in question are vote brokers known locally as *tiau-a-ka* ("pillars") who distribute money and goods to voters on behalf of candidates (Bosco 1994; Rigger 1994). Typically, campaigns assign vote brokers to small circles of relatives, friends, and neighbors. In one rural township in southern Taiwan, for instance, each broker was assigned to an average of only seven households (Wang 2001, 26). This form of vote buying was widespread at least through the mid-1990s. Indeed, various surveys conducted in the early 1990s found that at least a quarter of the population accepted cash or goods from candidates or their agents.[10]

In 1993, President Lee Teng-hui appointed as justice minister a young firebrand named Ma Ying-jeou, who made a crackdown on electoral corruption his highest priority. Under his direction, prosecutors indicted more than half of the members of the Taoyuan County assembly for selling their votes when electing the speaker and vice speaker of the assembly in early 1994. Investigations spread to other counties. Within five months, 436 politicians were indicted, including 341 of the 858 newly elected councilors nationwide, and half of those indicted were convicted. These prosecutions sent a strong signal to politicians that a new era had begun, especially since almost all of those indicted belonged to Ma's own Kuomintang (KMT) party, including all of the 17 assembly speakers and 15 deputy speakers brought to court.

By 1995, the crackdown extended to popular elections. In Tainan County, a record 981 people were convicted in a single case of vote buying during the 1996 legislative elections. The candidate himself was sentenced to four and a half years in prison, while two of his campaign workers received sentences of over two years.[11] Between 1995 and 1998 prosecutors won 4,375 local court convictions on charges of vote buying in southwest Taiwan alone, and 95 of those convicted were sentenced to prison. While political interference led higher courts to overturn convictions of several prominent KMT members during this period, many convictions stood (Wu and Huang 2004).

The campaign against vote buying picked up even more steam in 2000 with the defeat of the KMT presidential candidate by Chen Shui-bian, the Democratic Progressive Party (DPP) leader who rode to power partly on his pledge to root out political corruption. Vowing in his inaugural address to "eliminate vote buying" and make "rule by the clean and the upright" his "topmost"

---

10. See note 13.
11. "Court Convicts Record Number for Vote Buying," Associated Press, June 29, 1996.

priority, he appointed as justice minister Chen Ding-nan, a former magistrate and legislator so respected for his integrity that he became known as "Mr. Clean." Under Minister Chen's watch, prosecutors made frequent use of wire-tapping and forensic accounting techniques to track unusual movements of cash. They also expanded the role of local police in investigating suspected cases of vote buying and provided rewards to arresting officers.[12] Among the most effective tools, according to one Ministry of Justice official, was rewarding private citizens for information leading to the conviction of vote buyers (Chan 2003). For the 2001 elections, rewards went as high as $285,000. Among the most famous and successful informants was Tsai Pai-hsiu, a water vendor and DPP activist who earned enough money to buy diamond rings, a Rolex watch, and three Mercedes Benzes.

These aggressive tactics led to rising prosecution rates. During the first three years of the DPP administration (June 2000–July 2003), the number of vote-buying cases prosecuted almost quadrupled, and the number of people prosecuted more than doubled over the last three and a half years of KMT rule (1997–May 2000) (Chou 2003, 5). As for the number of people convicted, it was 74 percent higher during the first two full years of the DPP administration (2001–2) than for the last two full years under the KMT (1998–99) (DPA 2003).

Did the mounting attack on vote buying after 1995 have an impact on the incidence of this practice? Survey data are too incomplete to draw any quantifiable conclusions.[13] Nevertheless, both foreign and Taiwanese election watchers on the ground reported a decline in vote buying during the latter half of the 1990s and into the 2000s, while many observers proclaimed the 2001 elections as the "cleanest in Taiwan's history."[14] Opinion polls, too, indicated a widespread perception that vote buying was on the decline.[15]

Ethnographic studies confirm these observations. Perhaps the most careful and detailed study was conducted by sociologist Chin-shou Wang, who gained

---

12. "Ministries Cooperate in Crack-down on Vote-Buying," *Taipei Journal,* October 5, 2001.

13. There were two national surveys conducted prior to the 1995 crackdown. One survey found that 30 percent of the respondents were aware that vote buying was taking place in their neighborhoods during the 1991 National Assembly election (Chu 1994), while a 1992 survey found that 24 percent of the respondents had accepted money (Yang 1994). Neither survey provided city or county breakdowns. Still another survey, from Kaohsiung City only, found that 45 percent of the respondents had accepted money in 1992 (Ho 1995). From the post-1995 period, I am aware of only two surveys, neither of which allows satisfactory comparison since they do not cover the same geographic areas as the pre-1995 surveys. A survey in Chiayi County found that fewer than 1 percent of the respondents were offered money in 1998 (Wu and Yen 2000), while in Taiwan's third-largest city, Taichung, and its surrounding county, 27 percent of a random sample of eligible voters reported in 1999 that they had accepted cash during any electoral campaign in the past (Cheng, Wang, and Chen 2000).

14. See, for instance, Moon and Robinson (1998, 145); Rawnsley (2003, 769); "Anti-Vote-Buying Drive Gets Credit for 'Clean' Election," *Taipei Times,* December 5, 2001.

15. "Minister Hails 'Cleanest' Legislative Election," *Taipei Times,* December 14, 2004.

the trust of KMT organizers in one southern county. He was able to follow their activities for a number of years. Prior to the 1995 crackdown, Wang observed, brokers perceived little danger as they went about their business of buying votes. Brokers he interviewed in 1993 from one rural township "had no fear of being caught, since the police were not assumed to be diligent at this task. Also, since almost all candidates . . . conducted vote buying, few feared that they would be singled out" (Wang 2001, 28–29). The situation, however, changed for candidates and brokers in this township in the mid-1990s:

> In one local case in 1995, a young prosecutor's investigation managed to keep a powerful legislator from buying 50,000 votes; he only bought 30,000 votes, and was so shaken that he refused to run for reelection again. After the DPP won the 2000 presidential election and announced that it would investigate vote buying actively and seek jail time for brokers during the 2001 elections, some brokers panicked and abandoned vote buying campaigns. Some campaign managers dared not hold broker meetings or discuss vote buying by telephone. (Wang and Kurzman 2007, 72)

Brokers in other parts of the country were similarly deterred, in large part because it was on such go-betweens that prosecutors focused their attention.[16]

It is interesting to note that voter turnout in the township studied by Wang declined sharply after the 1995 crackdown. In the 1993 local election, turnout was above 73 percent. By 1997, it had dropped almost ten percentage points (Wang 2004). This slide mirrored the decline in local election turnout nationwide that began immediately after the crackdown. Between 1994 and 1997, turnout in various local elections dropped by an average of 10 percent and for the most part continued to fall thereafter (see figure 2).

It is also noteworthy that with the 1995 crackdown on vote buying came an explosion of political advertising, especially on television. In the 1992 legislative elections, parties bought a total of 261 minutes of advertising. In the 1996 presidential and legislative elections, it jumped to 12,290 minutes. By the 2000 presidential race it climbed to 33,627 minutes (Fell 2002, 15). Fell explains the partisan context for this sudden rise:

> In the [1991, 1992, and 1993] elections the DPP actually invested more in newspaper election ads than the KMT, while since 1994 the KMT has vastly outspent the DPP on newspaper ads and since 1996 on TV ads. In the [2000 election] the KMT had almost double the amount of TV and newspaper ads. This was because in the early 1990s the KMT felt that elections could still be won with what is known as the "organization" battle, which involved mobilizing of KMT affiliated

16. "Anti-Vote-Buying Drive Gets Credit"; "Minister Says That Anti-Vote Buying Effort Is Successful," *Taipei Times*, December 1, 2001; Göbel (2001, 8); Horng (2003).

groups, such as farmer's associations, local factions, veterans, and vote buying, however, by the mid 1990s even the KMT admitted the need to invest more in the "propaganda" battle (16).

Political advertising had been important to the DPP since the early 1990s, but it became suddenly and increasingly important to the KMT in the mid-1990s, at precisely the moment when vigorous prosecutions made it more difficult for KMT vote brokers to mobilize their supporters with gifts and money.

Observers of Taiwanese politics are in general agreement that vote buying is more important to local elections than to national ones. (This may be because the total number of votes cast in local elections is typically smaller, and thus each vote—and each vote bought—carries more weight.) It is thus not surprising that prior to the 1995 crackdown, as figure 2 shows, turnout in local elections was higher than in national elections. Vote buying, after all, was a more effective mobilization tool in local elections than in national ones. Local elections, in which candidates rely on face-to-face networks of vote-buying brokers, had a higher turnout than national elections, in which candidates relied more heavily on mass media campaigning.[17] After 1994, the situation reversed: turnout for national elections exceeded turnout for local elections. This reversal, I suggest, was due in part to a decline in vote buying that affected turnout in local elections more than national ones and in part to the novelty and drama of presidential elections (1996 was the first), which drew turnouts of 76 percent in 1996, 83 percent in 2000, and 80 percent in 2004.

Both the timing of the decline in turnout and differences in turnout trends between local and national elections map closely onto patterns of vote buying, efforts to curb it, and the rise of mass media political advertising. Still, it is worth considering other possible explanations for the drop in turnout, the most compelling of which is that elections lost their novelty. Just as turnout has declined in established democracies over time, turnout in Taiwan was bound to decline as elections became routine.[18] There are two problems with this explanation. First, it assumes that the decline in established democracies is the natural result of a long experience of voting. But there are other factors involved, among them changes in how elections have been administered and how parties have campaigned. The imposition of cumbersome registration procedures in some places and the rise of impersonal strategies of mobilization

17. The total amount of newspaper advertising bought by candidates in the national 1992 legislative elections, for instance, was more than twice the amount bought by candidates in the local 1993 county magistrate and provincial municipality mayoral elections (Fell 2002,15).

18. Brown, Moon, and Robinson (1998, 573) lay out the logic of this explanation, though they find the evidence for it mixed.

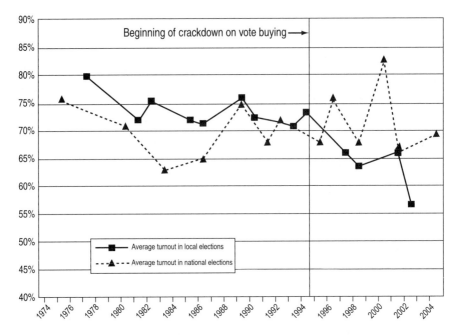

Figure 2. Turnout in local and national elections, Taiwan, 1975–2004.

Sources: Schafferer (2003, 65, 66, 94, 98, 101), Central Election Commission and National Chengchi University Election Databank (vote.nccu.edu.tw/engcec/vote4.asp).

Note: National elections include presidential, legislative *yuan,* and national assembly elections. Local elections include urban and rural township and county municipality chief elections, county magistrate and provincial municipality mayor elections, and county and provincial municipality assembly elections.

almost everywhere have both helped to generate "apathy" (Rosenstone and Wolfinger 1978; Piven and Cloward 1988; Wattenberg 2000). Second, the explanation fails to account for the timing of the turnout decline in Taiwan. Voters have been going to the polls since the 1950s. Multiparty competition emerged in the late 1980s and reached a plateau in 2000 with the election of a non-KMT president. The 1990s was thus a decade of intense political change and rising partisan competition. It seems unlikely that apathy would set in, suddenly, in the middle years of this transformation.

One final comment on the relationship between turnout and vote buying is in order. It would be wrong to assume that most Taiwanese who accept money go the polls to uphold their end of a vote-buying contract, for many people who accept money do not vote as instructed. As early as 1977, one anthropologist proclaimed the "decline of honest bribery" when he observed that

30 percent of the people in the village he was studying did not vote for the candidates who gave them money (Jordan 1977, 13). A survey of 1,263 people in Kaohsiung City following the 1992 legislative elections found that of the 45 percent of the respondents who accepted money, only 10 percent voted for the candidate on whose behalf it was given (Ho 1995, tables 7, 23).

Similarly, Wang (2001, 37, 54) compared the number of votes garnered by the KMT candidate in the rural township he studied to the number of voters who received money from KMT vote brokers (which Wang was able to determine by gaining access to the actual lists of names used by the vote brokers themselves). Sixty-seven percent of the eligible voters in the township received money from KMT brokers in the 1993 elections, but a full 45 percent of the people who received money did not vote for the KMT candidate. Still, turnout for the election was over 73 percent. Turnout was heavy even though almost half the people who received money did not vote for the candidate on whose behalf it was given.[19]

A high turnout of people who accept material rewards can be explained by a combination of factors. For sure, some people may feel compelled to vote for the candidate who pays them, but not all payment-accepting voters go to the polls simply to uphold their end of a vote-buying contract. Recall that 45 percent of the people in the township studied by Wang did not vote for the KMT candidate on whose behalf money was given. For these people, going the polls may have instead provided cover. If they had stayed home, vote buyers would have known for sure that they did not vote for the candidate on whose behalf they were given money. By going to the polls, the recipients at a minimum kept vote buyers guessing, since vote secrecy is by and large respected. Face-to-face invitations probably mattered as well, as they did in the field experiments conducted by Gerber and Green. In Taiwan, offers of money are made personally by neighborhood vote brokers. Material offers, in other words, are not simply monetary incentives; their individualized disbursement also constitutes a form of personal, face-to-face canvassing.

To conclude, available evidence suggests that the post-1994 decline in Taiwanese voter turnout is most directly attributable to the crackdown on vote buying and the concomitant rise of impersonal, mass media-centered campaigning.

19. I thank Chin-shou Wang for giving me access to the unpublished raw numbers from which I have calculated these figures. Interestingly, these numbers roughly mirror statistics from the Philippines on the impact of vote buying on turnout in the May 2001 elections. According to the Pulse Asia survey module that I commissioned (see chapter 2, note 38), 78 percent of the respondents who received no material offers went to the polls. But of those respondents who accepted money or material things on behalf of a candidate, an astounding 92 percent voted. Not all payment-accepting voters went to the polls simply to uphold their end of a vote-buying contract. A full 35 percent of them did not vote for the candidate(s) on whose behalf money was given.

Disrupting the practice of vote buying has not only lowered the number of voters who turn out to fulfill their end of a vote-buying agreement but has also made face-to-face, personal mobilization less common.

CONDITIONS THAT FACILITATE CUTTING OUT THE GO-BETWEEN

What conditions facilitate cutting out the go-between? To answer this question it is helpful to pose two more specific questions. First, what kinds of parties and candidates rely most heavily on personal mobilization and grassroots workers, and in what kinds of contexts? Second, under what conditions do parties sometimes support reforms that cut out go-betweens, reforms that undermine the parties' own ability to get out the vote?

As we have seen, face-to-face contact has become relatively unimportant in many industrial democracies today. Not all parties rely heavily on personal modes of mobilization and legions of grassroots workers. In determining which ones do, it is helpful to distinguish between electoral campaigns that are "programmatic" and those that are "clientelist" (Kitschelt 2000). Programmatic campaigns appeal to voters on the basis of policy achievements and promises of future programs. They distribute benefits to the electorate at large or to generic categories of voters (e.g., health insurance for the elderly, tax cuts for the middle class). Clientelist campaigns, in contrast, attract voters by distributing more targeted benefits (jobs, money, services) to individual voters. While programmatic campaigns tend to use television ads, speech making, and mass mailings to publicize policies and programs, clientelist campaigns must rely instead on networks of grassroots campaign workers to personally deliver material rewards. In other words, clientelist campaigns tend to require more face-to-face contact than do programmatic ones; they are thus more personal than programmatic campaigns. Why do parties and candidates rely more heavily on clientelist campaigns in some places than in others? Space permits only a few cursory remarks on this large topic. Much interesting work has been produced in recent years on the types of electoral rules that promote personal election strategies such as clientelism. One factor that appears salient, for instance, is strong intraparty competition, which prevents candidates from using party achievements (policies, programs) to differentiate themselves from other candidates. Intraparty competition, in turn, is often the product of particular electoral systems, such as the single nontransferable vote (SNTV), in which each voter casts one ballot for only one candidate in a multiseat district. SNTV is used, for instance, in Taiwan (Liu 1999).

Also salient is the size of electoral districts. The smaller the district, the less costly it is to distribute rewards to individual voters. When districts are large, the distribution of individual benefits becomes more costly, and candidates may turn to programmatic appeals, which are more cost-efficient. Indeed, it is for this reason that clean election reformers in some countries have sought to enlarge the electorate as a way to reduce vote buying. In Thailand, for instance, voting was made compulsory in 1997. Reformers reasoned that an expanded electorate would make buying votes prohibitively expensive (Schaffer 2004, 85). Similarly, in nineteenth-century England "when Parliament sought to deal with bribery that had become too extensive, their method was often to expand the offending boroughs so as to include more electors" (Cox 1987, 56). The importance of district size also helps explain why clientelist practices such as vote buying are often more important for local elections than for national ones. In the Philippines, for instance, candidates who run in local districts (for positions such as mayor, city councilor, or House district representative) are far more likely to offer gifts and money to supporters at election time than are candidates, say, for the Senate, who run in districts that are nationwide.[20]

It is, nevertheless, important to note that even within electoral systems shot through with clientelism, not all parties depend on it in equal proportions. Often, opposition parties unable to compete with rich incumbents in the distribution of material rewards adopt programmatic strategies (Hicken 2007a). In Taiwan, the KMT has been much more reliant on clientelism than has the DPP, at least until recently. In the 1992 Kaohsiung City survey, for instance, KMT candidates were found to be ten times more likely than DPP candidates to offer gifts and fourteen times more likely to offer money (Ho 1995, tables 14 and 15). The same is true in Brazil, where the Brazilian Workers' Party relies on clientelism less than other parties do. Because it "was not linked to government, was not formed from within the Congress, did not have an established team of well-known politicians, and generally lacked financial resources, it could not compete on the same turf as the other parties by using similar tactics" (Samuels 1999, 512).

Brazil is also interesting because levels of electoral clientelism vary considerably across subnational units with nearly identical electoral institutions. In wealthy Brasília clientelist mobilization was nearly nonexistent in the 1990s, while in poverty-stricken Piauí it was common. In this case, socioeconomic factors appear to have been more important than institutional ones in explaining the importance of clientelist forms of electoral mobilization (Desposato 2007).

Cultural factors, such as preexisting norms of gift giving, may also be important. In Taiwan, for instance, a culture of benevolence has made the distribution

20. According to the Pulse Asia survey module I commissioned (see chapter 2, note 38), 51 percent of the material offers made in 2001 came from candidates for mayor, 24 percent for city councilor, and 20 percent for House district representative, but only 6 percent for senator.

of money and goods a socially sanctioned method to build up personal networks. As Rigger explains, gift giving by vote brokers at election time in Taiwan became the norm because "Taiwanese custom requires a guest to greet his or her host with a small gift.... Gift-giving... demonstrates respect for the recipient; to give someone a gift is to give that person face" (Rigger 1994, 219; see also Jordan 1977, 15–19; Bosco 1994, 39–41).

Clientelism, along with the cultural, socioeconomic, and institutional conditions that promote it, is not the only feature of political life that can increase the reliance of parties and candidates on personal mobilization and grassroots workers. Sometimes it can be something as simple as ballot design. In the Philippines, for instance, the dependence of party leaders on local officials and workers is exacerbated by the use of blank write-in ballots. The government introduced this type of ballot during the early postwar era as a way to increase the independence of voters who, under the old block system of voting, were encouraged to vote for party slates (Landé 1996, 99). The blank ballot had, however, other unforeseen consequences. Many ordinary citizens had a difficult time remembering the names of all the candidates for whom they wanted to vote (some elections call for voters to write in more than forty names). Candidates, in response, began producing "sample ballots" that people could take into the voting booth to use as guides when voting. Exit polls indicate that a large number of voters still rely on these sample ballots: about half of those surveyed reported using them in the 1998 elections.[21]

The process by which candidates get their names listed on a sample ballot is complex. As Carl Landé (1996, 100), an expert on Philippine elections, explains:

> Typically, a senatorial candidate pays for the printing of sample ballots listing his own name—usually in extra-bold letters—as well as the names of other national candidates whom he wishes to help. These may or may not be the names of fellow candidates of his party. At this stage, the spaces for candidates for provincial and local offices are left blank. The senatorial aspirant must then find influential political leaders in as many provinces as possible, who are willing to pass on his ballots to the local leaders in all the municipalities of the provinces. Before distributing them downwards, each provincial and local leader can have printed onto these ballots the names of the provincial and local candidates whom he chooses to support. If and when the ballots finally reach the voters, they may show the distinctive type fonts of several printing presses.

The blank ballot and the use of sample ballots to which it has given rise have had the effect of strengthening the position of subnational leaders vis-à-vis elected officials at higher levels of government who must rely on these leaders to get

---

21. "Characteristics of the Vote," *Manila Standard,* May 25, 1998.

their sample ballots into the hands of voters (101). Subnational leaders, in turn, have also become more dependent on local operatives, known as *liders,* and *liders* have come to depend more heavily on the grassroots workers they hire. The number of grassroots workers employed today can sometimes be high. In the vote-rich poor neighborhoods of Metro Manila, it is not unusual for a mayoral or congressional candidate to deploy up to one worker for each forty registered voters in the constituency.

There is, in sum, a range of factors that encourage face-to-face mobilization. Even in this brief discussion, we have seen that go-betweens tend to be more important under some circumstances than others. Their importance in electoral mobilization seems to be greatest where there exist certain kinds of parties (incumbent, clientelist), certain kinds of party systems (candidate-centered, such as the SNTV), certain kinds of elections (local), certain socioeconomic conditions (namely, poverty), certain kinds of culture (gift giving), and even certain kinds of ballots (blank). And this list of conditions is by no means exhaustive. It also follows that the effects of clean election reforms that cut out go-betweens are likely to be felt unevenly, even within a single country. Turnout for local elections is typically hit harder than that for national ones. Turnout for parties that rely more heavily on clientelism is usually affected more than turnout for parties that rely on programmatic appeals.

For various reasons, certain kinds of parties, and parties in certain kinds of electoral systems, are more reliant than others on personal modes of mobilization. We have also seen that an array of clean election reforms—ranging from the strict enforcement of electioneering rules to the introduction of preprinted ballots to the vigorous prosecution of vote buyers—can undercut the ability of parties to use personal modes of mobilization. When these kinds of clean election reform disrupt face-to-face mobilization, why do party leaders—who are after all often legislators or government officials as well—sometimes acquiesce or indeed participate willingly in this disruption?

On this question, late-nineteenth-century New Jersey provides important clues. Recall that in New Jersey, ballot reform was a deliberately devised legislative strategy on the part of Republican and Democratic leaders to cut out go-betweens whom they saw as treacherous. In this regard, Taiwan appears quite different, to the extent that the crackdown on vote brokers appeared to have been more of a judicial matter, one directed by the minister of justice and carried out by prosecutors and the police. Indeed, when Justice Minister Ma launched the initial investigation of vote buying among newly elected assembly members in the 1994 assembly speakers' elections, "some disgruntled legislators...threatened to slash the justice system's budget in an effort to stop the probe."[22]

---

22. "Taiwan Cracks Down on Vote Fraud," Associated Press, March 31, 1994.

Here, however, the difference between New Jersey and Taiwan is more apparent than real, especially after the focus of prosecution shifted from politicians to voter brokers in subsequent elections. In Taiwan, operatives who broker votes sometimes defect to the campaigns of rival candidates, just as they did in New Jersey (Rigger 1994, 143–44, 177). Vote brokers also embezzle money or distribute it to family and friends, even to those who have no intention of voting for the candidate (Wang and Kurzman 2007). Candidates often complain privately that they cannot afford the high cost of vote buying and that they are unable to trace where the money goes. Still, they feel pressure to continue the practice because voters expect it. Many politicians have thus welcomed the crackdown on vote brokers as long as their own campaigns are not singled out for investigation (Horng 2003). In this context, it is interesting to recall, first, that prosecutors in Taiwan have gone after vote brokers more vigorously than they have candidates or vote sellers, and second, that the crackdown was directed, from 1995 to 2000, by a KMT minister of justice and netted many brokers for KMT candidates.

National political figures in the Philippines, to cite another example, also have reason to regard the local agents that they rely upon as unreliable, and this suspicion of local agents may have been one factor in building political support for reforms that may cut them out. As in late-nineteenth-century New Jersey, factional rivalries motivate local officials, *liders,* and campaign workers to shift their loyalties, and even to alter sample ballots. "By the time the ballots reach their final recipients, Landé explains, "the name of the national candidate who had paid for the initial printing may have been blocked out and replaced by that of one of his rivals" (1996, 100). I myself collected dozens and dozens of sample ballots doctored in this way during the 2001 and 2004 elections.

In this environment, national leaders find it necessary to constantly exhort local party officials and workers to support the national ticket. Shortly before the 2001 elections, for instance, the coalition party of President Gloria Macapagal Arroyo, LAKAS NUCD UMPD, took out newspaper ads with a message from the secretary general of the party:

ATTENTION!
ALL
LAKAS NUCD UMPD
OFFICIAL CANDIDATES NATIONWIDE

On this last week of the campaign for National and Local elective officials, may I enjoin all of our LAKAS NUCD UMPD official candidates nationwide to close

ranks by in turn enjoining your organizations, constituencies, supporters, and voters to vote for a complete and straight ticket of all of our LAKAS NUCD UMPD
official candidates. . . .

FOR YOUR COMPLIANCE.
Heherson T. Alvarez

More private forms of entreaty and coercion are used as well.

National politicians in the Philippines have also considered various legislative measures to discipline local officials, operatives, and workers or to
diminish their roles in election campaigning. There are draft bills in circulation, for instance, to provide state assistance to political parties so that they
become less dependent on the funds of large donors and, more to the point
for this argument, the organizations of local bosses. Other measures have
already passed into law. In 2001, Congress crafted legislation to lift the ban
on political advertising in the mass media, enabling politicians to reach voters
directly. Even more salient to the themes of this book, in 1997 the legislature passed a law that mandates the replacement of blank write-in ballots
with machine-readable preprinted ones. The primary objective of the law
was to reduce opportunities to manipulate the vote tally by speeding up the
counting process. But the introduction of preprinted ballots also promises to
alter the relationship between national candidates and local operatives. To the
extent that these ballots reduce the importance of sample ballots to voters,
national candidates may find themselves less dependent on unreliable local
intermediaries and freer to use their resources to run mass media campaigns
targeted directly at voters.

To date, the preprinted ballots and counting machines have not yet been
used, except for a few limited pilot tests. The original plan was to introduce
them nationwide for the 1998 elections. For political, bureaucratic, and financial reasons, implementation was pushed back to 2001, then to 2004, and then
still again to 2010. Since the law has yet to be implemented, we do not know
what consequences it will have. However, it seems possible, if New Jersey is
any guide and if automated counting is indeed adopted, that fewer grassroots
workers will be deployed to get out the vote, and turnout as a consequence
may decline.

To conclude, there are circumstances in which partisan legislative leaders may
support or even initiate clean election reforms that disrupt the electoral campaigns of their own grassroots workers. Specifically, legislators are more likely to
go along with, or help craft, plans to curtail the activities of local agents when
they perceive these local agents as unreliable.

From Mobilization to Deliberate Demobilization: Buying Abstention

When faced with new clean election reforms, candidates may also deliberately adopt campaign strategies designed to keep opposition supporters away from the polls. What we might call "buying abstention" or "negative vote buying"—paying voters to stay away from polls—is the most obvious and common. By paying voters to abstain from voting altogether, a candidate can prevent them from casting ballots for his or her opponent. In this section, I examine negative vote buying first in late-nineteenth-century rural New York and then in contemporary Africa and the Americas. Afterward, I identify conditions that facilitate this form of deliberate demobilization.

Buying Abstention in Late-Nineteenth-Century Rural New York

Negative vote buying first appeared widely with the advent of vote secrecy. Here I examine briefly the case of late-nineteenth-century New York, where, as in New Jersey, ballot reform was crafted to prevent the treachery of urban machine operatives and had a similar effect of cutting out the go-between (Bass 1961; Reynolds and McCormick 1986). And as in New Jersey, the Australian ballot in New York was introduced at the same time as ballot secrecy. In rural New York, however, ballot secrecy had a distinctive, apparently unanticipated effect. Because it made it more difficult for people to supply proof to vote buyers of how they voted, the reform pushed rural operatives from both the Republican and Democratic parties to rely more heavily on negative vote-buying strategies. Instead of paying for votes, operatives paid their opponents' supporters to abstain (Cox and Kousser 1981). As the state chairman of the New York Democratic Party explained in 1900, "under the new ballot law you cannot tell how a man votes when he goes into the booth, but if he stays home you know that you have got the worth of your money" (quoted in Cox and Kousser 1981, 656). A study of New York newspaper stories on electoral corruption from 1879 to 1908 revealed that the relative magnitude of negative vote buying (what Cox and Kousser call "deflationary fraud") grew dramatically after the advent of secret balloting in 1890:

> Rarely mentioned before 1890, explicitly deflationary fraud mushroomed to a quarter of the total after that date.... Moreover, if the ballot reformers sought to decrease corruption, they apparently failed, for the total number of corrupt events reported was considerably higher in the four secret-ballot than in the four party-ballot elections. (656–57)

The introduction of secret balloting in Maryland at about the same time produced a similar shift in tactics among party operatives, though comparable statistics are unavailable (Argersinger 1987, 234).

BUYING ABSTENTION IN AFRICA AND THE AMERICAS

Later innovations in election safeguarding around the globe ironically provided vote buyers the ability to *guarantee* that vote sellers would stay away from the polls once they were paid. To prevent fraudulent voting, for instance, citizens in many countries today are required to present a special identity document to vote. In places where only one type of identity document is acceptable, party workers can pay a voter to surrender the document for the duration of election day and thus make it impossible for that person to vote. Thus for the 1997 general election in Guyana, the Elections Commission required voters, for the first time, to present voter identification cards at the polling station. The response of agents campaigning for the ruling party was to buy the cards of the opposition's supporters, paying around $30 each.[23]

In Mexico, the government began to issue photo credentials in 1992 in preparation for elections in 1994 (Carter Center 1993, 18). By the 2000 elections, local Partido Revolucionario Institucional (PRI) officials were already adept at "renting" them to keep opposition supporters away from the polls. A national postelection survey conducted by a Mexican academic institution found that, as reported by Wayne Cornelius (2004, 53), "5 percent of the 5 percent of respondents who had been exposed to some form of vote buying or coercion had experienced it in that particular form." Thus, roughly ninety-four thousand potential voters had their abstentions bought.

There are other contemporary cases of negative vote buying worth mentioning as well, even if they resulted from procedures first established prior to the 1991 to 2006 period that is the focus of this study. Voters in Venezuela have long been required to present their identity cards in order to vote. Party workers often buy the cards of opposition voters, for about $25 each, during local and regional elections. Since electoral districts in these elections are smaller than for national elections, each abstention bought has a greater weight. One seasoned party leader explained:

> In the national election, [buying identity cards] would have been a useless expenditure of precious money. But when it comes to governors or mayors, and opinion

---

23. "Guyana: Voter Identification Cards for Sale," Inter Press Service, November 12, 1997; "4 Arrested for Tampering with Voting Before Guyana Election," *Dow Jones International News*, November 7, 1997.

polls predict a tight race, it is easy for them to buy 500, 600, or 800 identity cards to modify the results. . . . Some candidates have said with much cynicism "I prefer to keep my millions of bolivars for the purpose of buying 800 or 1000 or 1500 identity cards than to pay for newspaper inserts or radio campaigns that do not produce the same results." (Kornblith 2002, 12. My translation)[24]

Under such circumstances the demobilization of a small number of voters is more cost-effective than trying to mobilize support through the mass media.

Buying identity documents is also practiced in several African countries. In the 2002 presidential election in Kenya, one reporter observed that "if a . . . candidate finds his campaign lagging, he typically sends his agents out with a stack of cash to buy up the voting cards of people inclined to vote for his opponent. The going rate varies but can be as little as $1.50."[25] In Zambia, party operatives have also bought up the voter cards of opposition supporters and then returned them once the polls were closed (Gwenani 2001, 7). During a by-election in one Lusaka constituency, election monitors from Transparency International found that about 10 percent of all vote buying took the form of purchasing abstention—though the monitors did not report the overall level of vote buying they detected (TIZ 2001). Data are somewhat better for Malawi. There, a university research center surveyed 767 people from five constituencies in different regions of the country. When nonvoters were asked their reasons for not participating in the 1993 referendum on the introduction of multiparty democracy, more than 5 percent of the voting-age respondents reported that they had sold their voter certificates (Mvula and Kadzandira 1998, 50).

There are, it is worth noting, other election safeguards that vote buyers have used to gain some assurance that once paid, opposition voters will stay away from the polls. To prevent double voting, for example, voters in many countries are required to dip their fingers in indelible ink after casting their ballots. In the Philippines, party workers have exploited this requirement by paying registered voters to disqualify themselves from voting by staining their index fingers with ink prior to the opening of the polls.

There is little evidence, however, that this strategy is used widely in other countries, perhaps because of the many cases around the world of voters reportedly being able to remove the ink stains with bleach, abrasives, or just soap and water. Allegations of removal have been made in Kenya, Mexico, Pakistan, Djibouti,

24. This statement was made in January 2001, when 1 million bolivars was worth a little more than $1,400. Consequently "millions" of bolivars equaled "thousands" of dollars.

25. "Panel Tries to Keep Kenya Vote Aboveboard," *New York Times,* December 23, 2002.

Sri Lanka, Panama, Namibia, Guatemala, Afghanistan, and Papua New Guinea, among other places. It is also something I observed personally as an election monitor in Senegal in 1993.

Where candidates and operatives have doubts about the indelibility of ink, they may find preelection staining to be a relatively risky strategy when other means to keep voters away from the polls are available. Even in the Philippines doubts about ink indelibility are voiced periodically, which may explain why party workers who want to keep opposition voters away from the polls often prefer to hire buses to take them on out-of-town excursions on election day.[26]

Buying identity documents is superior to ink staining in another way. When a candidate or agent pays a registered voter to stain prior to election day, it reduces turnout for the opposition by one vote. When a candidate or agent buys a voting credential, that credential can then be used fraudulently (something that happens frequently in Venezuela, for instance). Consequently, this method subtracts one vote for the opposition and at the same time adds a vote to one's own total.

CONDITIONS THAT FACILITATE BUYING ABSTENTION

Two conditions that facilitate postreform negative vote buying are particularly important to single out for discussion: uncertainty about the vote buying contract and knowledge about the partisanship of voters.

Uncertainty. Particular conditions must prevail for vote buying (in either positive or negative forms) to be a worthwhile strategy for candidates and their agents to pursue. In the first place, vote buyers must have confidence that vote sellers, or some proportion of them, will in fact vote as they were paid to do. Actually monitoring how each voter casts his or her ballot provides one means.

When balloting is secret, however, uncertainty is introduced, and vote sellers are forced to fall back on other strategies. One such strategy is to monitor the aggregate turnout of villages or neighborhoods. This strategy is especially relevant in places where candidates or their agents offer material incentives to entire villages or neighborhoods, as happened in parts of England after the introduction of the secret ballot in 1872, and in Thailand in the 1990s (Seymour

---

26. Buying voting credentials is not a viable option in the Philippines, for there is no single document or form of identification that voters are required to produce when voting, and poll workers often do not request any form of identification at all.

1915, 438; Callahan and McCargo 1996, 383). It also takes place today in India and Senegal, among other places (Subramanian 1999, 65–68; Salem 1992). The strategy is particularly effective when votes are counted at the precinct level, as in India, Senegal, and Thailand prior to 1997 (Schaffer 2002, 78–79; 1998, 136; Callahan 2002, 7).

Alternatively, agents might try to instill in recipients a sense of personal obligation to vote for the candidate. One way a candidate can produce such a feeling is to recruit givers who are respected members of their communities, or other intermediaries to whom recipients feel bonds of personal accountability. This tactic has been commonly employed in Thailand. In the 1992 elections, for instance, campaign workers for one candidate sought in each village "to recruit the person best placed to deliver support, generally someone with significant social status in the village. Other qualifications include being respectable, well-known, a local leader (either official or unofficial), the candidate's relative or close friend, as well as having other special characteristics that would make people honour their vote promises" (Callahan 2000, 25).

Neither of these alternatives, however, provides a guarantee that vote sellers will hold up their end of the deal. Therein lies the comparative advantage of negative vote buying: it is easy to monitor whether a voter goes to the polls, even when balloting is secret. The advantages of negative vote buying are magnified when clean election safeguards such as voting credentials or indelible ink can be exploited to guarantee that the voter cannot vote once he or she is paid, thus eliminating both uncertainty and the need for election day monitoring.

Not all antifraud safeguards work equally well as vote-buying guarantees, but typically the better the safeguard works against fraud, the better it works as a mechanism for negative vote buying. Candidates and their agents, for instance, would prefer to purchase abstentions in an election where ink is truly indelible and applied to all voters than in an election where the ink can be removed or in which poll officials neglect to check prospective voters for ink stains. Purchasing abstention is more likely when only one form of voting credential is accepted at the polls (typically a voter's card) than when several forms of identification are acceptable (voter's card, passport, driver's license, and the like). It is for this reason that election officials in Zambia, after receiving numerous reports of negative vote buying, announced days before the 2001 polls that voters would be allowed to vote without their voting cards as long as they could produce their national registration card along with the official form issued to them when they registered to vote.[27] Multiplying the forms of acceptable identification so close to election day removed the guarantees on which vote buyers had counted.

---

27. "ECZ Counters Voters Cards Buying," *Monitor,* December 25–December 27, 2001.

Knowledge. A more careful look at England after the passage of the Ballot Act of 1872 reveals another condition that promotes postreform negative vote buying. As in rural New York, vote buying was common in certain English boroughs prior to reform. And as in New York, the secrecy provision of the Ballot Act had the effect of making it more difficult for party operatives to observe how people voted. The response of operatives in these English boroughs was, however, unlike that of their counterparts in rural New York. As one historian of electoral reform in England noted:

> The chief effect of the [secret] ballot was merely to decrease the price of votes, which in some places fell from five pounds to five shillings. In constituencies of this type…every election was conducted upon corrupt methods, and the evil rather increased after 1872. The Macclesfield commission reported in 1881 that while it seemed doubtful whether any election in the borough had been fought on really pure principles, "the corruption of the last election was far more widespread and far more open than had been the case at any previous parliamentary election, at all events of recent years, though the bribes were in most cases trifling in amount."…At Boston the agents felt it necessary to make more corrupt bargains than had previously been the case, when the exact number that could be counted upon was known. (Seymour 1915, 434–35)

Electoral agents newly constrained by the secrecy law spread money widely, hoping for a return on some small portion of their investment. New York party agents chose instead a strategy that would provide a more guaranteed return. What accounts for this difference?

Electoral agents in England chose their strategy because they knew little about the preferences of the many people newly enfranchised by the Reform Act of 1867, which nearly quadrupled the size the electorate (Helmore 1967, 7). Candidates and their agents had not yet, by the 1870s, figured out how these new voters were likely to cast their ballots. In this environment, as one historian remarked, electoral agents "might think twice before spending large sums on doubtful voters but would not mind risking a few shillings" (O'Leary 1962, 102). Rural New York party agents, in contrast, had intimate knowledge of their electorate. Communities were stable, party workers were themselves community residents, and these workers were able to conduct thorough preelection canvasses. With these canvasses in hand, party agents could identify exactly which voters they needed to keep at home (Baker 1984, 179, 190 n. 55).

We might expect negative vote buying in today's reforming democracies, then, only in places where parties can easily identify rival supporters. The fact that partisanship in Guyana is largely race-based certainly facilitated that kind of identification. Electoral agents of the Indo-Guyanese ruling party could easily pick out Afro-Guyanese supporters of the opposition. Similarly, partisanship in Kenya, Zambia, and Malawi tends to run along ethnic or regional lines (Wiseman 2000, 638; Burnell 2003, 390–91; Ndegwa 2003). The demographics of partisanship and its relationship to negative vote buying are more complex in both Mexico and Venezuela, though scattered evidence suggests that indigenous communities, where partisanship and ethnic identity tend to overlap, are particularly prone to having abstentions bought (Kornblith 2002, 14; Hernández Carrochano 2003, 2).

It should be noted, however, that strong regional patterns of partisanship may also limit the magnitude of negative vote buying. When opposition partisans are clustered in discrete geographic locales, buying abstention can be dangerous for the operatives who are actually charged with seeking out people willing to sell their voting credentials, since it requires venturing into towns or villages that may be hostile to them and their party. In Kenya, armed youths in one constituency assaulted six agents of the then-ruling Kenya Africa National Union days before a by-election. As reported by the BBC, the agents "were believed to have been offering people money in exchange for their voting cards when they were attacked."[28] In another incident, a Nairobi politician was almost killed during the 2002 election campaign "when a mob beat him for allegedly buying voters cards" (CDU 2002, 42).

Other Cases of Partisan Demobilization?

In the 1991 to 2006 data set of clean election reforms, I discovered no instances of partisan demobilization beyond the cases I have discussed in this chapter. I suspect, though, that there may have been instances that went unnoticed by the journalists and election observers whose accounts I surveyed. It is, after all, the *response* of parties to clean election reform that causes this form of vote depression. Because of this indirect impact on turnout, partisan demobilization—especially in its unintended form—may be more obscured from view than either legal disenfranchisement or administrative exclusion. Certainly it is a phenomenon to which we should be more attentive.

Candidates are often forced to alter their campaign strategies when new clean election measures are undertaken. Sometimes the new strategies they adopt have a demobilizing effect. This demobilization can be either intentional

28. "Violence at Kenya Polls," BBC News, January 12, 2001.

or unintentional. It is intentional when candidates choose to keep the support-ers of their opponents away from the polls. It is unintentional when candidates are forced to shift from more effective strategies of personal, face-to-face mo-bilization to less effective strategies of impersonal mobilization that rely heavily on the mass media.

These two forms have different facilitating conditions. Intentional demobili-zation—buying abstention—tends to occur when other vote-buying guarantees prove ineffective and when candidates can easily identify supporters of rival can-didates. Like the intentional variants of legal disenfranchisement and administra-tive exclusion, buying abstention requires in-depth knowledge about voters. All three intentional variants, in addition, tend to occur where there is organizational strength, be it in the legislature, administration, or political party.

In contrast, unintentional demobilization—cutting out the go-between—is most likely to occur where reforms restrict or disrupt personal mobilization strategies; and these reforms are most likely to be acquiesced to, or pushed, by parties that have weak control over their local officials and workers. Like the unintentional variant of administrative exclusion, then, cutting out the go-between is most likely to occur where there is organizational weakness—in this case, indiscipline within the party.

Focusing exclusively on such differences, however, obscures important points of commonality. One theme implicit in the discussion of both the intentional and unintentional variants of partisan demobilization is thus worth articulat-ing explicitly: parties do not necessarily have an interest in high turnout. This is self-evident in the case of negative vote buying, but it is sometimes also true when one's own potential supporters are kept away from the polls. As Watten-berg (2000, 76) explains:

> As individual office-seeking organizations, there is unfortunately little reason for parties to be concerned about poor turnout levels. In fact, it is more efficient for a party to win an office with fewer votes. This would be akin to General Motors making just as much money with the sale of fewer cars.

The intuition here is that parties may well prefer lower aggregate turnouts and smaller electorates when having fewer voters translates into substantially lower campaign costs. This is particularly true in places where voter mobilization re-lies heavily on the widespread distribution of gifts and money.

While low turnout may be in the interest of parties, it is important to em-phasize that it not good for the legitimacy of parties, for the vibrancy of the party system, or for the inclusiveness of participation. Does this chapter, then, argue in defense of dirty but mobilizing electoral practices such as vote buying?

To be sure, positive vote buying is effective at getting people to the polls, even people who do not vote for the candidates who gave them money. Giving money to individual voters is, after all, a form of face-to-face mobilization. To stay at home is to shun a personal invitation and to elicit approbation or retribution.

That vote buying boosts turnout does not, however, make it a benign practice. It can compromise democratic accountability (Stokes 2007), intensify economic inequalities (Baland and Robinson 2007), and fuel organized crime (Schaffer 2004, 84). Consequently, the argument here is not that reformers should turn a blind eye to it. The point, rather, is to understand how the practice of vote buying gets people to the polls so that we can better identify the ways in which anti-vote-buying efforts sometimes depress turnout. This information can be used to design measures that offset the demobilizing impact of anti-vote-buying reforms.

For example, compulsory voting—as practiced today in Belgium, Australia, and Uruguay, among other places—might be gainfully bundled with other anti-vote-buying reforms. It furnishes an alternative set of private incentives for people to go to the polls—most commonly, to avoid fines or to become eligible for certain government services. Compulsory voting also provides an institutional disincentive for vote buying: by expanding the electorate it makes vote buying more expensive. The fines or other penalties associated with nonvoting also offset the gains voters might receive for selling their abstention.

Of course, compulsory voting may not always achieve these goals. For it to work, both enforcement and supportive social norms must be strong (Hill 2004, 492–95; Hill and Louth 2004, 12–14). The problem is that vote buying tends to be most rampant in places where both law enforcement and civic-mindedness are weak. Consequently, the imposition of compulsory voting where enforcement and norms are weak is unlikely to be effective. Indeed, by law voting is already mandatory in the Philippines, but this legal provision has had no detectable impact on levels of vote buying or turnout because it goes completely unenforced. Compulsory voting may thus be most viable for a country like Taiwan, where vigorous law enforcement has been the cornerstone of its anti-vote-buying campaign and where a growing economy promises to enlarge a presumably civic-minded middle class.

The main point here is that if clean election reformers, or the people who watch over them, can be made more aware of how reforms affect the mobilization strategies of parties, they might consider antidotes to keep turnout from falling.

5

Civic Educators

Disciplinary Reaction

E lection watchdog groups, public-minded corporations, government election bodies, reformist political parties, and other civic educators sometimes try to clean up dirty electoral practices by teaching ordinary voters to change their behavior. The goal of this education, typically, is to convince people to obey existing election laws, whether it be to vote secretly, to refrain from selling their votes, or to resist the temptation of voting more than once.

To the extent that civic educators wish to train voters to act "correctly," their efforts have a disciplinary component. This reality suggests a need to understand how people who are the target of educational reform experience and react to these disciplinary efforts. Whether voters spurn, absorb, ignore, or misunderstand specific educational messages will have significant implications not only for the effectiveness of the education campaign but also for the quality of the resulting democracy.

Rarely has civic education been studied as a disciplinary project, so empirical data on such reactions are scarce. For this chapter, I thus found it necessary to gather evidence on the ground. Among countries instituting clean election reforms, the Philippines stood out as a promising research site since civic education is a major component of reform there. In this chapter, then, I examine in some depth the case of the Philippines, drawing on mass surveys as well as open-ended interviews I conducted or supervised with ordinary voters, politicians, civic educators, and advertising executives. As we shall see, unanticipated reactions to civic education campaigns in the Philippines resulted in iatrogenic harm, alienation in particular. Before turning to this analysis, however, a few words are in order to put the Philippine experience in its proper comparative context.

Education Campaigns around the World

Among the behaviors that civic educators around the world single out for reform, vote buying appears to be the most common, perhaps because educators believe it to be particularly amenable to change and perhaps, too, because it is so widespread. Credible reports of vote buying have come from all corners of the world, and in many countries the scale of this practice has been huge (Schaffer 2007, 2–4).

In trying to convince voters to refrain from selling their votes, many civic educators have kept the message simple and palatable: accept the money, but vote your conscience. In Bulgaria, the party representing the Roma told their supporters to "eat their meatballs, but vote with your heart" (Pinto-Duschinsky 2002, 74). Civil society groups in Zambia urged voters to "eat widely but vote wisely" (Gwenani 2001, 9). Jaime Cardinal Sin, archbishop of Manila during the twilight years of Marcos, advised voters to "take the bait but not the hook" (Youngblood 1993, 199).

Other civic educators have taken other tacks, perhaps realizing that this kind of message may encourage voters to ask for money. Prior to elections in 1989, reformers in Taiwan produced stickers with the message "My family doesn't sell votes" and asked voters to display them on their houses (Rigger 2002, 5). In Brazil, the slogan of a national ad campaign was "Votes don't have a price, they have consequences" (Desposato 2003). In Mexico, Catholic bishops distributed pamphlets informing parishioners, "Your vote is free...it cannot be bought or sold."[1] Radio spots broadcast in Guinea told voters, "Your voice is sacred, so no material goods should influence your choice" (NDI 1999b). Civic educators in South Africa advised, "Do not vote for a party which offers money or food for exchange for your vote. One who tries this is corrupt" (NDI 1995).

How have voters responded to these educational campaigns? Empirical data are scattered and thin, but what we do know is not encouraging. A researcher in Taiwan discovered that not everyone reacted to the "My family doesn't sell votes" sticker as civic educators had anticipated:

> In 1991 I interviewed an opposition party activist in a southern Taiwanese village who said she wouldn't dream of using the sticker, which she found embarrassingly self-righteous. She gave me the sticker as an example of how out of touch activists in Taipei were with conditions in the countryside. (Rigger 2002, 5)

---

1. "Mexican Church Urges Catholics to Vote Their Conscience," Associated Press, May 4, 2000.

In Thailand, voter education campaigns also produced unintended consequences. During the 1995 election, for instance, public service ads inspired the
very behaviors they were trying to discourage—in schoolchildren no less. One
observer explained:

> To promote the elections, mock polls were organized in many schools. But in one
> primary school there were unexpected results: "one team bribed the others with
> candy, while another straightforwardly stuffed papers with their candidate numbers
> into the hands of younger pupils." This was not seen as a natural thing for Thais
> to do. Rather, as the assistant principal told the press, it was the product of modern
> media culture: "They did not know they were doing anything wrong. They saw
> anti-vote-buying advertisements on TV but did not get the whole message. They
> thought bribery might help them win, so here we got plenty of candy today."
> (Callahan 2000, 133)

Children were not the only ones to draw the "wrong" lesson from voter education campaigns. A network of Thai election monitoring organizations hosted
a series of educational forums in Chiang Mai province in anticipation of the
2000 elections, with funding provided by the National Democratic Institute
for International Affairs. A primary goal of the forums was to teach voters not
to sell their votes. After interviewing some 1,700 attendees, evaluators found
that, perversely, "there was a slight increase after the forum in the number of
participants who believed that it was wrong to sell their votes and not vote for
the buyer" (Thornton 2000, 29). In other words, the forums, like the anti-vote-
buying ads to which the schoolchildren were exposed, reinforced or produced
the very beliefs they were designed to dispel.

During the lead-up to the 2001 elections in the Philippines, poll-watching
groups like the National Citizens' Movement for Free Elections (NAMFREL)
and the Parish Pastoral Council for Responsible Voting (PPCRV) sponsored
a variety of radio, television, and newspaper public service ads on the evils of
vote buying. They also distributed flyers, pamphlets, and posters, while several corporations placed their own newspaper ads. One NAMFREL handout
challenged voters, "Ask yourself, why is the candidate treating your vote as a
commodity or an item in a sari sari [corner convenience] store?" A NAM-
FREL newspaper ad reminded voters, "Your vote is valuable. It does not have
a price." Still another asked "Do you love the country or the money?" A
full-page newspaper ad placed by 3M Innovation (the maker of Post-Its) told
voters, "Don't be blinded by money. Vote with your conscience." Another
newspaper ad paid for by Red Horse Beer warned voters: "A little pocket
change won't put you ahead. Don't get bribed. Vote for the right candidate."

Pagbabago@Pilipinas—a group of artists, educators, businessmen, and professionals dedicated to social reform—distributed a song through NAMFREL and parish offices called "You Can't Buy Me" (*Hindi Mo Ako Mabibili*). The song contained the following lyrics: "You can't buy me. I won't make that mistake again. You think because I'm poor, you can fool me.... What do you think, I don't have self-respect? No, you can't buy me."

To gauge the effectiveness of this kind of advertising, I put together a team of interviewers. We showed three print ads to 160 randomly selected voters in five communities around the country where vote buying is common.[2] Only 29 percent of the respondents, we found, thought that someone in "a community like theirs" would change his or her mind about accepting money from a candidate upon seeing the 3M "blinded by money" ad. For the Red Horse Beer "pocket change" ad, that figure dropped to 22 percent, and it was a mere 14 percent for the NAMFREL "your vote is valuable" ad. The ads, furthermore, elicited strong negative reactions among many respondents, making nearly one in five feel, in their words, "manipulated," "humiliated," "insulted," and the like. Also worth noting is that a number of respondents thought that some of the ads would encourage, not dissuade, people from selling their votes. Typical is the reaction of a farmer who remarked that "this ad says not to accept pocket change, so it means: go for the highest bidder!"

When we asked another fifty-four voters in Metro Manila (including twenty-four who had accepted money in elections past) whether seeing the ads would have had an effect on *their own* behavior, only one man said that seeing these ads would have changed his mind about taking money (but not about his choice of candidates).[3] All others responded that the ads would have had no effect whatsoever. Indeed, nineteen of the fifty-four people (35 percent) had seen one or more of these ads during the 2001 election campaign and reported that the ads did not influence their choices at that time. Just as significant, one of every five voters—and one of every three voters who did not accept any money—were downright offended by the ads, calling them "hurtful" or "insulting." One indignant retiree snapped, "They think I can be bought for pocket change? Don't they know I wouldn't accept even a large sum of money?"

Anti-vote-buying education campaigns, as far as we can tell, have not proven to be tremendously effective in either the Philippines or Thailand, nor is the anecdotal evidence from Taiwan auspicious. In the rest of this chapter, I explore

2. These communities were located in the National Capital Region and the provinces of Quezon and Catanduanes in Luzon, Iloilo in the Visayas, and North Cotabato in Mindanao.

3. In addition to the NAMFREL "Your vote is valuable," the Red Horse Beer "pocket change," and 3M "Don't be blinded by money" ads, interviewees were asked to comment on the NAMFREL "Do you love the country?" ad.

some of the reasons that education campaigns have not only failed but also had unintended damaging side effects. I focus on the Philippines, where, unlike Taiwan or Thailand, voter education has been the cornerstone of efforts to curb vote buying.[4]

To preview the argument, I make the case that it is in part the class character of the civic education movement in the Philippines that has both hamstrung efforts to convince poor voters to stop selling their votes and alienated many of these voters. Civic education campaigns present an upper- and middle-class view of vote buying that does not match up well with how the poor themselves experience it.

These differences in how the higher and lower classes view vote buying are embedded within larger differences in how the rich and poor see each other and their respective roles in democratic politics. To understand how class affects the effectiveness of civic education, it is thus necessary to first examine these broader differences.

Class in the Philippines

Because class is a key category for this analysis, a few words on its meaning in the Philippine context and its relation to civic education are in order. Class distinctions are important and real to most Filipinos, though precise class boundaries are hard to delimit. There is a long-standing debate among academicians about the structural attributes of "the middle class," or "the bourgeoisie." Opinion pollsters and market researchers distinguish five classes: A (very rich), B (moderately rich), C (middle class), D (moderately poor), and E (very poor). Estimates of the class composition of the Philippines using this schema vary somewhat. Depending on the survey, classes A, B, and C—the middle and upper classes—together make up between 7 and 11 percent of the population, class D between 58 and 73 percent, and class E between 18 and 32 percent.

The use of these lettered categories has, notably, spread beyond the polling and marketing industries. Journalists writing for the daily papers regularly talk about the "ABC crowd." People in urban centers sometimes also use these categories to designate themselves and others. Residents of Metro Manila (the city of Manila itself plus surrounding cities and towns) are familiar enough with these categories that pollsters can ask interviewees to place themselves in one of them.

---

4. On the significance of vigorous law enforcement in Taiwan see chapter 4. On the importance of institutional reform in Thailand see Hicken (2007b).

There are, of course, still other categories that ordinary Filipinos use to designate class. When speaking about wealth, speakers of Tagalog, the most widely spoken language in the country, sometimes distinguish *mayayaman* (the rich) from *mahihirap* (the poor). When speaking of politics and social order, they might differentiate *elitista* (the elite) from *masa* (the masses). In the realm of taste or culture they differentiate those who are *burgis, sosyal,* or *coño* (from the upper class but more broadly, classy, smart, chic, snooty) from those who are *jologs* (crass, low class) or *bakya* (literally "wooden clog," meaning poor, tacky, cheesy, old-fashioned). These categories, to be sure, are not completely overlapping. Not everyone who is wealthy is a *coño* sophisticate. Not everyone who is poor has provincial *bakya* taste. It is also noteworthy that an awareness of "middleness" is growing, no doubt because the number of managers, teachers, and other white-collar workers has itself grown in the past few decades.

For the purposes of this analysis, the middle and upper classes—however loosely we must content ourselves with defining them—will be grouped together. One reason is that the number of people who belong to these classes is relatively small. Consequently, pollsters typically group the rich A and B classes together with the middle C class when presenting their findings. The few quantitative data that are available thus do not often permit finer distinctions.

Another reason for grouping the middle and upper classes together is that civic educators tend to be drawn from both strata. Among the most active participants in election watchdog groups are middle-class white-collar workers, educators, and church leaders; upper-class local capitalists and corporate managers who perceive their business interests to be damaged by the lack of transparency and accountability in government; and middle- and upper-class students attending elite universities or private high schools.

The two most prominent voluntary organizations involved in cleaning up elections are NAMFREL, which conducts a "quick" parallel vote count to deter and detect vote padding and other forms of "wholesale" cheating, and the PPCRV, which fields poll watchers on election day to deter intimidation, vote buying, and other forms of "retail" malpractice. In the 2001 elections, NAMFREL claims to have fielded more than 150,000 volunteers nationwide, while the PPCRV reports that it fielded more than 450,000. Both organizations also engage in voter education.

While a wide array of civic associations and church groups—from the Women's Action Network for Development to the National Council of Churches in the Philippines—belong to NAMFREL, big business plays the leading role. The general secretary of NAMFREL in 2001, Guillermo Luz, was also the executive director of the Makati Business Club, whose membership consists of senior executives from the largest corporations in the country. The national chairman of NAMFREL at the time, Jose Concepcion, Jr., was also chairman of the board of the Concepcion family-owned RFM Corporation, the country's second-largest food and beverage conglomerate. The national secretariat of NAMFREL, tellingly, is located in the RFM corporate headquarters. The list of business and professional associations that have donated labor, money, and materials to NAMFREL reads like a who's who of the Philippine corporate world. Among them are the Philippine Chamber of Commerce and Industry, the Management Association of the Philippines, the Bankers Association of the Philippines, the Integrated Bar of the Philippines, and the Federation of Philippine Industries. Business and professional organizations have leadership roles in the organization's most dynamic provincial chapters as well. As one observer noted, "'[F]ree and fair elections' is the new business of business" (Hedman 1998, 166; see also Hedman 1999).

As for the PPCRV, its origins can be traced to a small breakfast hosted by the archbishop of Manila in 1991. Among the guests were Haydee Yorac, board member of the Commission on Elections (COMELEC), and Henrietta de Villa, national president of the Council of the Laity of the Philippines. As the conversation turned to the upcoming 1992 elections, those present decided to initiate, in words attributed to Yorac, a "big organized systemic endeavor" to "repel the evil" of goons, guns, and gold (Bacani 1992, 40). The PPCRV was officially launched five months later by the archdiocese of Manila, and it soon spread nationwide. While the seven members of the board of advisers are all bishops or archbishops, the PPCRV is a lay organization. The national chairman comes from the laity, as do most members of the national executive board. The PPCRV relies, furthermore, on the lay pastoral council of each parish to supply coordinators and volunteers.

The lay membership of the PPCRV is disproportionately middle-class. As the PPCRV noted in its report to COMELEC on the 1992 elections, "the involvement of the poor, as deduced from the data, was not clearly manifested" (de Villa 1992). The same concern—that "volunteers belong to the middle class, less from grassroots"—was echoed in a 1996 national conference report (PPCRV 1996).

If civic educators come mostly from the middle and upper classes, vote sellers are concentrated among the poor. According to a national survey module I commissioned,[5] in the 2001 national and local elections 8 percent of voting-age adults in the ABC classes were offered money, as were 9 percent of the D class and 7 percent of the E class. Though people in each of these three categories received offers in roughly the same proportion, there are far more people in

5. See chapter 2, note 38.

the D and E classes, which together make up no less than 89 percent of the population. Thus, in absolute numbers, many more poor people were offered money. The poor were also more likely than the better-off to accept what was offered: 68 percent of class D respondents and 75 percent of class E respondents accepted, compared with only 38 percent of ABC respondents.

Philippine Democracy Viewed from Above

It might not be an overgeneralization to say that many in the middle and upper classes find elections to be a source of both frustration and anxiety. Election after election, politicians whom they perceive to be inept, depraved, or corrupt are returned to power. Actors, entertainers, and sports heroes with little or no experience in politics routinely do well in the polls. In the 2001 elections, a child rapist serving a life prison sentence won a congressional seat, as did a candidate fighting extradition to the United States on charges of wire fraud, tax evasion, illegal campaign contributions, and conspiracy to defraud the government.

Consequently, many in the middle and upper classes are left with a feeling of electoral powerlessness. The ABC classes, when grouped together, make up no more than 11 percent of the electorate, which means they do not often decide electoral outcomes. Whoever wins the vote of the D and E classes wins, period. Such was the (successful) strategy of presidential candidate Joseph "Erap" Estrada, who ran in 1998 on the platform *Erap para sa mahirap* (Erap for the poor). Winning 38 percent of the class D vote and 48 percent of the class E vote, he was not hurt by weak support among the ABC classes (only 23 percent). Going into the election, Estrada knew that he did not need their votes, and therefore he did not court them. Some ABC voters were reported to have said that they would leave the country if Estrada were to win. His reply, broadcast on national television, was an indifferent "they can start packing" (Laquian and Laquian 1998, 111). Even the politics of Makati City—financial center of the Philippines and home of some of the poshest residential subdivisions in the county—is determined largely by the vote of the poor. When Makati's elite opposed Mayor Jejomar Binay's bid for reelection in 1995, he told them disdainfully: "[Y]ou only compromise five percent of the people here, and when it comes to votes, yours don't matter, we can even do without counting them" (Gloria 1995, 83). His assessment was correct, and he won.

Most politicians thus work hard, as Binay and Estrada did, to cultivate the poor vote. They sponsor community "projects" such as school building, street lighting, well digging, and drain cleaning. They also provide more direct payoffs to voters by supplying potential supporters with food, money, free medical care, scholarships, discounted funerals, and the like. To protect this pool of votes, politicians also take measures to prevent the relocation of poor voters to areas outside their bailiwicks. In Quezon City, for instance, a congressional representative tried to postpone the completion of a major roadway until after the election so that "his" squatters would not be resettled elsewhere.

Many in the middle and upper classes are troubled by the kind of patronage politics that results. They are also troubled by the pivotal role played by poor voters who allow themselves—in the words of one editorialist—"to be herded, fed, and paid."[6] As a result, many better-off Filipinos not only feel contempt for dirty or incompetent politicians, they also have misgivings about the poor who keep reelecting them. Not *all* wealthy Filipinos possess such feelings, of course. Crony capitalists who bankroll clientelist politicians and members of the higher classes who distance themselves from reform groups, among others, surely hold different opinions. Still, misgivings about the poor can be heard in sitting rooms, coffee houses, and office buildings across the country and read in almost all of the major newspapers.

These apprehensive feelings toward the poor intensified during the turbulent five months leading up to the legislative and local elections of May 2001. The period began with an aborted impeachment trial of President Estrada on charges of graft, bribery, and corruption. A massive popular demonstration soon followed, which resulted in his forced resignation and subsequent arrest. This provoked a large counterdemonstration in his support, which culminated, just two weeks before the elections, in a violent attempt to storm Malacañang Palace and remove the new president, Gloria Macapagal Arroyo, from power. Underlying this tumult was a gaping class divide: those who sought to remove Estrada from the presidency were drawn largely from the middle and upper classes, while those who tried to defend or reinstate him were for the most part poor.

Middle- and upper-class apprehensions found a particularly high-tech but lowbrow outlet during the pro-Estrada demonstrations, commonly referred to as "Edsa 3,"[7] in text messages exchanged by people who disapproved. Text

6. Rene Espina, "Minding Other People's Business," *Manila Bulletin*, May 20, 2001.

7. Edsa is the main thoroughfare that runs though Metro Manila. It was the site of the mass demonstrations that culminated in the ouster of Marcos in 1986, an event commonly referred to as "Edsa 1." It was also the focal point for the disproportionately middle- and upper-class "Edsa 2" protests that led to the ouster of Estrada in January 2001 (a Pulse Asia survey found that 65 percent of the adults who rallied at Edsa 2 came from the ABC classes; if those in class D with some college education or middle-class occupations are included, then the total middle- and upper-class representation jumps to 74 percent [Bautista 2001, 8]). And it was there again that the poor gathered in late April and early May 2001 to protest Estrada's arrest; this gathering is usually called "Edsa 3."

messaging is wildly popular in the Philippines among those wealthy enough to afford cellular telephones, and during the Edsa 3 demonstrations the many critics of Estrada exchanged an enormous number of messages containing disparaging jokes about the poor who attended.[8] Even though I did not engage in politics while in the Philippines, I myself received dozens. Many were also reprinted approvingly by newspaper columnists.

Some messages questioned the motives of those who went to Edsa 3 by mocking their hunger and poverty. One message read: "Edsa 1: free the nation from a dictator. Edsa 2: free the nation from a thief. Edsa 3: free lunch, dinner, breakfast and snacks too...let's go!" In other words, those who participated in Edsa 1 and Edsa 2 were moved by their principles; those who gathered at Edsa 3 were there for the handouts. Other messages derided those who went to Edsa 3 for being stupid: "The world's looking at the Philippines again. The rally at Edsa will be in the Guinness Book of World Records for the largest gathering of fools, idiots and imbeciles ever." Still other messages disparaged those at Edsa 3 for being unclean: "Calling all the filthy and ignorant, the toothless and unclothed, let's prove we have no brains—go to Edsa, please pass." This form of derision was not confined to texting. In the Tagalog-language media, the poor who rallied at Edsa 3 were referred to as *mabaho* (smelly) and *hindi naliligo* (unbathed). In the English-language media, the poor were called, more poetically, "the great unwashed."

This focus on dirt reveals the journalists' and texters' class anxiety rather than their powers of observation.[9] As anthropologist Mary Douglas (1966) has taught us, "dirt" is something that is not in its proper place. In the eyes of many better-off voters, the poor have been literally out of place—both at Edsa and in the electoral arena. It is because the poor hold undue influence, many of the better-off believe, that politics is stinking and rotten.

The power of this "dirt" construct can be seen in the skewed reaction of President Arroyo to organizers of the Edsa 3 protest, who played over loudspeakers a well-known, ribald drinking ditty called *"Gloria Labandera"* (Gloria the Laundrywoman) in an attempt to mock her. To their surprise, the president embraced the image. With pride, she revealed to the nation that she was, in fact, the granddaughter of a laundrywoman. Soon after, the National Food Authority began selling discounted rice and sugar from Gloria Labandera rolling

8. In 2001, subscribers sent at least 70 million messages daily, and more than 60 percent of those subscribers belonged to the ABC classes.

9. Class anxiety was reflected in the use of terms such as "dirty" and "smelly" to describe the poor in early-twentieth-century Sweden and pre–World War II England as well. See Frykman and Löfgren (1987, 261–62) and Orwell ([1937] 1958, 127–36).

stores. A detergent manufacturer even proposed to the president using the name Gloria Labandera for a new line of soap.

The new president, in a metaphorical sense, was poised to launder the "dirty" nation (see figure 3). But getting rid of dirt requires more than metaphorical cleansing or promotional gimmicks. Cleansing requires real action. "Filth is precisely that which we are taught to renounce and repel forcefully," writes Filipino scholar Vicente Rafael, "while the inability to separate oneself from it is taken to be a pathological sign of immaturity and perversion that requires corrective intervention."[10] As Rafael suggests, there are at least two ways to clean what is morally dirty: it can be repelled or corrected. Middle- and upper-class reformers in the Philippines have contemplated both strategies.

To repel dirt is to push it back to where it belongs. For instance, some in the Philippines have suggested barring the poor, or some portion of the poor, from participating in elections at all—an idea that has even attracted the attention of the lofty Newsmakers Breakfast Forum. One proposal is to disenfranchise those who do not file tax returns; another is to require voters to pass

Figure 3. President Gloria Macapagal Arroyo, "This is what I use!" Cartoon from the *Philippine Daily Inquirer*, July 24, 2001.

10. Vicente L. Rafael, "Dirty Words," *Philippine Daily Inquirer*, July 24, 2001.

a competency test to limit the franchise to the better educated, who also happen to be the better-off.

Neither of these solutions has been tried. Nor is it likely that either will be implemented anytime soon, since each would face serious political and constitutional challenges. Thus most reformers—for practical, political, or ethical reasons—have banked on a different way to put the poor in their place: corrective intervention. That is, they have tried to discipline the poor, to train them to vote "correctly." As one columnist observed, "We call the poor dumb for not voting wisely, which is just another way of saying for not voting the way we want them to."[11]

Voter education, however, requires knowledge about those who are to be educated. To effectively teach people how to vote "wisely" requires understanding the reasons why they vote "unwisely." After Edsa 3, there was a new awareness among members of the middle and upper classes that they did not really understand those whom they wanted to educate. "Isn't it amazing that in this day and age there still exist undiscovered islands in our archipelago?" wrote one commentator. "In early May we discovered one such island: a colony of smelly, boisterous and angry people. They are the poor among us."[12]

Philippine Democracy Viewed from Below

How, then, do the poor—this "undiscovered colony"—understand Philippine democracy and their place in it? To explore this question, I and two research assistants conducted 139 interviews in 2001 with a random sample of registered voters in four areas of Barangay Commonwealth, Quezon City.[13] Quezon City, located within Metro Manila, is the largest city in the country. It has a population of over 2 million (the population of Manila itself is only 1.5 million). Barangay Commonwealth is the largest barangay in Quezon City, with a population of about 120,000. (A *barangay*, or community, is the smallest administrative unit in the Philippines.) The people who live in Barangay Commonwealth are predominately poor. The four areas in Commonwealth under study, with a total population of about 14,000 registered voters, have no class A or class B residents, and only 10 percent belong to class C. The vast majority fall

---

11. Conrado de Quiros, "Tongues on Fire," *Philippine Daily Inquirer*, May 1, 2001.

12. Leandro V. Coronel, "Discovering the Poor," *Philippine Daily Inquirer*, May 19, 2001.

13. We chose at random from the voter registry 2 percent of the people who were listed as living in each of the four areas. Of the people who actually still lived there—many had moved abroad or to the provinces after registering, and a few had died—our response rate was 81 percent.

within the D and E classes. Barangay Commonwealth is thus a typical urban-poor community.

What we learned from the interviews was that to many residents of Barangay Commonwealth, a major problem with Philippine democracy is that the poor are not shown kindness or respect, that those with power and money act in ways that are rude, hurtful, or unlawful. As a dressmaker explained to us, "There is no democracy at this time because they [the rich] don't listen to the poor. The way they look at us is really ugly." One woman described her own personal experience:

> The rich treat us so inhumanely. They look at us as if we were rats. When I used to work as a house helper my employer used to beat me. ... Someone called on the phone, and she accused me of giving out the number. She started hitting me all over. She was rich so she felt she had the right to do that.

This kind of treatment understandably leads to feelings of insult and indignity. Such feelings help explain why Edsa 3 received such widespread support from residents of Barangay Commonwealth. To them, the demonstrations represented above all a plea or demand on the part of the poor to be noticed, to be heard, and to be treated with humanity.

In terms of electoral politics, this moral calculus leads many voters to choose candidates whom they perceive to be caring, kind, and helpful, candidates who respect their *kapwa*—their fellow human beings—especially those who are poor.[14] It is not that issues and policies are irrelevant to poor voters, but even abstract concerns often get translated into a language of personalized care. It is this language of caring that so many people in Commonwealth use, even when talking about politics in general. One housewife, for instance, explained to us that "a politician who treats other people [*kapwa*] well will always win." A low-level accountant similarly told us that "when we vote for a person...he should do good things for us. He should be able to help us if we're in need. If there is a disagreement among us, he should show us that he's concerned." Not surprisingly, many people we spoke with judged candidates on their concrete acts of caring. The reasons offered by one unemployed elderly widower for voting for then congressman Sonny Belmonte to be mayor of Quezon City were typical:

> He's very helpful to fellow human beings. He helps the poor. He helped me personally. When my wife was dying, I asked for his help. I told him I didn't have the money to pay the hospital bills, and he gave me five thousand pesos. I had first gone

14. On the meaning and significance of *kapwa* see Enriquez (1986).

to [congressman] Liban [another candidate for mayor]. The people in his office told me to go to the Quezon Institute, or to go ask Belmonte. They told me to go here; they told me to go there. My gosh, they made me feel so stupid!

This man chose not to vote for Liban because Liban's staff had refused his request for assistance. Worse, they had given him the runaround. To him it had been humiliating and shaming. Belmonte, in contrast, had helped the man and had treated him with dignity.

Politics, then, for many among the poor in Barangay Commonwealth, is a politics of dignity. Bad politics is a politics of callousness and insult, while good politics is a politics of consideration and kindness. In contrast, many in the upper and middle classes tend to view bad politics as a dirty politics of patronage and corruption, while they see good politics as a clean politics of issues, accountability, and transparency. Interestingly, the personalized distribution of material rewards from candidate to voter figures prominently in both lower- and upper-class characterizations, but while it is lauded in the first one, it is reviled in the other.

Class and the Meaning of Vote Buying

From this perspective, it becomes easier to see how the fight against vote buying—and more broadly the effort to replace dirty politics with clean politics—is disproportionately a middle- and upper-class project. What is less obvious is that this class character of reform has consequences. Perhaps most important, it has led reformers to misunderstand the electoral practices they seek to curtail.

Many in the middle and upper classes share the opinion, voiced here by a newspaper editorialist, that "the *masa* [masses] treats elections as mere fund-raising circuses."[15] Votes, in this view, are simple commodities that the poor exchange for money, without any moral or political reflection. Ignorant voters literally chase after the money of corrupt politicians (see figure 4). It follows that an important way to combat vote buying is to provide poor voters with a moral education to, in the words of one journalist, "rescue" them "from the bondage of ignorance."[16]

Many of the 2001 advertisements discussed at the beginning of this chapter—ads that exhorted the poor to vote their conscience, love their country, or have self-respect—issue from the same worldview. Moreover, these public service

15. Jarius Bondoc, "It's Not Just Erap, It's the System," *Philippine Star*, April 1, 2000.
16. Belinda Olivares-Cunanan, "Students Should Help Educate Voters," *Philippine Daily Inquirer*, March 13, 2001.

Figure 4. Cartoon from the *Philippine Star,* July 1, 2002.

ads echo, although in a more polite form, the same assumptions present in the derogatory Edsa 3 text messages. The poor, in both cases, are presumed to be desperate, shortsighted, and lacking in moral or political discernment. Just as the text messages assume that the poor went to Edsa for the free meals and not out of principle, these ads assume that the poor participate in elections simply as a way to come into some fast money.

But do the poor—even those who accept money from candidates—really use their votes in that way? I was able to place a few questions on the topic of vote buying in a 2001 national postelection survey of 1,200 Filipinos.[17] Responses from that survey show that "vote selling" is more complex than a simple exchange of votes for money—and this should come as no surprise if we remember the language used by the residents of Barangay Commonwealth.

17. See chapter 2, note 38.

In the national survey, only 38 percent of poor voters (classes D and E) who accepted money reported voting for the candidate, or roster of candidates, on whose behalf the money was offered. Of those 38 percent, one in five said he or she would have voted the same way even without being offered anything. Thus money appears to have influenced decisively the vote of only about 30 percent of the poor voters who accepted it. In other words, most voters who received money still apparently exercised their freedom of choice.

Furthermore, those who accepted money had mixed sets of motives for doing so. To be sure, economic motives are sometimes powerful. In the national survey, 29 percent responded that they accepted the money because they needed it. But there were other, more morally saturated reasons as well, including a desire not to embarrass the person who did the offering (9 percent) and a belief that candidates have an obligation to give money or things to their supporters (9 percent).

When these survey responses are put into the context of the open-ended interviews we conducted with poor voters in Barangay Commonwealth and other areas of Metro Manila, a still more complex picture emerges. There we found that many people accept money because they do not see all forms of money giving as attempts to purchase their votes. Local operatives who actually distribute the money often say it is simply a "handout" that does not obligate the voter to the candidate. Indeed, many voters that we talked to distinguished giving money with strings attached (what they called "vote buying") from giving money without such strings (what they called "goodwill" money). And most people we spoke with saw goodwill money as less problematic than vote buying. In the words of one unemployed voter, "It's definitely not OK to buy votes! That's against the law. But to spend money for the purpose of spreading the candidate's name and goodwill, I guess that's OK."

Goodwill money is given as a gesture of generosity on the part of a candidate. It carries no explicit understanding that the voter will cast a ballot for that candidate. What it may do is demonstrate to the voter that this is indeed a candidate who cares, who pays attention to the poor. It seemed to have this effect on a laundrywoman we interviewed, who explained to us that "there were no conditions attached to the money that they gave me so I didn't feel I had any obligation to them. But I voted for them just because they bothered at all to give me something."

It appears, then, that to many urban poor voters the moral calculus involved in deciding whether to accept money or gifts is embedded within, and derived from, the politics of dignity described above. It is all right to accept gifts if they come from candidates who are showing consideration, paying attention, and offering help. A similar calculus appears, furthermore, to be used by the rural poor. Indicative is how voters in the village of San Isidro, Bataan, reacted to reformist candidates who ran on a platform of clean politics and elections.

To distinguish themselves from corrupt traditional politicians, they refused to distribute money or even to shake people's hands. To voters this refusal signaled an unwillingness to "be in solidarity" with the community. As a result, the reformists fared poorly on election day in San Isidro (Alejo, Rivera, and Valencia 1996, 108–9), as they have in other rural parts of the country for apparently similar reasons (Hawes 1989, 17).

These observations suggest that voter education materials that tell people not to treat their votes like commodities miss the mark since most poor voters do not think of their votes in that way. The resulting friction between reality and representation generates much of the antipathy felt by many poor voters across the nation toward the education materials:

> I find this ad irritating; they think that when I vote it's because of the money. (Small-town market woman)
> Automatically this ad impresses upon you that you can be bribed. I find that insulting. (Nurse in Quezon City)
> This ad makes it seem that elections only focus on vote buying. It is insulting to those who don't accept money. (Village fisherman)
> The words hurt; they see voters as greedy. (Domestic helper in Manila)

An anthropologist who studied the urban poor of Metro Manila provides an explanation for why these voters may have felt so offended:

> What matters most to people...is the way others attribute or deny value to them as human beings. It is primarily in this context that wealth differences are to be understood. Indeed, it is the common burgis [bourgeois] tendency to portray the lives of the poor purely in terms of material deprivation that people...find so degrading and shaming. Seen as eking out a bare hand-to-mouth existence, they are effectively denied their own humanity and culture. (Pinches 1992, 174)

It is precisely this *burgis* portrayal of the poor as people driven only by material need, as people without principles, that provided the basis for voter education in 2001 and that seemed to pique so many of the respondents.

The Damage to Democracy: Alienation

Most poor voters that we interviewed do not like the feeling of being bought. Their reasons for accepting things from candidates are complex and are often tied to their vision of what good politics ought to be or how good politicians ought to behave. Voter education materials that ignore this reality and instead reproduce middle- and upper-class stereotypes of the poor do not appear likely to change the behavior of those who accept money from candidates.

Such attempts at voter education, to make matters worse, are insulting to many poor voters, especially to those who do not engage in vote selling at all. Recall that 35 percent of the registered voters we interviewed in Metro Manila immediately after the 2001 elections were exposed to education materials during the campaign and that 20 percent of all respondents and a third of the non-vote-selling respondents found such materials offensive.

This offensiveness is damaging to democracy. Most directly, the education materials alienate the poor from the poll-watching organizations that produce and distribute most of the advertisements. The ire of many of the people that we interviewed, after all, was directed not only at the ads themselves but at the people who put them out. As two of our interviewees commented, *"They* see voters as greedy" and *"They* think that when I vote it's because of the money."

This anger and alienation partially explain why PPCRV and NAMFREL officials complain regularly that they have difficulties recruiting volunteers among the poor. In Quezon City, for instance, recruitment by the PPCRV was twice as efficient in wealthier neighborhoods as in poor ones for the 2001 elections. Data I collected from seventy-five precinct territories spread over seven barangays and encompassing more than 113,000 registered voters show that the PPCRV attracted one volunteer for every 119 registered voters from predominantly middle- and upper-class neighborhoods (70 or more percent ABC classes) but only one volunteer for every 240 voters from predominantly poor neighborhoods (70 or more percent D and E classes). Even though many among the poor support several core goals of the PPCRV and NAMFREL—such as reducing the incidence of intimidation, vote padding, disenfranchisement, and ballot box snatching—they are not joining these organizations in large numbers.

Therein lies the problem for democracy. Groups like the PPCRV and NAMFREL engage not only in civic education but in poll watching as well. They are the watchdogs charged with safeguarding the honesty of elections—by monitoring or participating in all stages of the election process, from registration to voting to counting to tabulation. Thus the quick count of NAMFREL helps deter politicians and their confederates from padding and shaving vote tallies, while PPCRV volunteers who staff voters' assistance desks in polling centers around the country help thousands of voters find their precincts, thereby reducing the number of people unable to vote. The less grassroots support these volunteer organizations receive, the less able they are to do their job. By alienating the poor, civic education materials designed to reduce electoral fraud have thus had the ironic and unintended effect of diminishing the ability of poll watchers to guard against malfeasance and administrative neglect.

We can see this dynamic most clearly at the grassroots level, especially with regard to the PPCRV. During the run-up to the 2001 elections, many alienated parishioners in Barangay Commonwealth stopped participating in church activities, including those sponsored by the PPCRV. Even some neighborhood leaders of the church distanced themselves from the PPCRV, refusing to help recruit volunteers for the 2001 elections.

Intensifying the alienation of Commonwealth residents was the bundling of the 2001 campaign against vote buying with partisan attacks on former president Estrada. This politician, to reformers, represented the worst kind of dirty politics. Indeed, both the national chairman of NAMFREL and its general secretary were, in the months and weeks leading up to Edsa 2, among the most highly visible and vocal figures calling for Estrada's resignation, as were the archbishop of Manila, the honorary chairman of the PPCRV, and other officials of the Catholic Church. In reaction, many Catholic parishioners in Commonwealth disassociated themselves from the church, citing the frequent "political" and "anti-Erap" sermons of the parish priest and the archbishop of Manila as their reasons. Even national leaders of the Catholic Church acknowledge that many among the poor have distanced themselves from mainstream Catholicism. In the words of Father Anton Pascual of the Church-operated Radio Veritas, "We saw in Edsa 3 that the poor [are] no longer with the Church" (Rufo 2001, 8). The loss here is not only to the Catholic Church. Democracy also suffers to the extent that one of the national organizations most important in ensuring honest polling is losing credibility among the poor.

The effects of alienation ripple beyond poll watching. It also deepens the rift between rich and poor, for the offensiveness of voter education is, to borrow a phrase from the sociologists Richard Sennett and Jonathan Cobb (1973), an "injury of class." Many among the poor experienced the education materials, after all, as an attack on their dignity. This idea was expressed obliquely by a health care worker, who explained to us that "many are vulgar when they speak. They don't mind if what they say is hurting other people." Where the poor feel disrespected, even small acts of class ridicule take on big meaning. One Commonwealth resident explained how, while he was at the Edsa 3 protest rally, "some cars of wealthy people passed us by and they threw coins at us. In their eyes we are not worth any more than pocket change. It's because of things like that that emotions ran high." To many of the poor we interviewed, the contempt shown by throwing change from a window was little different from the contempt expressed in the voter education ads. Both issued from a mind-set that conceives of the poor as ready to dive or vote blindly for a handful of coins.

Where class sensibilities are so brittle and where civic educators (among others) keep inflicting injuries of class both small and large, outbreaks of class rage become a dangerous possibility. It makes emotions run high, as we saw when rioting broke out around the presidential palace during the climax of Edsa 3. The tendency toward violence only increases where the poor believe that the rich manipulate the rules of the democratic game to their own advantage. In the words of one food service worker we interviewed, "The law is for those who have money. If you are poor, they just kill you." When people lose faith in the law, it becomes difficult to contain demands and grievances within the confines of lawful democratic procedure.

It is thus not surprising that the commitment of the poor to procedural democracy is shaky. National surveys consistently show that significant numbers of the poor are not fully convinced that democracy is best for them. Among the recent polls: one in five class D and E members surveyed in 2001 disagreed with the statement that "democracy may have problems but it's better than any other form of government" (SWS 2001). In 2003, 18 percent of class D respondents and 24 percent of class E respondents believed that "under some circumstances, an authoritarian government can be preferable to a democratic one," while another 20 percent of class D respondents and 22 percent of class E respondents felt that "for people like me, it does not matter whether we have a democratic or a non-democratic regime" (SWS 2003).

We must be careful, of course, not to overstate the role of civic education in generating this indifference to, or suspicion of, democracy. It is, after all, nearly impossible to measure directly and accurately the impact of voter education campaigns on the value that poor people attach to democracy; there are too many other factors that also shape opinion. Indeed, the small injuries of class inflicted by individual voter education advertisements may be of little consequence on their own. But repeated many times over and combined with other injuries of class, these education materials may well be eroding the commitment of the poor to democracy in their own small but diffuse ways.

Comparative Perspectives

Under what conditions are middle and upper classes likely to embark on anti-vote-buying civic education campaigns? Under what conditions are such campaigns likely to fail or backfire? Let me provide here only two comparative reflections.

First, reformers typically turn their attention to the behavior of individual voters only when elections are truly competitive. Where the middle class—or fragments of the middle class—are still fighting for competitive democracy, their reformist energies tend to be focused more on loosening administrative restrictions or curtailing government abuses than on changing the behavior of the poor.

To limit our focus to Southeast Asia, this fight for democracy is still ongoing in both Malaysia and Cambodia and was only recently (and provisionally) won in Indonesia. Consequently, groups like the Malaysian Citizens' Election Watch or the Cambodian Committee for Free and Fair Elections (COMFREL) have not really devoted their resources to voter education (though COMFREL did distribute in the run-up to the 2003 elections copies of a leaflet called "The Consequences of Vote Buying"). In Indonesia, election watchdog groups are still in the early stages of organizing themselves, most having had experience only with the 1999 and 2004 polls.

Within Southeast Asia, Thailand and the Philippines are the countries where electoral competition has been the most open (until a 2006 coup put an end to democratic rule, at least temporarily, in Thailand). So it is not coincidental that the most aggressive voter education campaigns have been mounted in those two countries.

Interestingly, in Thailand it was the middle class that worked most actively to promote clean elections. PollWatch, by far the largest poll-watching group in the country, drew most of its volunteers from this class: one survey found that 64 percent of PollWatch volunteers in the 1992 elections belonged to the middle class (LoGerfo 2000, 228–29). Indeed, PollWatch preferred to recruit its members from the middle class. As one scholar observed during the 1995 elections, "Since low education levels are seen as one of the main supports of election fraud, PollWatch actively recruited 'educated people'—students, teachers, business people, lawyers, civil servants—to work at the volunteer level" (Callahan 2000, 9). Thus, as in the Philippines, there was a class dimension to clean election reform: urban middle-class organizations such as PollWatch tried to discipline how the rural poor vote. As one scholar commented on the 1992 election, "These middle-class stalwarts were acting to ensure that Thailand's largely rural electorate would choose only 'good' politicians who did not buy votes" (LoGerfo 2000, 229).

As in the Philippines, the poor in Thailand sometimes reacted to the educational efforts of PollWatch and other civic educators in ways unanticipated by reformers. Recall the reaction of schoolchildren to the anti-vote-buying television ads and the reaction of those who attended the educational forums in Chiang Mai province. Both the forums and the ads generated the very beliefs and behaviors they were designed to forestall.

The second comparative point is that voter education seems most likely to have unintended consequences when it is undertaken by middle classes in formation, by people who are trying to define themselves in contrast to the poor. Such was the case in both the Philippines and Thailand.

Class, it is important to recall, is in part a cultural construction that requires the active work of self-definition. While class no doubt involves wealth and one's place in the economy, it is also constructed out of shared values, tastes, habits, and (most important for our inquiry) political commitments (Bourdieu 1984). The problem is that the task of self-definition often becomes transformed into a project of hegemony as new classes attempt to impose their recently created "superior" lifestyle on the poor (Frykman and Löfgren 1987). In this context, then, we should note that sizable middle classes in both Thailand and the Philippines are fairly new, products of the Asian miracle of the 1970s–1990s (Hewison 1996, 139–45; Pinches 1996, 115–23). As a consequence of this newness, the middle classes in both countries are culturally inchoate. In the Philippines, "the newness of the middle classes gives rise to *homines novi* in search of a format and a culture" (Mulder 1997, 115), while in Thailand, "diverse fragments and diverse constructions...have not yet been conflated into a single social class" (Ockey 1999, 245).

The incipient nature of middle-class culture has led to much storytelling by middle-class intellectuals in both countries as they try to work out what it might mean to belong to the middle class. In Thailand, such cultural work has resulted in an ongoing effort "to construct the Thai middle class in terms of political practice and ideology" (Ockey 1999, 240). In the Philippines, it has produced what one historian called "'burgis [bourgeois] projects'—efforts on the part of middle upper class intellectuals to construct and display Filipino society and culture mainly to themselves" (Cullinane 1993, 74). As in Thailand, there is a strong political and ideological component in that construction.

Public service ads that describe the evils of vote buying appear to be part of these middle-class storytelling projects. Political education campaigns, in other words, might not just have been intended for the poor; they may also have served to remind middle-class Thais and Filipinos of who they are and how they are different from—and morally or politically superior to—the poor. One scholar thus described the drive to curb vote buying in Thailand as an unintended form of "middle-class cultural imperialism" that has resulted from attempts to construct a class ideology. "The unfortunate side-effect of these attempts," he wrote, "has been to consolidate a conviction among the middle classes that democracy belongs to the middle class, and that the lower classes are incapable of effective participation in a democratic system. The middle-class frustration with the common practice of vote-buying is the most dramatic indication of this attitude" (Ockey 1999, 245–46). The same could have been written of the Philippines.

It may thus not be coincidental that in the Philippines, many of the anti-vote-buying print ads produced for the 2001 elections ran just as frequently in the English-language newspapers, which are read mostly by the middle and upper classes, as they did in the less expensive Tagalog-language tabloids. The ad placed by the makers of Red Horse Beer appeared, tellingly, only in English-language newspapers (even if the ad itself was in Tagalog). It is also suggestive that the agencies involved in crafting the Philippine ads did not, as they usually do, submit their ideas to focus group testing. Instead they relied, as an ad executive who coordinated the NAMFREL campaign told me, on their "own observations and personal experiences." This comment shows the extent to which the ad makers relied on their own conventional views of "the poor" when crafting their messages. Whatever the intent, the effect was to communicate higher-class sensibilities to a variety of class audiences. The problem, of course, is that the resulting stereotyped images, however reaffirming to the self-image of higher-class Filipinos, stood little chance of changing the behavior of the poor and sometimes aroused instead their indignation and resentment.

Other Cases of Disciplinary Reaction?

To the extent that clean election reform in general and anti-vote-buying campaigns in particular have been undertakings of middle and (sometimes) upper classes around the world today—from Taiwan to Brazil to Mexico—the problem of class-bound misperception (and the alienation of voters or proliferation of cheating that can result) may be widespread. Certainly this problem was present during earlier eras of reform. During the progressive period in the United States, for instance, "contemporary observers of fraud were predominantly middle- and upper-class native-born elites who confused the issue of illegal voting practices with their own moral beliefs about how citizens should exercise their rights to vote" (Mayfield 1993, 62; see also Allen and Allen 1981, 171–76; Altschuler and Blumin 2000, 257–58). Nevertheless, for the contemporary period we know little about the intersection of class and clean election reform or about the ways in which class-based misperception can undermine even the most well-intentioned reforms. These dynamics deserve far more careful scrutiny than they have so far received.

Efforts to clean up elections through voter education are disciplinary projects that sometimes go awry. In Thailand, attempts to educate voters left people more likely to engage in vote selling. In the Philippines, such attempts handicapped the poll-watching groups charged with safeguarding the integrity of elections and may have further estranged the poor not only from the rich but from democracy itself. Unanticipated reactions to civic education, to put it another way, caused two distinct forms of iatrogenic harm: alienation and the proliferation of election cheating.

As we have seen, these unhappy consequences can result from, among other things, a clash of moral codes, especially ones that pit higher-class reformers against lower-class "wrongdoers." Such class-based clashes are likely to originate, it appears, in attempts of new middle classes to build a political culture of their own, and in the distorting effect that this culture building project has on how higher-class reformers perceive, and act upon, the poor and their politics.

Even where anti-vote-buying campaigns are not class projects, this examination of civic education in the Philippines and Thailand highlights the importance of adequately understanding the practices one wishes to reform. Vote buying carries different meanings to different people, and these meanings can vary not only by class, but also by religion, ethnicity, levels of education, and the like. Civic education campaigns will be unlikely to succeed if they are not sensitive to this fact.

No doubt, this variability of meaning raises a set of thorny questions. Should reformers be aiming to "correct" voters, to eliminate vote buying, if indeed it is not the amoral, shortsighted economic transaction they imagine it is but rather something involving moral judgment and political reasoning? Has vote buying really been a serious defect of the Philippine and Thai electoral systems, or have efforts to discipline vote sellers reflected instead middle-class fantasies and anxieties blown out of proportion? One scholar went so far as to argue that in Thailand "vote-buying itself is not as big a problem as is our obsession with it" (Callahan 2002, 24). Could he have been right?

Different types of vote buying surely have differential implications for various aspects of democracy, not the least of which is accountability. There is a difference between a candidate who literally purchases votes and a candidate who performs favors as an ostensible gesture of caring. In the former case, accountability may run no deeper than the demand for a periodic electoral payoff. In the latter case, it can take the form of ongoing demands for help. Certain forms of vote buying, then, impose a kind of accountability on politicians and provide important sources of help for poor and vulnerable people. These forms of vote buying may well be more consonant with norms of democracy and social welfare than are vote-for-cash market transactions.

Still, no matter what meanings people attach to vote buying, or how much accountability it might entail, or how much help individuals receive, there are certain ills that typically go along with vote buying that make it a less than benign practice. To give but one example, in both Thailand and the Philippines, vote buying has been tied intimately to organized crime. Politicians need to raise large sums of money to buy votes, and because vote buying is illegal, the sources of those funds must remain clandestine. Often politicians turn to smugglers, gambling kingpins, drug syndicates, and kidnap-for-ransom rings to provide those untraceable funds. In Thailand, much of the money has come from provincial, mafia-like "godfathers" (Ockey 2000). In the Philippines, the chairman of the House Committee on Dangerous Drugs estimated in 2003 that one-quarter of all elected officials received money from drug barons.[18] The number of bank robberies, illegal gambling operations, and kidnappings for ransom in that country spikes just before the beginning of each election season.[19]

If vote-buying candidates who raise funds in such ways are elected, criminals get their financial support repaid in cash, cronyism, and protection. Vote buying thus not only fuels robbery, murder, and trafficking but also extends the reach of organized crime by expanding the political influence of the criminal financial backers on whom candidates rely. Thus, whatever benefits may accrue to individual voters or whatever moral rationality they may be exercising, the criminality and the criminalization of politics caused by vote buying impose heavy societal costs that may well justify efforts to curb it. The open question is whether civic educators—working within a logic that makes sense to the poor and respects their dignity, principles, and autonomy—can find ways to convince those who accept money that vote selling is not in their own, or their community's, best interest.

18. "Lawmaker: One-fourth of Public Officials Funded by Drug Barons," *Philippine Star,* June 26, 2003.

19. "'Jueteng' Return Driven by 2004 Polls," *Philippine Daily Inquirer,* October 7, 2002; "Solon Sees Link Between Bank Heists, 2004 Polls," *Philippine Daily Inquirer,* September 14, 2003; "President Orders: 'Go After Politicians Behind Kidnaps,'" *Philippine Daily Inquirer,* October 31, 2003.

6

Remedies

In this book I have explored how clean election reforms—reforms designed to reduce fraud and error in the casting and counting of votes—have sometimes damaged the quality of democracy in a range of cases, both historical and contemporary. I found, in fact, three broad ways in which reform can harm democracy.

Clean election reform can result in *vote depression* when it causes a drop in the number of people who register, turn out to vote, or have their votes count. It is the form of iatrogenic harm that has received most attention in the book because it is the easiest to observe and quantify. This type of harm can be inflicted either intentionally or unintentionally and takes three characteristic forms, depending on the actors who induce it. Legal disenfranchisement is caused by lawmakers who draft depressive reforms, as we saw in places such as Chicago and South Africa. Administrative exclusion is caused by the mismanagement or manipulation of reform by election officials or workers, as in Florida and Venezuela. Partisan demobilization is caused by parties, candidates, or their agents who alter their electoral strategies in reaction to clean election reforms, as in Taiwan and Guyana.

Clean election reform can also cause the *proliferation of cheating*. Proliferation can be brought about by different actors with varying levels of intentionality. Civic educators can unintentionally promote vote fraud when their educational efforts go awry, as happened in Thailand. In this instance, proliferation was an unexpected response of voters to the disciplinary efforts of educators. Election administrators can also be centrally involved in cheating. This typically occurs when the unintentionally chaotic implementation of clean election reforms by top election officials affords local election workers new opportunities to cheat—often in cahoots with partisan accomplices, as we saw in the schemes to hoard registration forms in Nigeria, double-mark ballots in Venezuela, and pad votes in the Philippines. Sometimes, too, clean election reforms can provide candidates, parties, and their agents new means by which to cheat, means that do not require the cooperation of partisan election officials. Voter identification requirements, we saw, allowed partisan operatives to engage in novel forms of negative vote buying in Mexico and Guyana.

Clean election reform can, finally, result in *alienation,* in disaffection toward various stakeholders in the electoral system, other citizens in the polity, or democracy itself. One could imagine scenarios in which alienation is the intended effect of clean election reform (as an indirect way, say, to depress the turnout of particular groups of voters). Nonetheless, in all the cases I discovered, alienation was an unintended consequence of reform. In the Philippines, it was an unexpected reaction against ill-conceived civic education campaigns. In Zambia, Malawi, and post-soviet Georgia, it was an unanticipated reaction of voters or political parties to the gross mismanagement or manipulation of clean election reform by election administrators.

In sum, the three forms of "treatment-induced" iatrogenic harm can, to varying degrees, be either the intended outcomes or the unintended effects of clean election reform. It matters whether the harm is intended, especially when it comes to contemplating remedies, the topic of this concluding chapter.

Motive, Knowledge, and Power

A variety of factors make clean election reform more prone to iatrogenic harm in some contexts than in others. These factors range from intense partisanship to the availability of detailed knowledge about the electorate to the absence of effective safeguards against negligence and abuse. Many factors apply to more than one set of actors. For instance, in the case of vote depression, knowledge about the electorate was used to craft disenfranchising legislation (by lawmakers in South Africa), to administratively exclude voters (by election officials in Florida), and to demobilize voters (by party operatives in Guyana).

Many factors are also common to more than one type of iatrogenic harm. In fact, vote depression, the proliferation of cheating, and alienation often have a common set of causes. Consequently, from a long list of specific factors that make particular instances of clean election reform prone to harm, we can extrapolate three broad facilitating conditions. When harm is intentional, actors typically have a strong *motive* to gain electoral advantage by manipulating clean election reforms; they must also possess sufficient *knowledge* to successfully manipulate the reforms to their advantage and have the *power* to act on that knowledge. Even when harm is unintended, a motive of electoral victory can drive the actions of reformers, but more commonly, unintended iatrogenic harm is caused by reformers' lack of knowledge and their inability to match means to ends.

Let us examine in turn each of these three conditions—motive, knowledge, and power—to help us identify broadly applicable ways to reduce or prevent iatrogenic harm. (Readers seeking a condensed summary of the remedies may wish to skip ahead to table 1 on page 188.)

MOTIVE

Acts taken to intentionally disenfranchise, exclude, or demobilize voters arise most obviously from a desire to win elections. Lawmakers in South Africa, election officials in Florida, and party operatives in Quebec all used clean election rules to gain partisan advantage because they believed that electoral defeat was a real possibility. The closer the election and the higher its stakes, the stronger the motive to "fix" it. Where outright fraud or overt manipulation is not possible (usually because laws guaranteeing political equality and fair competition are more or less enforced), partisans may use cleaning up elections as a pretext or opportunity to boost their electoral prospects.

Even when iatrogenic damage to democracy is unintended, a motive of electoral victory can stand behind it. It was, after all, in part a desire to use clean election reform as a vehicle to rein in unreliable party operatives, and thus make parties more competitive electorally, that motivated party leaders in 1890s New Jersey and 1990s Taiwan to introduce the Australian ballot and crack down on vote buying, respectively. In neither place did party leaders foresee the likely impact of those reforms on voter turnout.

Are there any measures that might allay feelings of electoral uncertainty or lower the stakes of an election and thus reduce the likelihood of iatrogenic harm? Certainly there are ways to reduce the risk that those who hold elected office will lose their bids for reelection. Districts might be redrawn to protect incumbents by dispersing supporters of a rival party among several constituencies where they will always remain a minority—a tactic used widely in the United States and known as "gerrymandering." Proportional representation systems might include high electoral thresholds to prevent smaller parties from taking away seats from larger parties, as in Poland, where a party must win at least 7 percent of the vote before it can be awarded a seat. Legislative seats can also be reserved for members of particular groups, as they have been in various countries for ethnic minorities, women, or sector representatives.

There are also ways to soften the impact of losing an election. A variety of institutional setups can, for instance, protect the rights and interests of losing (ethnic or religious) groups. National pacts, such as the one negotiated in Lebanon in 1943, can reserve key government posts for representatives of each group. A mutual veto can provide each group guarantees that one group will not impose its will on the other when its vital interests are at stake, as provided by the 1970 constitution of Belgium. Regional or cultural autonomy can be granted to various groups, as in India or Switzerland.

For a variety of reasons, such remedies are less than optimal cures for the kinds of iatrogenic harm that are focus of this book. In fact, some may clearly cause more problems than they solve. Gerrymandering, for instance, can dilute group representation and thereby compromise democratic inclusiveness.

In addition, what counts as "winning" or "high stakes" is highly subjective and can vary by type of election or electoral system. Winning a referendum or first-past-the-post race typically means receiving a plurality of votes. But what counts as winning an election in a proportional representation system can vary with the specific goals of the party. Indeed, at the extreme, African National Congress (ANC) officials in 1999 South Africa defined winning as the ability to secure a two-thirds majority in the National Assembly, which would have given them the power to amend the constitution unilaterally. In this case, stronger constitutional guarantees of minority group rights might only have intensified the desire of the ANC to win big. After all, the ultimate goal of party strategists was to reduce constitutional constraints on their own power. Because "winning" and "high stakes" are so context-bound, and might vary so much from election to election, it may be difficult to craft universal rules that alter durably and benignly the incentive structure of candidates, parties, and partisan election administrators.

Furthermore, to the extent that each of these motive-based remedies has broad implications for the distribution and limits of power as well as the competitiveness of elections, each will have wide-ranging effects on the political system, with consequences that ripple far beyond administering elections. From this perspective, the remedies are all too systemic to allow us to predict reliably how they will affect the overall quality of democracy.

Finally, not all iatrogenic harm is motivated by a desire to win elections. There are, after all, other less overtly political motives that can give rise to inadvertent harm. One worth mentioning is an appetite for private financial gain. The apparent misappropriation of funds by COMELEC employees in the Philippines, as we saw in chapter 3, hampered the electoral body's ability to complete its new precinct-mapping registration program and resulted in the administrative exclusion of many young voters. Where the financial motives of those who implement reforms are powerful, effective safeguards against unintended iatrogenic harm might include measures to reduce bureaucratic corruption—from incentive bonuses to credible monitoring to stiff penalties (Rose-Ackerman 1999, 39–88).

In sum, with the exception of measures that alter the financial incentives of election officials and workers, reforms that target the motives of clean election reformers tend to be overly blunt, potentially injurious, and possibly ineffective. It is therefore difficult and perhaps undesirable to alter the bedrock political motives of those involved in clean election reform.

KNOWLEDGE

When reformers effect changes based on faulty or incomplete assumptions about how voters, party operatives, or local election workers are likely to respond, iatrogenic harm may result. In the Philippines and Thailand, civic activists did not anticipate that their anti-vote-buying education campaigns would alienate voters or convince them to honor vote-selling agreements. In Taiwan, law enforcers did not anticipate that cracking down on vote buying would lead party organizers to adopt demobilizing campaign tactics. There are at least two knowledge-gathering strategies that might help prevent or mitigate this kind of unintended iatrogenic harm: performing preliminary evaluations and running pilot tests.

Preliminary Evaluations. Evaluations performed before reformers commit themselves to programs, campaigns, and systems can reveal how people who are the subject of reform are likely to respond to the planned changes. The Malawi focus group study discussed in chapter 2—which revealed voter suspicions about how the government would use photo IDs—is instructive because it demonstrates that it is possible, with the right kind of research tools, to anticipate the reaction of voters to specific clean election reforms (Mvula and Kadzandira 1998). The field experiments conducted by Gerber and Green (2000) and Green, Gerber, and Nickerson (2002) on the impact of different forms of partisan mobilization on voter turnout in the United States, as reported in chapter 4, are similarly revealing.[1]

---

1. Since these field tests involved real candidates and real elections, it is unclear whether they more appropriately belong to this category of preliminary evaluations or to the category of pilot tests discussed below. For the purposes of this discussion, it does not really matter.

I was personally involved in this kind of preliminary evaluation research when I helped NAMFREL in the Philippines prepare its anti-vote-buying education campaign for the 2004 elections (Schaffer 2003).

Several months before the elections I, with the help of a team of Filipino researchers, crafted a number of sample ads to test different kinds of messages and then solicited the reactions of randomly selected voters in five communities around the country where vote buying is widespread. Some of the results were consistent with the voter attitudes I reported in chapter 5. For instance, poor respondents from all five communities judged one ad—which focused on the corrupt motives of vote buyers—as unlikely to alter the behavior of people in a community like their own. The ad showed a fat-cat politician standing atop a ballot box, throwing money into the air and saying, "It's OK if we spent a lot of money, it'll be easy to recoup our expenses if we win!" The caption on the bottom of the page read, "Now that he won, how will he get back what he spent? Graft? Corruption? His campaign handouts are more expensive than you think." The idea behind the ad was that funds dispensed for vote buying tend to be recouped through graft and corruption and thus diminish the quality of public goods (nice streets, good health care, clean water, etc.) that communities might otherwise receive. Because graft, corruption, and other dimensions of "dirty" politics tend in the Philippines to be issues of higher concern to the middle and upper classes than to the poor, we anticipated significant class differences in how people judged the effectiveness of this ad. True to our expectations, the ad was deemed to be moderately effective by middle- and upper-class respondents but ineffective by poor respondents, who constitute the vast majority of vote sellers.

In contrast, the ad judged by far to be the most effective (and least offensive) by poor voters around the country was one that reflected the concerns voiced by the residents of Barangay Commonwealth I had interviewed and mirrored the language of dignity they had used. The idea behind this ad was that vote buying is sometimes effective because poor voters think that people who give money are making a concrete and genuine gesture that they care. But buying votes, we thought, might be framed alternatively as a gesture of disrespect; from this perspective, a politician who truly cares would refrain from buying votes. This ad thus showed a child standing in front of a shanty and contained the following text: "Mr. Candidate, are you really pro-poor? Show that you care about the poor. Don't buy votes. Help build the country instead." Of all the ads that we tested, as we had expected, this ad was judged by poor voters to be the most effective. Couched in a language likely to resonate with poor voters, the ad was able to challenge beliefs without offending.

Despite the confirmation of several of our key assumptions, we did nevertheless fail to anticipate accurately the full range of reactions to particular ads. One ad, for instance, focused on the idea that vote-buying candidates often get their money from drug and gambling lords or other criminal gangs; thus to accept money is to put innocent people in harm's way. This ad showed a gun in the background and contained the following text: "Dangerous Money. It's election time. It's time to give out cash. Where does the money come from? Kidnapping? Robbery? Drugs? Don't put people's lives in danger. Don't accept money from candidates." Whereas young urban poor respondents judged this ad to be highly effective, to our surprise some respondents from rural communities understood a different message than the one intended. To these respondents, the message of the ad was, "You had better accept any money offered to you, or else your own life will be put in danger." These respondents thus felt the ad would promote rather than deter vote buying. What we did not realize when crafting this ad, but what seems obvious in retrospect, was that in rural communities with high levels of political intimidation, raising the connection between violence and vote buying might make voters more likely to do whatever vote-buying politicians ask.

When we evaluated various themes before committing them to an ad campaign, then, some ideas that initially appeared promising to us were dropped because of their potential to generate iatrogenic harm. We feared these ads might reinforce the very behaviors that civic educators sought to curtail. The broader point is that preliminary evaluation research—whether it probes voter reactions to civic education campaigns, new identification requirements, or mobilization techniques—can catch problems *before* new initiatives are launched. This kind of evaluation research, of course, can be used to investigate the reactions of party agents and grassroots election workers as well.

Pilot Tests. Another way to compensate for gaps in knowledge is to conduct pilot tests—real-world trial runs that permit the small-scale implementation of new procedures and systems to test the reliability and accuracy of new technologies, check assumptions about voter, party, and poll-worker reactions, and the like. If pilot tests do not go well, they can lead electoral authorities to modify or abandon plans that exhibit serious defects.

In the Philippines, troubling pilot test results led electoral authorities to drop plans to use nationwide automated counting machines, which, during the bidding process, had appeared to meet the country's needs. For the pilot test, forty-two optical scan counting machines supplied by American Information Systems (AIS) were used for the 1996 elections in the Autonomous Region of Muslim Mindanao (ARMM). Although the machines were able to count ballots far faster than was previously possible by hand, the new equipment proved to be ill adapted to the human and environmental realities of Philippine elections. Heavy rains, lack of air conditioning, and crowded counting centers all raised humidity levels beyond the machines' tolerance. Sputtering generators were not able to supply steady power. Wetness, folds, ink stains, and food remains (from precinct workers eating their meals during long hours of uninterrupted work) made ballots unreadable. Locally printed ballots did not have fine enough perforations to allow smooth feeding into the machines. The physical placement of the machines and the ways in which local officials actually operated them made them vulnerable to fraud (AIS 1996, COMELEC 1996, CSER 1996).

When the machines were used again for the 1998 elections in the ARMM, many of the same problems recurred. Furthermore, lack of suitable storage facilities and poor maintenance led to their quick deterioration. By 1999, only two machines were still operable.[2] Growing skepticism about the automated counting machines among certain COMELEC commissioners blocked their nationwide deployment in 2001, and soon after the poll body decided to abandon the AIS machines altogether. Had COMELEC decided in the mid 1990s to forgo pilot testing and instead automate counting nationwide with the AIS machines, it would have squandered its limited budget and possibly caused electoral havoc. Pilot testing, in a word, functioned as an early warning system.

The Limitations of Preliminary Evaluations and Pilot Tests. Preliminary evaluations and pilot tests are valuable tools for those who genuinely seek to craft and implement salutary clean election reforms. Nevertheless, neither should be seen as a cure-all. First, reformers need the capacity to act on what they have learned. For resource-poor or low-capacity electoral bodies, watchdog groups, or civic education organizations, this can be a challenge. In Malawi, for instance, the electoral body was so dependent on funding from foreign donors that it had little leeway to override their wishes with regard to the use of photo identification cards. NAMFREL, in the Philippines, is a volunteer group that relies entirely on the donated time and expertise of advertising agencies to make its ads print-ready. Devoting much of their time to public health education during the SARS epidemic of 2003, these advertising agencies did not show much interest in helping NAMFREL in the months leading up to the May 2004 elections. Thus NAMFREL, despite the preliminary evaluation work already completed, was not able to put out any anti-vote-buying print advertising at all.

---

2. "Ballot-Counting Machines Can't Count Anymore," *Philippine Daily Inquirer,* March 9, 1999.

In addition, neither evaluation research nor pilot tests are foolproof. In South Africa the HSRC (1998a, 1998b) conducted a well-funded preelection study on who possessed which forms of identification and why. Yet this survey failed to detect the fear of bar-coded identification documents that kept a certain number of Pentecostal Christian villagers in Mpumalanga Province from registering for the 1999 elections. Evaluation research and pilot tests may thus not always have been fine-tuned enough—or directed at the right questions—to provide advance warning of particular hazards.

Evaluation research and test results can also be manipulated or misrepresented. In Ireland, an electronic voting system was pilot-tested during a general election and referendum vote in 2002. The government minister charged with managing the tests announced that the results were "very good" and gave the go-ahead to roll the system out.[3] The ministry, however, did not make public the full test results to back up this claim, and after nine requests under the Freedom of Information Act, it finally released data in 2004 that exposed serious flaws in both the accuracy and security of the system.[4] The lesson is that results that are not made available for public scrutiny are of questionable utility.

Finally, the relationship of knowledge to clean election reform is Janus-faced. On the one hand, new information put in the hands of well-intentioned reformers can remove the causes of iatrogenic harm. When advocates of voter registration in the early-twentieth-century United States became aware that women were sometimes uncomfortable disclosing their age to election officials and thus sometimes chose not to register at all, they adopted alternative ways to verify the identity and eligibility of registrants. In New York, for instance, registrants had only to declare that they were "over twenty-one" (Harris 1929, 171). In this case, new information allowed election officials to make simple but salutary changes in how clean election procedures were implemented.

On the other hand, knowledge about potential voters in the hands of partisan agents, lawmakers, or election officials can be used to suppress the vote of opposition supporters. In South Africa, the ruling party used the HSRC survey findings on possession rates of different forms of identification to enact registration reforms that reduced the participation rate of nonblack voters. In Guyana and Zambia, among other places, information about the partisan distribution of voters allowed party operatives to purchase the abstention of opposition supporters. In the United States, detailed knowledge about the political leanings of poor, minority, and absentee voters and data on the demographics

---

3. Quoted in "Electronic Voting 'More Efficient,'" *Irish Times,* November 1, 2002.
4. McCarthy (2004); "Better the Vote You Know Than the E-Vote You Don't," *Sunday Business Post,* April 18, 2004.

of photo identification possession allowed Republican legislators in Georgia, among other places, to tailor their voter identification laws in a way likely to depress the turnout of their opponents while minimizing the laws' impact on their supporters.

The vexing problem for those who wish to make elections both clean and inclusive is that there are no straightforward ways to keep information from being used for partisan purposes. In South Africa, the HSRC survey, which served as the basis for depressing the participation of minority voters in 1999, was originally commissioned by the IEC because it *feared* disenfranchising voters. After the fraud-plagued 1994 elections, the IEC came out in favor of allowing only those people with bar-coded identification cards to register. But nagging concerns about whether eligible voters actually possessed that form of identification led it to commission the survey (HAPC 1998). When the results showed significant racial disparities in rates of possession, the IEC reversed its position and argued in favor of allowing all forms of state identification for the purposes of registration. But legislators from the ruling African National Congress, who had initially opposed restricting registration to bar-coded ID holders, looked at the same survey results and enacted that restriction into law.

As the example of South Africa demonstrates, information intended to protect the inclusiveness of democracy can be used instead to curtail it. This danger is particularly grave when a single party (or bloc of parties) can unilaterally push through legislative changes or when the electoral administration falls under partisan control. Those who wish to make the electoral process both clean and inclusive should thus be particularly careful when conducting preliminary research or pilot tests under these conditions.

The bottom line: new information is potentially useful for avoiding unintended forms of iatrogenic harm, but such information also increases the danger of intended harm. Consequently, reforms that target knowledge, like those that target motive, may under unpropitious circumstances create as many problems as they solve. Reforms that focus on power—reigning in or building the capacity of those who are in a position to legislate, implement, or educate—perhaps hold more promise.

POWER

The concept of power, as I understand it, has two meanings. In the sense of "power over" it means roughly influence, domination, or the ability to have one's will prevail over others. In the sense of "power to" it means capacity or wherewithal (Pitkin 1972, 275–79). In searching for ways to prevent iatrogenic harm, one should consider both kinds of power.

To state it succinctly, the likelihood of iatrogenic harm increases when "power over" is too concentrated or when "power to" is lacking. That is, iatrogenic harm, when intentional, is typically made possible by a concentration of administrative or legislative power. Power, in this context, is the ability of partisan lawmakers to push through clean election legislation over the objections of legislatively weaker parties, or the ability of partisan administrators to implement clean election reforms with a clear bias toward a party or candidate. In contrast, when iatrogenic harm is unintentional, it typically results from bureaucratic, managerial, technical, or organizational incapacity. Lack of power in this context is an inability to relate means to ends.

To some extent, these different causes point toward different solutions. To overcome incapacity requires, among other things, developing professionalism, instituting a rational and realistic planning process, securing adequate funding, implementing safeguards against corruption, conducting evaluation research and pilot studies, and making sure that election officials have the right qualifications and that technicians are properly trained.

To reduce the incidence of deliberate partisan intervention, in contrast, requires diminishing the role that partisanship plays in elections. One obvious way to scale down the potential scope of partisanship is to make electoral administration more impartial.

Reducing Partisanship. This danger of partisanship was all too evident in Florida, as we saw in chapter 3. The administrative exclusion of eligible voters in 2000 occurred as a result of a directive given by the Republican secretary of state—a directive, by all appearances, intended to help the Republican presidential candidate in a closely fought election. Indeed, the partisan direction of electoral administration is a widespread problem in the United States, where chief electoral officers in thirty-three states are selected through popular, partisan elections (Hasen 2005, 51). It is thus not surprising that election officials in several states wear two hats at election time. As one *Los Angeles Times* reporter noted weeks before the 2004 elections:

> Ohio's Republican Secretary of State J. Kenneth Blackwell is co-chairing the president's reelection efforts there, while Republican Dean Heller of Nevada and Jan Brewer of Arizona are actively campaigning on Bush's behalf while fulfilling voting duties as secretary of state. Joe Manchin III, West Virginia's Democratic secretary of state, has pitched in to help Kerry, even while running for governor.[5]

---

5. "Key States' Ballot Officials Feel Glare of Critical Eyes," *Los Angeles Times,* October 22, 2004.

The potential for the kind of partisan manipulation we observed in Florida is by no means limited to that state.

There are, thankfully, other models of electoral administration that may be less vulnerable to partisan meddling at the top. India, Canada, Australia, and Costa Rica, among other places, have nonpartisan electoral chiefs, while New York State has experimented with a bipartisan board of elections.[6] Some of these arrangements have worked better than others. In New York, bipartisanship has not been very successful, with deleterious consequences for the quality of elections (Hayduk 2005, 75–80). As a 2004 editorial in the *New York Times* explained:

> The State Board of Elections is a case of noble intentions gone terribly awry. In an effort to put elections above politics, it was made bipartisan, with two Republican commissioners and two Democrats. But this has simply led to a constant war to subvert the structure and gain partisan advantage.
>
> Gov. George Pataki recently waited eight months before reappointing one Democratic commissioner, a step that should be automatic. In the interim, his party had the upper hand. The board's top two staff positions are supposed to be split by the two parties. But the position of executive director has been kept vacant for a year, allowing the deputy executive director, a Republican, to run the agency. Democrats have not been blameless in this feud. They have tried to take advantage of a peculiar glitch in the law that allows Democratic chairmen of the board to hold their positions more than twice as long as Republicans.
>
> When everybody's in place and the board has been truly bipartisan, the result has been deadlock. The four commissioners, bitterly divided along party lines, have been unable to adopt even basic policies. Under federal law, for instance, New York must adopt a list of acceptable forms of voter identification, but three months before the presidential election, the Democrats and Republicans on the board are still fighting over it. Local election officials, who have already started preparing election materials and training poll workers for November, are rightfully unhappy. There is a very real possibility that eligible voters will be turned away this year because of all the confusion.[7]

A bipartisan solution, at least one modeled on the New York Board of Elections, may well produce iatrogenic illnesses of its own.

Nonpartisan election administration, at least for federal elections in Canada, has experienced far fewer problems. Some analysts have even proposed the

6. Other ways to classify electoral management bodies around the world can be found in López-Pintor (2000, 21–30); Massicotte, Blais, and Yoshinaka (2004, 83–101); and Wall et al. (2006, 5–19, 85–90).

7. "The Shame of New York," *New York Times,* August 10, 2004.

Canadian approach as a model for the United States to emulate (Pastor 2004, 586–87; Simon 2005; Massicotte 2005; Hasen 2005, 11, 63). Jean-Pierre Kingsley (2004, 406), chief electoral officer of Canada from 1990 to 2007, explains how independence from partisan influence is achieved:

> First, the Chief Electoral Officer is appointed by a resolution of the House of Commons. Although 50 percent plus one vote would be sufficient, all appointments since 1920 [the year the position was created] have been made by unanimous consent.... Once appointed, the Chief Electoral Officer reports directly to Parliament, and is thus completely independent of the government and political parties. He communicates with the Governor in Council (i.e., the Cabinet) through a designated Minister of Parliament and vice-versa. The normal term of office for the Chief Electoral Officer is until retirement at the age of 65. He can be removed from office only for cause—in other words, sufficient reason—by the Governor General following a joint address of the House and Senate. To preserve the nonpartisan nature of the Office, the Chief Electoral Officer is not permitted to vote in any federal election, by-election, or referendum.

The Australian Electoral Commission, too, has received high praise for its independence and neutrality (Maley 2001; Hughes 2003).

The track record of (at least nominally) nonpartisan electoral administrations around the world is not, however, uniformly good. Electoral commissions in both Venezuela and the Philippines are, on paper at least, independent and nonpartisan. Yet high election officials in both countries have acted less than impartially. In the Philippines, a COMELEC commissioner orchestrated in 2004 an extensive vote padding and shaving scheme—caught on secretly recorded telephone conversations—that may have altered the outcome of the presidential race.[8] In Venezuela, the Consejo Nacional Electoral (CNE) took a number of dubious actions in 2004 to undermine the efforts of opposition parties to gather enough signatures to trigger a referendum vote on recalling President Hugo Chávez. Miriam Kornblith (2005, 127–28) describes one of these acts:

> Of the multiple irregular and arbitrary actions that the CNE took during this phase, the most egregious was the use of a highly questionable technicality to invalidate more than a million signatures. The Council retroactively applied a norm—it dated only from late February 2004—in order to rule inadmissible all signature coversheets on which someone other than the voter had filled in voter-identification details such as name, identity-card number, or date of birth. No

---

8. A transcript of the conversations, as well a reconstruction of how the fraud was perpetrated, can be found in the Philippine Center for Investigative Journalism (2005).

exception was to be allowed even for coversheets that bore the unique signature and thumbprint of the voter. Such coversheets were designated "blank," "with dissimilar handwriting," or "assisted." The CNE refused to recognize the validity of the signatures associated with such coversheets, even though none of the original norms intended to regulate the process expressly forbade such a practice.

What was going on was clear enough: As the signature-verification process got underway with the original criteria in force (even if partially and arbitrarily applied), it was becoming obvious that the recall had drawn enough signatures to meet the legal requirement. That was when the government fabricated its post hoc coversheet rules as a fallback device to justify the wholesale tossing out of signatures.

In the end, this move was not enough to thwart the signature drive. The referendum was held, and voters chose not to oust the president. Playing no small part in Chávez's victory, again, was the manipulation of referendum rules by the CNE—from delaying the referendum vote until the president's polling numbers were on the rise to keeping the voter rolls open beyond the legal closing day so that more of his supporters could register (132–33).

Not all "nonpartisan" (or "bipartisan") electoral bodies are, then, equally independent and neutral. National differences in overall levels of government professionalism and the rule of law are certainly germane and may help explain why the chief electoral officer of Canada is more widely believed to be impartial than his counterpart in the Philippines, land of "goons, guns, and gold." Also pertinent are the personal character and competence of the election officials themselves. Differences in these qualities might explain why COMELEC in the Philippines enjoyed a reputation of relative impartiality under Christian Monsod or Haydee Yorac but not under the direction of Benjamin Abalos.

Differences in institutional design are certainly also relevant. As we saw in New York, some designs may be simply ill conceived. In the wake of Florida 2000, American legal scholars and other stakeholders have proposed a variety of alternatives. Law professor Richard Hasen, for instance, has suggested the following setup to replace the current procedure of selecting the chief elections officer in California through partisan popular election:

California's Constitution should be revised so that the chief elections officer (who may or may not be the secretary of state) is appointed to the position for a fixed term of, say, 10 years. He or she should be nominated by the governor and approved by a 75% majority of the Legislature. Such a supermajority requirement would ensure that only a consensus candidate who could achieve broad support from both parties would be chosen for the office. The Constitution should also guarantee some independence for the budget of the office and provide that the chief elections officer can be removed only through a difficult impeachment procedure. In addition, the Legislature should pass tough conflict-of-interest provisions.[9]

Former California state senator Barry Keene (2005) fears that Hasen's proposal will establish a "10-year dictatorship" and argues instead that "transparency and an unpaid bipartisan board, appointed by the Governor subject to Senate confirmation, for staggered terms, to select and oversee a chief elections officer that serves at the pleasure of a majority of the board is the intelligent way to go."

Such proposals merit serious consideration and debate, a process that is only now beginning in the United States. This statement should not, however, be taken as an endorsement of either Hasen's or Keene's plan. To mention but one concern, the potential pitfalls of bipartisanship are all too evident in the experience of New York, while the quest for a supermajority can also result in deadlock, with similarly damaging consequences. It did at least in Venezuela. In 2003, as Kornblith (2005, 124–26) explains:

> The Supreme Court named a new person to fill each of the five seats on the CNE board, following a long and tortuous process in which the National Assembly failed to secure the requisite two-thirds majority to confirm the nominations. Although the constitution and laws state that the CNE is to be an independent, apolitical body, three of the new board members were government sympathizers, while the other two were identified with the opposition.

With a majority of seats on the council, the pro-Chávez faction was able, as we have already seen, to bend the recall referendum rules to the president's advantage.

There are, then, competing imperatives that must be balanced carefully if an electoral administration is to operate in a truly impartial fashion. First, the ideal of neutrality must be balanced against the need for effectiveness. If groups with competing political interests cannot reach a consensus on a "neutral" chief election official, or if members of an election committee are chosen to represent and balance out these competing interests, there is a danger that the result will be not neutrality but stalemate and partisan jockeying. The mechanisms for ensuring neutrality cannot be so onerous or the balancing of partisan interests so even that the whole business of administering elections bogs down.

In addition, the need for independence must be balanced against the need for accountability. To ensure neutrality, electoral authorities must be given independence, but independence can also make officials unaccountable. On the

---

9. Richard L. Hasen, "Taking the Politics Out of Elections," *Los Angeles Times,* February 8, 2005.

one hand, the threshold for what counts as "reasonable cause" to remove election officials cannot be so high or the procedures so demanding that even blatantly incompetent or partisan officials remain in power. On the other hand, the threshold cannot be so low or the procedures so slack that impartial and capable election officials can be removed for defying the wishes of influential politicians and power brokers.

This treatment of competing imperatives is necessarily incomplete, and it, like the discussion leading up to it, focuses only on the impartiality of top-level electoral officers. It should not be forgotten that partisanship can also inhabit the lower echelons of an electoral administration. Even Elections Canada—that exemplar of impartiality—has problems when it comes to midlevel returning officers, who are appointed by the cabinet and are not entirely free of partisan commitments (Kingsley 2004, 411; Massicotte 2005). A more complete discussion of nonpartisan electoral administration would thus have to take into account the entire electoral management body from top to bottom.

Be that as it may, focusing only on institutional design at any level sidesteps a glaring problem with proposals to put in place neutral electoral bodies—the problem of getting there from here. Where partisans control both the legislative agenda and the electoral administration, why should lawmakers agree to relinquish their party's control over the electoral administration? The short answer is that they might do so if they fear that the legislative balance of power will soon change or that the electoral administration may fall into the hands of an opposing party. In such circumstances, the uncertain electoral prospects of a party may provide a window of opportunity for change. Fearing what might happen if the electoral administration were to be captured by their opponents, lawmakers might agree to "tie the hands" of future electoral administrators. As we saw in chapter 3, something like this happened in Quebec when Union Nationale and Liberal Party legislators—both unsure of their future electoral prospects in a newly competitive electoral environment—agreed in 1936 to a bipartisan method of appointing poll workers. Similar considerations led Republican and Democratic Colorado lawmakers in 2005 to join together in passing a law barring the secretary of state from heading the electoral campaign of any candidate running for state or federal office.

Lawmakers might also relinquish their party's control over the electoral administration to bolster their own legitimacy. During the "third wave" of democratization that began in the 1970s, many hegemonic regimes felt intense domestic and international pressure to open up their political and electoral systems (Huntington 1991). Countries in which opposition parties attracted large followings but in which the ruling parties nonetheless clung to power by rigging or manipulating the vote saw elections lose credibility. To make elections appear fairer, shore up their legitimacy, and protect themselves in the event of electoral loss, those in power sometimes agreed to make electoral administration more neutral. This happened in both Mexico and Senegal in the 1990s. Ruling parties in both countries acquiesced to opposition demands and transferred authority over electoral administration from the executive branch to an independent body—and soon after were voted out of power (Eisenstadt 1999, 87–92; Vengroff and Magala 2001, 132).

Nonpartisan electoral bodies might be established by other means as well. In Costa Rica, reform followed from a traumatically fraud-ridden election and the revolutionary transformation it sparked. Explains one scholar:

> Electoral fraud in the 1948 Costa Rican election provoked a revolution by José Figueres, a young social democratic leader. After his army overthrew the government, Figueres dismantled the armed forces, allowed elections for a constituent assembly, and handed power back to the legitimately elected president. The new constitution gave responsibility for conducting the entire election to a new institution, the Supreme Electoral Tribunal (TSE), a fourth branch of government (Pastor 1999, 78).

In Ohio, Democratic-leaning activists pursued instead a populist strategy. They successfully filed a petition with 521,000 signatures to put a measure on the November 2005 ballot that would have created an independent state board of elections to take over the election responsibilities of the (then Republican) secretary of state. Even though voters rejected the proposal, which had many problems, the exercise demonstrates that there are multiple roads to increasing the neutrality of election management bodies.

Shared Remedies: Ways to Manage Both Incapacity and Partisanship. Summing up this discussion of power, we can say that reducing the danger of unintended harm brought about by a lack of capacity requires training, resources, and safeguards against corruption, among other things; reducing the danger of intended harm brought about by partisan meddling requires limiting the scope of partisanship, by making electoral administration, for instance, more impartial.

There are, in addition, several strategies that can do double duty. They can help both manage incapacity and keep partisans honest. To the extent that some electoral systems are vulnerable to both intended and unintended harm at the same time—Venezuela, the Philippines, and the United States come immediately to mind—measures that protect against both are all the more welcome. Such dual-purpose strategies include implementing reforms slowly, keeping technologies and elections simple, making election bodies operate transparently, and forcing them to take remedial action in the event of impending harm. Let us examine each of these four strategies in turn.

Taking it Slow. Lawmakers and election officials often push clean election reforms in response to crisis or scandal. Too often the stopgap measures that result are ill planned and thus have harmful consequences. Baby steps can help work out kinks that result in unintended harm before large-scale changes are implemented. Baby steps can also reduce levels of chaos and mismanagement that are sometimes exploited by those who wish to manipulate elections.

India is one example of a country that proceeded in small, incremental steps. Indian electoral authorities rolled out electronic voting over a period of many years. Planning and design of the new EVMs began in the late 1970s. By 1982 a locally produced prototype was developed and pilot-tested in fifty polling stations in one constituency. After this successful test, the machines were tried out in nine more constituencies around the country. In the late 1980s and early 1990s, the use of the machines was put on hold as the Election Commission of India (ECI) worked out the legal framework for their use and as concerns by various stakeholders were investigated and addressed. EVMs were then reintroduced to sixteen constituencies in the state elections of 1998. One in eleven constituencies used them in the 1999 general elections, and around half used them in the 2000 state elections. It was not until 2004 that the entire country used the EVMs—more than twenty years after the first prototypes were built. At many points in this long process, the ECI conducted or commissioned studies on the machines' reliability and resistance to tampering, as well as on their reception by voters. The machines, in a word, were tested thoroughly and their performance studied intensively before their full-scale, nationwide deployment.

It is thus not surprising that this deployment in 2004 came off without many hitches. As an editorial from a leading newspaper gushed:

It is clear that the Election Commission of India's bold and progressive decision to shift exclusively to the use of Electronic Voting Machines (EVMs) across the length and breadth of a huge country has come off splendidly. At every stage after the first field experimentation in 1982, the EVM faced prejudices and inhibitions revolving round the fear that a system of electronic vote registration could not possibly be made tamper-proof. Commendably, those in charge of conducting elections were not put off by the objections but worked with indigenous companies to come up with what is now claimed to be the world's best electronic voting machine. After a series of tests, reviews, improvements of the product, and, most important of all, persuasion of political parties, EVMs were introduced incrementally in different types of elections. It required courage and confidence in the country's technological as well as grassroots democratic capabilities to make the big jump in 2004. This has also meant a big financial outlay, meticulous planning, strenuous training, and a mass awareness programme to educate voters, especially the overwhelming majority of them who live in the countryside. It is remarkable that after three major phases of polling, there has been no problem with the EVMs worth speaking about (when the rare technical snag surfaced, technicians lost no time in putting the machine right to the satisfaction of all).[10]

By taking it slow, the ECI was able to work out kinks and bugs, build consensus, train election workers, and educate voters. As a result, the first nationwide test—involving more than 389 million voters and over a million machines—came off well.[11]

Contrast Poland, where an electronic tabulation and transmission system was hurriedly put into place for the 2002 elections. With just five weeks to implement the project, managers had no time to test it under real-life conditions. On election day, the system crashed. Although apparently no votes were lost, announcement of the election results was delayed almost a week (Pawłowska 2004, 176–77).

Contrast, too, Venezuela, where electoral authorities chose and put in service an automated vote-counting, tabulation, and results transmission system for the entire country in just fifteen months. Poll body officials went out for bids in September 1997, reached purchasing agreements in July 1998, and used the system for elections in November and December. They then used it for another election and two referendum votes 1999. The ballot configuration for each of these votes was relatively simple, and the new equipment appeared to work relatively well, though some machines did malfunction. Preparations for the 2000 mega-elections, however, went terribly wrong when the new system proved too unwieldy and bug-ridden to handle the many different ballot configurations required. Just days before the elections, the Supreme Court ordered the postponement of the vote. By the time the new presidential election was held two months later, partisan operatives had already tampered with the stored blank ballots, resulting in the exclusion of up to 5 percent of the electorate.

Contrast, finally, the United States, where local authorities have scrambled to quickly modernize election systems around the country in the aftermath of

---

10. "In Praise of Electronic Voting," *Hindu*, June 5, 2004.

11. This is not to say that the EVM is without its critics—some experts are rightly concerned about the impossibility of conducting software-independent vote recounts. More on this in the "Making it Transparent" section of this chapter.

the Florida 2000 fiasco, often making choices of questionable wisdom. Federal lawmakers, in the wake of the disputed 2000 presidential election, passed the Help America Vote Act (HAVA) in October 2002. Among other things, this legislation provided federal funding for local governments to replace their out-moded punch card and lever voting technologies. To avail themselves of the money, however, local authorities had to buy the new equipment before January 1, 2006—leaving a maximum period of only three years to choose, test, and purchase the new technology.

The actual window of opportunity was substantially shortened by foot drag-ging at the highest levels of government. As a 2004 editorial in the *New York Times* explains:

> The Election Assistance Commission [EAC], which is charged with administer-ing the act, was appointed nearly a year after the legal deadline. It was given only $2 million for its operating expenses this year, not the $10 million it was due. As a result, it works in borrowed offices, with a skeletal staff. Hundreds of millions of dollars have been allocated for making improvements at the state level, but the commission is too short on cash to distribute it. By law, the money cannot be dis-bursed until the states' plans appear in The Federal Register, and the commission cannot afford the $800,000 publishing cost.[12]

Although the U.S. General Services Administration disbursed $300 million "early" funding in 2003 before the EAC became operational, the EAC itself did not begin distributing funds until June 2004 (EAC 2004b; 2005a, 9–10).

Local authorities scrambled to meet the 2006 deadline, replacing old punch card and lever voting systems with "state of the art" optical scan or direct-recording electronic (DRE) machines. With optical scan machines, voters use a pen to mark a preprinted ballot, often by filling in bubbles; the ballot is then fed into, and read by, an electronic scanner. With DRE machines, voters enter their choices directly onto an ATM-style touch screen, or they use a wheel or buttons to select the names of candidates that appear on an electronic screen. In the 2000 elections, only 42 percent of all registered voters nationwide used optical scan or DRE machines; by the 2006 elections, the number jumped to 87 percent (EDS 2006). Unfortunately, the new voting technologies—especially DRE machines—have proven to be unreliable and glitch-prone:

- Pollwatchers monitoring 108 (of 1,787) Maryland precincts in 2004 re ported 201 problems with the state's DRE machines. These problems

---

12. "Budgeting for Another Florida," *New York Times*, February 8, 2004.

included system crashes, screen malfunctions, vote switching, and encoder failures. Because it was not possible to conduct software-independent vote recounts, we do not know the impact of these glitches on electoral outcomes (TrueVoteMD 2004).

- DRE machines in thirteen of Mercer County, Pennsylvania's one hundred precincts malfunctioned in 2004 as a result of a coding error, preventing many votes from being recorded correctly. Faulty machines in two precincts recorded only 20 to 30 percent of the votes cast for president of the United States. Countywide, at least four thousand votes were lost. The absence of paper backup receipts meant that these votes could not be recovered (Independent Election Committee 2005).

- Fifteen of Florida's sixty-seven counties switched to DRE voting after the 2000 election debacle. Machine malfunctions spanning several elections raised many concerns about their reliability. After a report disclosed that the vote count of one machine in Miami-Dade County had been added multiples times to the vote tally after its software had become corrupted, the county elections supervisor pushed to mothball his county's machines only three years after purchasing them for $24.5 million.[13]

- Machine malfunctions resulting in voter exclusion were also reported in Wake County, North Carolina (November 2002), Muscogee County, Georgia (November 2003), Fairfax County, Virginia (November 2003), and San Diego and Alameda counties, California (March 2004) (VerifiedVoting.Org n.d.).

- In 2004 alone, the Verified Voting Foundation (2004) received reports of more than 1,800 machine malfunctions, nearly half involving paperless DRE machines.

Despite the well-known shortcomings of these newer technologies, the tight schedule imposed by the 2006 deadline left little time for local electoral authorities and other stakeholders to adequately test and evaluate new systems, while the underfunded federal EAC failed to provide much guidance. Although HAVA included a $10 million budget for pilot-testing new technologies, no funds were appropriated for the program (EAC 2007). HAVA also mandated the creation of a Technical Guidelines Development Committee to draft voting equipment standards, but this committee was not formed until June 2004 and did not deliver its first report until May 2005 (EAC 2004a, 2005b). Consequently, as Keith Cunningham, president of the Ohio Association of Election

---

13. "Machine Counted Votes Several Times," *Daily Business Review*, May 12, 2005; "Florida County Urged to Ditch Voting Machines," *New York Times*, May 28, 2005.

Officials, explained as the deadline loomed close, "The people who are trying to get this done at the local level are just running blind."[14] By 2007, state officials in Florida, Maryland, and Virginia began to consider scrapping their newly purchased equipment.

A desire to prevent a recurrence of Florida 2000, along with tight federal deadlines and inadequate EAC funding, pushed local authorities to quickly put in place new voting systems that had not been adequately tested and evaluated. The modernization of American elections has consequently become haphazard and contentious, as watchdog groups file lawsuit after lawsuit to prevent the adoption of questionable technologies. In the meantime, many voting systems (both old and new alike) remain vulnerable to the twin dangers of fraud and error.

When compared to the hurried and ill-planned adoption of new election technologies in Poland, Venezuela, and the United States, the slow and deliberate introduction of the EVMs in India must be considered a success. The automation of polling in India was, of course, not glitch-free. During the nationwide rollout of EVMs in 2004, for instance, machines from some constituencies were mistakenly interchanged.[15] The EVMs also made possible a reduction in the number of polling booths, leading to the reallocation of some voters, which caused confusion on election day.[16] The EVMs also did not totally eliminate the problem of "booth capturing," for which they were designed as an antidote.[17] Furthermore, the EVMs lack an important safeguard—software-independent verification of the vote totals that would allow the electronic tallies to be audited. So far, however, there has been no large-scale failure or massive cheating, as in Venezuela, or reports of irrevocably lost votes, as in the United States.

The main point is that major overhauls in the mechanics of voting are complex undertakings that require long-term planning, extensive testing, and consensus building. To anticipate and rectify areas of potential iatrogenic harm, such reforms are best accomplished in a series of baby steps rather than in one giant leap.

Keeping it Simple. Many clean election reforms being contemplated or introduced around the world today involve technological fixes designed to

---

14. Quoted in "Push to Replace Voting Machines Spurs Confusion," *USA Today,* May 8, 2005.
15. "Repolling in Binnypet, Hoskote Booths," *Times of India,* April 21, 2004.
16. "Probe into Missing Names in Karnataka's Voters' List," *NewKerala Online Daily,* April 22, 2004, www.newkerala.com.
17. "On New Voting Machines, the Same Old Fraud," *New York Times,* April 27, 2004.

reduce the scope for human error or manipulation. These technologies include such things as tamper-proof biometric voter identification cards, computer registration databases, and various electronic forms of voting. There are a number of challenges associated with these technological fixes.

First, such systems tend to come bundled together, and their components are more tightly interlocked than they were with older technologies. The issuing of new voter identification cards typically goes hand in hand with the creation of a centralized database of registered voters; the use of electronic voting machines is often coupled with an electronic system to transmit results, and the like. The danger here is that the more complex a system—the more interaction there is between tightly connected parts—the more likely it is to suffer a catastrophic failure, since a failure of any one part may bring the whole system down.

This danger of failure only increases when reforms are undertaken by electoral bodies lacking the experience, resources, or expertise to manage change effectively. In the Philippines, the registration of first-time voters in preparation for the 2001 elections became dependent upon the successful delineation of new precincts boundaries since electoral authorities decided to use the house-to-house enumeration needed for precinct mapping as an occasion to inform first-time voters of new registration deadlines and procedures. When the process of delineation bogged down because of poor planning and a lack of technical expertise, so did efforts to register first-time voters, resulting in the administrative exclusion of as many as 3 to 6 million people. In Venezuela, a freshly appointed electoral body struggled in 2000 to manage a new automated election system that required that a new candidate database, ballot configurations, and flash card software all be in sync. When troubles arose in preparing the database, such as mistranscribed names and the use of different parameters in different parts of the country, it became impossible to prepare the flash cards in time for the scheduled elections.

In both the Philippines and Venezuela, it was because parts of the electoral system were "tightly coupled"—to use the language of systems theorist Charles Perrow (1984, 4)—that iatrogenic harm was inflicted. That is, there were no mechanisms in place to prevent a failure of one part of the system (precinct mapping, preparation of candidate database) from compromising another part (voter registration, flash card programming). When electoral bodies proved unable to manage one part, the other part suffered as well.

Tight coupling can also facilitate large-scale cheating. Someone who gains access to any number of vulnerable access points can, after all, manipulate the entire system. A computer security firm hired by the state of Maryland in 2004 to evaluate its new $55 million electronic voting system found out how easy it was to alter the electoral outcomes for the whole state by intercepting just one telephone call. As team director Michael Wertheimer explained:

> At the end of the day, these machines aggregate all their votes…and one of the machines is connected to a modem—a regular telephone line and a modem like on your home laptop. And it phones in all the results of the precinct in that county. We discovered…because the cryptography and the authentication [were] not put in properly, that we could intercept that call, as it were. In other words, we could have the machine call our computer, and when it called our computer we asked it, "What's your name and your password?" and it was happy to tell us. We changed the votes that it was sending to us and then we transferred them to the county computer—which was a mock-up, which was actually a computer sitting in our spaces, of course. And we changed the election results on the fly. Everyone on my team feels they could actually log in and change an election in a state using one of these machines. It's a spectacular statement…by people who are not prone to exaggerate. (Quoted in Lurie 2004; see also Wertheimer 2004)

In some places, the danger is more than hypothetical. In Australia, a hacker was able to break into and gain "superuser" status in the Sequent Computer System used by the Australian Electoral Commission (AEC) just three months prior to the 1993 federal election. As one journalist explained, this system is "the AEC's nerve centre and controls the electoral rolls, the election management system and the election process" (Glancy 2000, 2). Eventually the police tracked down and arrested the hacker. But much to the alarm of civic watchdogs, the AEC never disclosed what he did while he had access to the system. Tight coupling in both Maryland and Australia, at a minimum, provided an opportunity to commit fraud on a massive scale.

There are a number of strategies that might be put in place to reduce the dangers posed by unfortunate combinations of tight coupling with administrative incapacity or partisan meddling. Perhaps the most obvious is to choose reform strategies and new technologies that simply do not require tight coupling. That is, dangers of wholesale failure or manipulation will be reduced if parts of a new electoral system can be arranged so that they operate independently, so that the smooth or honest operation of one part is not dependent on the smooth or honest operation of another. In India and Argentina, for instance, electronic voting machines are literally left uncoupled, since they are not networked together. The isolation of each machine prevents the kind of systemic fraud to which the Maryland electronic machines are vulnerable.

In the Philippines, to give another example, it would have been easy to decouple precinct mapping from the new voter registration information campaign.

The two projects could simply have been administered separately. Thus the Philippine COMELEC might have followed the example of Election Canada, which uses mass mailing to inform newly eligible voters of their right to vote. Prior to the 2004 federal elections, for instance, the chief electoral officer of Canada sent registration forms to some three hundred thousand Canadians who had turned eighteen after the 2000 elections (Elections Canada 2004). In the Philippine case, killing two birds with one stone was the wrong way to go.

When it is not possible to decouple reforms or technologies, it might be wise to introduce changes sequentially. Thus in Venezuela, it might have made sense for election administrators to work out all the kinks of the candidate database before introducing electronic counting machines into the new system. Baby steps, in a word, can be an effective tool to manage complexity.[18]

Not only is it advisable to keep reforms and technology as isolated and manageable as practicable, but it also helps to keep the elections themselves simple. A major reason for the failure of the May 2000 mega-elections in Venezuela was the sheer complexity of the exercise. Simultaneous elections were planned for all elected positions in the country: president of the republic, National Assembly deputies, legislative deputies, state governors, mayors, and parochial board and local community council members, as well as Latin American and Andean parliamentarians. The exercise thus required 1,371 different ballot configurations to accommodate some 33,000 candidates. In addition, 11,200 ballot changes had to be made to reflect shifting partisan alliances in the weeks preceding the elections. This complexity proved too much for novice electoral authorities to handle—especially when it came to inputting the data into the glitch-prone candidates' database. Just three days before the scheduled date of the elections, these technical difficulties forced the Supreme Court to order the postponement of the vote—and provided an opportunity for partisans to tamper with the stored ballots. Had elections for the various posts been split up and held on two or more dates, spread far enough apart to allow adequate preparations for each, such a massive failure (and subsequent fraud) might have been averted. Indeed, the same automated election system had been used in two referendum

---

18. Some systems theorists propose redundancy as another strategy to reduce the dangers posed by tight coupling (Roberts 1990, 168). Although some forms of redundancy in the context of electoral administration do make sense (spare voting machines, extra ballot papers, provisional ballots, software-independent vote recounts), there are drawbacks to adding redundancy to all tightly coupled electoral systems. For one thing, redundancy can sometimes cause failure by encouraging laxness and risk taking (Snook 2000, 119–35). Furthermore, redundancy seems to work best in organizations marked by high levels of technical competence and ample funding (Frederickson and LaPorte 2002, 36–38). Electoral bodies, however, often lack the financial or human resources to manage the primary components of an electoral system, let alone the added burden of a redundant one. In a context of managerial incapacity, redundancy may actually increase the chances of failure.

votes and three (more limited) elections during the preceding eighteen months, without major incident.

This last recommendation, however, needs qualification. If it is wise to avoid holding electoral exercises that are so large that they become unmanageable, it is also advisable to avoid holding many separate elections held too close together in time. For one, a quick succession of elections may also overburden an electoral body. In addition, frequent elections can cause voter fatigue and thus depress turnout (Boyd 1981; Jackman and Miller 1995, 482–83). A balance must thus be achieved so that neither the capacity of the electoral body nor the enthusiasm of voters is overly taxed.

It should, finally, be noted that catastrophic failure and massive fraud are not the only dangers presented by complex election systems. Some technologies may also be prone to more hidden forms of error or manipulation. Indeed, if electoral components are too new or too complicated for electoral authorities to adequately test and evaluate, design flaws or security breaches might go undetected, leaving open the possibility that the system may be operating incorrectly even when it appears to be functioning as intended (Moynihan 2004, 519–21). To avoid such problems, election administrators might do best to steer clear of systems that are too complex or too new to evaluate adequately, as electoral authorities eventually did in Ireland. These authorities, as mentioned above, had pilot-tested an electronic voting system in 2002 and planned to use it nationwide in 2004. After being forced to release data exposing problems with the 2002 test, however, they created an independent body—the Commission on Electronic Voting (CEV)—to examine the system more thoroughly. Upon completing its investigation, the CEV recommended against deploying the voting machines nationwide because the need for many updates of, and revisions to, the complicated software code made it impossible to test the machines as they would actually be configured in the 2004 elections (CEV 2004, 74). Without the CEV's go-ahead, the government decided against using the system.

In sum, decoupling technologies, introducing changes sequentially, keeping electoral exercises as simple as possible, and staying away from technologies that are too new or complicated to test adequately are all ways to manage the complexity of newly designed election systems.

Making it Transparent. When the activities of election officials and the performance of new election systems are shielded from public scrutiny, glitches, bugs, incompetence, and deficiencies as well as outright manipulation are more likely to remain hidden sources of iatrogenic harm. In Venezuela, the Philippines, and Florida, the incapacity or connivance of election officials went undetected (until too late) because electoral bodies were allowed to operate in opacity. When electoral administration is more transparent, problems are more likely to be exposed. There are many ways to make elections, and electoral reform, more open to public scrutiny.

Perhaps the most comprehensive solution is to establish independent audits that assess the overall performance of electoral bodies as well as the integrity and impartiality of financial transactions, hiring decisions, and equipment purchases. In Australia, for instance, this task is performed by an independent government agency called the Australian National Audit Office (ANAO) (Wanna, Ryan, and Ng 2004). In recent years, the ANAO has audited both the integrity of the electoral roll and the management practices of the Australian Electoral Commission (ANAO 1998, 2002, 2004). In Mexico, a fairly comprehensive audit of the new computerized voter registry was conducted in 1994 by a consortium of international and Mexican companies—though it did not ask how many people were excluded involuntarily from the registry (Carter Center 1994).

Performance reviews, of course, presume the existence of a probing, neutral auditing body—whether it be a government agency such as the ANAO or an external authority such as the Mexican consortium. Such bodies are not, however, present in many electoral jurisdictions. Where auditing bodies are absent or ineffective, the media, civic gadflies, domestic poll watchers, and foreign monitors bear an extra burden to stay alert and dig deep. When they do, the glare of public attention may expose abuse or negligence that might have otherwise gone undetected.

Aggressive investigation by CNN and other news organizations, for instance, helped prevent a repeat in 2004 of the overzealous purge of felons that had taken place in Florida four years earlier. In preparation for the 2004 elections, Florida Secretary of State Glenda Hood produced a list of 47,763 possible felons and ordered county election supervisors to verify the convictions and remove all confirmed felons from the voters' database. And bolstered by a 2001 law passed by Florida's Republican-controlled legislature to limit the public's access to purge lists, her office refused to disclose the names on the new list. Despite the assurances of Jenny Nash, spokeswoman for Hood, that "we feel confident that the same mistakes made in 2000 will not be repeated," many news organizations and watchdog groups expressed concern that the purge list might again be used for partisan purposes.[19] CNN went a step further and sued the state to abolish the 2001 statute and obtain a copy of the new purge list.

19. Quoted in "State Wants Felons Purged from Voter List," Associated Press, May 6, 2004.

When a judge ruled that the statute was indeed unconstitutional and ordered the state to make the list public, the *Miami Herald* quickly discovered that it included the names of at least 2,119 Florida felons who had already had their voting rights restored through clemency.[20] Hood's immediate response was to justify their removal on the grounds that they had registered before they were granted clemency. But when the American Civil Liberties Union and the Florida Justice Institute threatened to sue and the controversy was picked up by news organizations around the country, Hood backtracked and allowed their names to be included on the voter rolls.

At around the same time, the *Sarasota Herald-Tribune* reported that Hispanics, who made up around 11 percent of Florida's prison population, constituted only one-tenth of 1 percent of the names on the purge list.[21] This disparity reportedly resulted from difficulties matching racial categories used in the two databases (the felon database had no Hispanic category, but the voter registry did). To the extent that blacks tend to vote Democratic while Florida Hispanics tend to vote Republican, the near absence of Hispanic names fueled suspicion that the lists were once again being manipulated for partisan purposes.[22] Days later, Florida election officials were forced to back down and announced that they would abandon altogether the disputed list of 47,673 possible felons. Aggressive investigation and reporting by news organizations, in this case, helped prevent a new round of discriminatory exclusion.

Independent audits, a watchful media, a vigilant civil society, and alert international monitors are especially important in places where electoral reform takes on a strongly partisan cast and where those who implement reform thus try to hide their partisan activities from public scrutiny. Where reformers instead share a commitment to inclusive and clean elections, there are ways that they, too, can enhance transparency—particularly in the realms of voter registration and ballot counting.

When voter registration procedures are reformed, there is a danger that eligible voters may be wrongly removed from the registry. As we saw in the Philippines, difficulties reconciling old and new registration databases led to the administrative exclusion of an estimated nine hundred thousand voters in the 2004 elections. When the risk of such exclusion is inadvertent, one way that electoral authorities or other stakeholders can reduce it is to make voters' lists

20. "Thousands of Eligible Voters Are on Felon List," *Miami Herald,* July 2, 2004.

21. "Hispanics Missing from Voter Purge List," *Sarasota Herald-Tribune,* July 7, 2004.

22. Indeed, reporters from the newspaper later discovered that state election officials had known since late 1997 or early 1998 that the procedures they had adopted would exclude Hispanics from the purge list. "State Knew of Felon-List Flaw," *Sarasota Herald-Tribune,* July 20, 2004.

available for public inspection well before the election. In the Philippines, COMELEC is required by law to post the lists fifteen days in advance at each local precinct. In practice, the lists are often put up late, if at all, and once posted, they are often torn down or blown away. In response, COMELEC has joined with civil society activists to find ways of making registration information more accessible to the public. Thus the Parish Pastoral Council for Responsible Voting has, with help of two private companies, set up an online election service called FindPrecinct.com, which enables voters to verify that their names are on the voters' list and to identify the precinct in which they should vote.

One problem with this kind of solution, of course, is that it requires Internet access, something that many voters in this predominantly poor country do not have. For this reason, the service has been set up to also allow voters to access information via telephone calls and text messaging. Organizers have also requested that the many neighborhood Internet cafes dotting the country make computers available for free to people who wish to locate their precincts. Another problem with this service is that it must rely on COMELEC to provide accurate information and to make it available far enough in advance of election day for voters to detect and rectify problems. In 2004, the voters' lists were a mess, and COMELEC was late in releasing information for about a quarter of the electorate, delaying the launching of the service. Nevertheless, as more and more voters become aware of the service, some of them at least may be able to protect their right to vote. In other places, it is worth noting, electoral authorities themselves have set up online sites where voters can verify their registration status. In the United States, for instance, state electoral authorities in Georgia, Virginia, and North Carolina have set up verification websites, as have many county election officials nationwide.

Many clean election reforms today involve the introduction of new electronic technologies for counting ballots. In such cases, transparency in counting can be enhanced by allowing inspection of the software source code that controls the machines. By making the code available for scrutiny to computer experts, and perhaps to political parties and the informed public as well, officials are more likely to catch bugs and glitches (Swire 2004; Hall 2006). When Australian electoral authorities made the code for its voting machines available for inspection on the Internet prior to the 2001 Australian Capital Territory elections, researchers at the Australian National University and National ICT Australia were able to find various bugs that were subsequently fixed.[23] Not

---

23. The code can be downloaded from www.elections.act.gov.au/Elecvote.html. The expert findings were contained in a report titled "Formal Methods Applied to Electronic Voting Systems," which can be found at www.users.rsise.anu.edu.au/~rpg/EVoting/index.html.

coincidentally, postelection evaluation of the machines found that they were quite reliable (ACTEC 2002, 1).

Making software source code available for inspection can also expose security vulnerabilities and reduce the risk that the vote will be hacked. When the proprietary software code for DRE voting machines manufactured by Diebold Election Systems was inadvertently leaked on a file transfer protocol site in 2002, outside computer experts discovered several serious security flaws. This report led the state of Maryland, which had just spent $55 million for sixteen thousand Diebold machines, to hire two companies to evaluate the new purchases (Kohno et al. 2003). One of the companies, RABA Technologies, set up the system as it would have been used in a real election and then tried to hack into it. As mentioned above, this firm discovered serious security flaws. Indeed, it found that election results for the entire state could be changed by intercepting just one telephone call. State electoral authorities and legislators, maintaining that the machines were nonetheless safe, did not require any security enhancements for the 2004 elections.[24] However, this new evidence immediately prompted the secretary of state in California (where several counties also used Diebold DRE machines) to require random testing of the machines, their disconnection from the Internet, and the posting of results for each machine at the precinct level. The state later sued Diebold, and as part of the settlement the company agreed to improve the security of the machines. When the company proved unable to fix the flaws, some counties returned to using paper ballots and optical scanners in 2006. In this case, the inadvertent release of the software source code and the public scrutiny that followed allowed California election officials to take protective measures.

Transparency in counting where DRE machines are used might also entail mechanisms to verify, independent of the machine's own software, the accurate recording of votes. To the consternation of many experts and citizens, some U.S. jurisdictions use DRE machines without any kind of verification mechanism, as do countries such as France, India, Kazakhstan, the Netherlands, and Brazil (which the exception of an experiment in 2002).[25]

But mechanisms for independent verification exist. The most common in the United States today is what computer experts call a "voter verifiable paper audit trail" (VVPAT), which provides a paper printout of each vote. The voter

24. Officials of Montgomery County—the state's largest jurisdiction—later reviewed the performance of the machines in the 2004 elections. They found that of the 2,597 units used, 189 failed, and another 122 were deemed "suspect" because they recorded a significantly lower number of votes than other units used in the same polling place (MCBE 2005, 11).

25. Rezende (2004); Ramachandran (2004); Carrier (2005); OSCE (2006, 9–10; 2007, 15–16); "Opposition to Electronic Voting System Grows in France," *New York Times,* April 4, 2007.

can see the printout in a window but not keep it (to prevent vote selling). In the event of malfunction or suspected manipulation, the paper votes can be compared against the electronically recorded votes. Nevada used VVPATs with mixed success in the 2004 elections (Selker 2004), and by the 2006 elections twenty-two states required them.

Given the ease with which the software of DRE machines can be tampered with and the relative frequency with which machines malfunction or are improperly operated, there is an emerging consensus among computer experts that some form of software-independent verification of vote counts is necessary. However, the use of paper printouts has proven to be difficult logistically. Paper jams, as well as crumpled, smeared, or blank printouts sometimes make the records unreadable. Of nine machines audited after the 2004 elections in Guilford County, North Carolina, four experienced printer problems, and 2 percent of the votes cast were not recorded (Gilbert 2007). A similar audit in Cuyahoga County, Ohio, found that almost 10 percent of the VVPAT ballots for the May 2006 primary elections were "destroyed, blank, illegible, missing, taped together or otherwise compromised" (Election Science Institute 2006, 6). In addition, election officials have found that manually counting paper printouts is cumbersome. It took 18 people 78 working hours to tally 976 VVPAT ballots from the 2006 elections in Cobb County, Georgia. Placed end to end, the printouts were longer than five football fields (State of Georgia 2007). There are other problems too. Voting technology expert Roy Saltman (2007) points out that many voters do not review their printouts; blind people cannot read them; and if a voter discovers an error when comparing the printout to the DRE screen, the secrecy of that voter's ballot will be violated if a poll worker or election official tries to confirm the discrepancy. These difficulties have led Saltman to recommend alternative independent verification mechanisms such as the use of optically scanned paper ballots, DRE-generated optically scanned ballots, or electronic independent verification devices. Such alternatives deserve serious consideration.

Whatever technology is used for independent verification, it is important that this verification actually take place. Mandatory audits for voting machines that produce extraordinary results (turnout in excess of 100 percent, a high percentage of blank votes, and the like) is one option. Another option is routine, mandatory auditing of election results from a random sample of voting machines, a procedure that, as of 2006, only twelve states required (BCTF 2006, 4). One advantage of routine audits, Stanford University professor David Dill (2006) explains, is that they "depoliticize recounts because they do not have to be requested by a candidate, and because they must occur regardless of whether an election is close or which candidate won. With routine audits, election problems can be discovered and addressed when the outcome of the election is not in dispute."

There is, then, an array of strategies available to expose glitches and manipulation that threaten the inclusiveness and integrity of elections. These strategies include performance audits of electoral bodies, aggressive news reporting, the wide publication of voter registration lists, public inspection of software code, and mandatory software-independent vote recounts. This list is not exhaustive, but it does illustrate at least a few concrete ways in which the process of reform might be opened to public scrutiny.

Forcing Remedial Action. Feedback from outside audits, civic groups, international observers, and the media can aid well-intentioned election officials or shame partisan officials into taking steps to avoid iatrogenic harm. But election officials—from either partisan motivation or administrative inertia—cannot always be counted on to act on the input they receive. For this reason, the dangers of iatrogenic harm can be further reduced if there are mechanisms in place to compel electoral authorities to take remedial action when there are clear dangers that vote depression or other forms of harm are likely to occur as a result of clean election reform.

Such mechanisms can take different institutional forms. Bundled with the reform of the electoral system in Mexico in the mid 1990s, for instance, was the creation of a nonpartisan electoral prosecutor's office, whose sole task it was to enforce the penal code with regard to any criminal election acts (Carter Center 1994).

The courts, too, can act as agents of accountability. In Ghana, the Supreme Court struck down a new voter identification requirement that threatened to administratively exclude up to 2.5 million voters in 2000 (Smith 2002, 625). There are, however, limits to the most common forms of judicial intervention. After all, in many places, including Ghana, court action is dependent upon the private initiation of litigation (in this case, the legal challenge was filed by a supporter of one of the political parties). But because electoral preparations are so often shrouded in secrecy, potential plaintiffs do not always become aware of problems far enough in advance to leave the courts with many options once lawsuits are filed. In Ghana, the court reached its decision only three days before the election, leaving it with only three real choices: cancel the election, uphold the identification requirement and strip millions of people of their right to vote, or strike down the requirement and make the election vulnerable to fraud. The court chose the last of these evils.

Similarly, Venezuelan electoral authorities repeatedly assured the public in the weeks before the 2000 mega-elections that preparations were going smoothly.

However, civil society groups, alarmed that the CNE had failed to inform voters about their choice of candidates, filed suit to suspend the elections (Neuman and McCoy 2001, 51). It was only during hearings before the Supreme Court—three days before the elections—that technicians disclosed how ill prepared the electoral body actually was, leaving the court with few real options other than to order the postponement of the elections.

Close-to-election-day court intervention can also create confusion among poll workers about which laws and procedures are in effect. In 2006, such confusion caused an unknown number of people to be turned away from the polls in both Georgia and Missouri after courts in both states put last-minute stops on new laws requiring voters to present photo identification in order to vote. In Missouri, the state supreme court struck down the photo ID law only three weeks before the November elections. Nevertheless, election workers in St. Louis County asked voters to produce photo identification.[26] In Georgia, a superior court judge issued a preliminary injunction to block the implementation of the new requirement a mere eleven days before the primary elections. Apparently unaware of the judge's order, some poll workers in Bibb County did not allow would-be voters to cast their ballots unless they could show a photo ID.[27]

The constraint of time is related directly to the nature of privately initiated litigation. Lawsuits can be filed only after harm has been done or the threat of harm has been discovered. Bringing a complaint to court is thus reactive. It is a *response to* dangers actual or emergent. But once plans are set or preparations are already under way for such a complex undertaking as an election, it is often too late for courts to impose any but the bluntest of remedies, which also risk sowing confusion among the poll workers charged with implementing the law.

A different, perhaps more successful, model of oversight is provided by the Voting Rights Act (VRA) of 1965, which established a set of proactive safeguards against vote depression in the American South. Mirroring the language of the Fifteenth Amendment, the act stated flatly that "no voting qualification or prerequisite to voting, standard, practice, or procedure shall be imposed or applied by any State or political subdivision to deny or abridge the right of any citizen of the United States to vote on account of race or color" (section 2). The act banned the use of any literacy, education, or moral character tests for voter registration as well as other discriminatory devices. Areas of the country where such tests or devices had been in place and where registration rates or turnout was especially low (below 50 percent) were subject to a special enforcement

26. "Secretary of State Blasts County on IDs," *St. Louis Post-Dispatch,* November 9, 2006.
27. "Not All Bibb Workers Knew Photo ID Not Required," *Macon Telegraph,* July 19, 2006.

provision. Under section 5 of the act, these jurisdictions could not impose any "voting qualification or prerequisite to voting" or alter any "standard, practice, or procedure with respect to voting" different from those already in place unless the proposed change received prior approval from federal authorities—a requirement that has come to be called "preclearance." In 1965, the covered jurisdictions were Alabama, Georgia, Louisiana, Mississippi, South Carolina, and Virginia, in addition to forty counties in North Carolina. There were two ways that electoral authorities in these jurisdictions could obtain preclearance. They could seek either the administrative approval of the attorney general or the judicial approval of a three-judge panel in the federal district court for the District of Columbia.

The act was initially set to expire after five years but was renewed by Congress in 1970 and 1975 (when the list of barred practices was expanded to include English-only ballots in places with sizable language minority groups) and then again in 1982 and 2006. As of 2007, the jurisdictions covered by section 5 include eight states and specific counties or townships in another eight. From 1996 to 2006, the civil rights division of the United States Department of Justice (DOJ)—to which the attorney general has delegated responsibility for section 5 oversight—reviewed fifteen to twenty-four thousand proposed voting changes each year and objected to about one of every one hundred submitted (DOJ 2007a).

Soon after its passage in 1965, the VRA was expanded to include the protection of not only the "right to vote" (the right to register and cast a ballot) but also the "value of the vote" (the right to have one's ballot count as much as anyone else's ballot) (McCrary 2003, 685–90). To prevent efforts to dilute the voting strength of minority communities, jurisdictions covered under section 5 have also had to obtain preclearance for all redistricting plans and changes to the method of election (from district to at-large voting, for instance). Among changes subject to section 5 preclearance, redistricting and new methods of election have attracted by far the most attention of legal scholars and political scientists. After a series of complex Supreme Court rulings and increasing ambiguity about how particular changes actually affect minority representation, some analysts have begun to ask whether section 5 in its current form has outlived its usefulness.[28]

The question of whether the continued application of section 5 to redistricting and methods of election actually enhances the representation of minority communities is outside the scope of this book. It should not be overlooked,

---

28. See, for instance, Issacharoff (2004); Abigail Thernstrom and Edward Blum, "Do the Right Thing," *Wall Street Journal*, July 15, 2005.

however, that section 5 covers many "right to vote" changes as well. Among the proposed changes found objectionable by the DOJ over the years have been poll list signature requirements, changes in the placement or number of polling places, the dates of elections, the use of particular kinds of voting equipment, and the purging and reidentification of voters, as well as certain residency requirements, multilingual election provisions, and registration and absentee balloting procedures. From 1965 to 2006, of the 458,217 proposed changes received by the attorney general, only 2 percent related to redistricting and fewer than 4 percent to method of election, while 24 percent related to polling place changes and another 11 percent to voting methods, voter registration procedures, or voter and registration purges (DOJ 2007b).

Even critics of section 5 acknowledge that the enforcement of the right to vote has "markedly transformed the political landscape."[29] It has greatly reduced the incidence of discriminatory electoral practices in the covered jurisdictions, contributing to the spectacular growth of registration rates for blacks. From 1965 to 1988, these rates jumped from 19 percent to 68 percent in Alabama, 32 percent to 77 percent in Louisiana, and 7 percent to 74 percent in Mississippi (Grofman, Handley, and Niemi 1992, 23–24).

For those worried about the discriminatory potential of clean election reform, there are several features of the VRA—at least with regard to its right-to-vote protections—that make it a model worth contemplating. One is the preclearance provision of section 5, which requires election officials to receive approval for any changes *before* implementing them. Preclearance is thus more effective than private lawsuits in anticipating and preventing vote depression. Indeed, the preclearance requirement is an effective deterrent against abuse to the extent that both local election officials and legislators must take into account the VRA rules when they begin contemplating making a change to voting procedures (Pitts 2005, 613–17). Preclearance, in this regard, provides protection against *both* legal disenfranchisement and administrative exclusion.

Another attractive feature of the VRA is the built-in protection it affords against the partisan manipulation of oversight. Imagine, for instance, that one party (say, the Republicans) controls the executive branch of the federal government, and thus the DOJ, while another party (say, the Democrats) controls the state or county reform agenda under review. Under these circumstances, there might be a danger of what former Department of Justice lawyer Michael J. Pitts (2005, 624) calls "intransigent partisanship." The Republican attorney general might well intransigently refuse to preclear a plan or delay its

---

29. Issacharoff (1992, 1833–34). Thernstrom and Blum, "Do the Right Thing," similarly argue that "the 1965 Act was amazingly effective."

approval only because it harms the electoral prospects of Republican candidates in that jurisdiction. Section 5 mitigates this danger by allowing local election authorities to submit their preclearance requests to either the attorney general or the federal court. While most local officials choose the quicker route of administrative approval by the attorney general, if they fear partisan intransigence in the DOJ, nothing stops them from seeking a declaratory judgment from the court instead. "In fact," Pitts explains,

> Democrats in several states have recently done just that. In the post-2000 redistricting cycle, Democrats controlled the legislative process in Georgia. Looking northward, they saw a Republican Attorney General. So the Democrats sued. The State of North Carolina, also controlled by Democrats, similarly chose a declaratory judgment action in the D.C. District Court rather than administrative preclearance by a Republican Attorney General. And in the end, Democrats emerged victorious, at least from a Section 5 standpoint, in both Georgia and North Carolina. (624–25)

The effectiveness of this safeguard against partisan intransigence is, of course, premised on the three-judge panel's acting in a collectively impartial way or with a bias (cloaked, to be sure) for the plaintiffs. If the court has the same partisan commitments as the attorney general, protection is obviously diminished. Multiple submission venues, nevertheless, offer a measure of protection against partisan intransigence that would otherwise not exist.

While the existence of multiple submission venues mitigates the problem of partisan intransigence, it does little to prevent what Pitts (2005, 624) calls "collusive" forms of partisanship. Imagine now that one party controls both the executive branch of the federal government and the state or county reform agenda under review. In this case, there is a danger that the attorney general might collude with local officials to approve a plan that is nonetheless discriminatory. Many observers, for instance, saw partisan politics at work in the DOJ's preclearance of Georgia's photo voter identification plan in 2005.[30] Even under these conditions, however, the VRA offers some protection, for wronged minorities can still file a lawsuit, claiming a violation of section 2. Democrats in Texas took this approach when the Republican attorney general in 2003 approved the congressional redistricting plan drawn up by Texas Republicans—though the court rejected the section 2 claims (627). Opponents of the Georgia voter identification plan also tried to block its implementation in 2005 by claiming, among other things, a violation of section 2. While they won a preliminary injunction, the court withheld judgment on the section 2 claims.[31]

---

30. "Criticism of Voting Law Was Overruled," *Washington Post,* November 17, 2005.

31. Common Cause/Georgia v. Billups, No. 4:05-cv-00201-HLM, slip op. at 105—16 (N.D. Ga. Oct. 18, 2005) (order granting preliminary injunction). Note that the lawsuit resulting in the 2006

Preclearance, along with reasonably effective safeguards against partisan manipulation, makes the VRA a valuable tool in the fight against discriminatory electoral reform. This is not, however, to argue that the VRA—even with regard to protecting only the right to vote—is without flaw.

One obvious limitation is that section 5 does not extend to the whole country. Ohio, for instance, is not covered. Thus when Ohio Secretary of State J. Kenneth Blackwell, a Republican, resurrected in 2004 antiquated rules about paper quality to justify the invalidation of thousands of new, mostly Democratic, registration applications, his directive was not subject to preclearance, even though it may well have been a racially discriminatory device. In this case, it was only intense media attention and loud public outcry that forced him to back down—but only after the order had been in place for three weeks and an untold number of applications rejected.[32]

Another problem is that the section 5 review process does not entirely prevent the use of discriminatory tests and devices, even in covered jurisdictions. The DOJ, as we saw, precleared Georgia's restrictive photo identification law in 2005, and the section 2 claim of the 2005 lawsuit did not prosper. Recall, too, from chapter 3 that the DOJ reviewed the clean election reforms passed by the Florida legislature in 1998. Although the federal reviewers blocked implementation of the absentee ballot provision because they feared it would disproportionately harm minority voters, they let stand the purge procedures and failed to intervene when the Florida secretary of state later expanded the purge parameters.

Still another limitation of section 5—at least as a mechanism to prevent a broad spectrum of ills that might result from electoral reform—is that it focuses too narrowly on racial and linguistic discrimination. There are, after all, other forms of discrimination (based on, say, party affiliation) and other ills (large-scale fraud, gross administrative bungling) that threaten the inclusiveness or integrity of elections and that could be prevented by a preclearance mechanism.

Thus a generic model of effective preclearance might include the following features:

- Coverage of all electoral jurisdictions
- Coverage for changes that might discriminate not only on the basis of

---

preliminary injunction, mentioned earlier in this chapter, did not address possible violations of the Voting Rights Act. In 2007 a judge allowed the plan to be put in effect.

32. "Blackwell Ends Paper Chase: Some Could Be Unable to Vote Because of Flap over Registration Forms," *Columbus Dispatch,* September 29, 2004.

race, color, or language but also according to partisan affiliation, gender, area of residence, and the like
- Coverage for changes that might facilitate large-scale fraud or result in election failure
- Multiple submission venues for preclearance requests to protect against the intransigent manipulation of oversight
- The right to file private lawsuits challenging approved changes as a way to prevent the collusive partisan manipulation of oversight

How likely it is that legislators would adopt such measures obviously depends on a number of factors, not least of which is whether lawmakers across the partisan divide perceive them as protecting their own interests. How well the oversight function would actually operate if implemented is also dependent on a number of factors, not least of which is the existence of government institutions capable of conducting serious, independent reviews. Not all countries meet both of these conditions.

Recap

A variety of remedies are available to reduce the dangers of unintended and intended harm presented by clean election reform. The menu of options is long and includes financial incentives to reduce bureaucratic corruption, software-independent vote recounts, and the use of decoupled technologies. As we can see in table 1, most of the remedies focus on the dimension of power—either limiting or augmenting the autonomy and capacity of key actors in the election process—rather than on the dimensions of motive or knowledge, where it is far more difficult to intervene benignly. We see also that some remedies are more appropriate to treating unintended harm (pilot-testing, evaluation research), others to intended harm (nonpartisan electoral administration), yet others to both (preclearance, taking it slow).

Different actors, to broach the subject from another angle, have different leverage points. Depending on the scope of their legislative authority, lawmakers with a genuine commitment to clean and inclusive elections can create incentives and provide the funding necessary to make election bodies more capable. They can impose higher standards for election technologies and mandate that they be both tested thoroughly and deployed in a measured fashion. They can pass laws to require routine software-independent vote recounts and to limit the number of individual election contests to be held on any given polling day. They can create independent auditing bodies and pass legislation

Table 1.　Remedies Recap

Intentional Harm to Democracy	Unintentional Harm to Democracy

Motive

Source of Harm

Desire of lawmakers, election administrators, and partisan operatives for electoral victory provides motive to suppress turnout of opponents' supporters or to engage in election cheating.	Desire of election officials and workers for illicit financial gain undermines capacity of electoral administration, resulting unintentionally in vote depression, alienation, or the proliferation of cheating.

Possible Remedies

Reduce the risk of losing reelection by imposing high thresholds or creating safe districts and reserved seats.* Soften the impact of losing an election by putting in place national pacts, mutual vetoes.*	Alter financial incentives (performance bonuses, stiff penalties) to reduce bureaucratic corruption.

Knowledge

Source of Harm

Information about the citizenry is used to suppress the vote of groups supporting one's opponents or to engage in election cheating.	Faulty or incomplete assumptions about voters, party operatives, and local election workers lead to unanticipated reactions to reform that result in vote depression, alienation, or the proliferation of cheating.

Possible Remedies

Refrain from conducting evaluation research or pilot studies on sensitive topics (when a single bloc dominates the electoral administration *or* legislative process).	Conduct evaluation research, pilot studies (when the electoral administration is impartial *and* the legislative process is not controlled by a single bloc).

Power

Source of Harm

The ability of partisan lawmakers to push through biased clean election legislation over the objections of legislatively weaker parties, or the unfettered ability of partisan administrators to implement clean election reforms in a biased way, results in vote depression, alienation, or the proliferation of election cheating.	Bureaucratic, managerial, or technical incapacity results in an inability to relate means to ends, resulting in vote depression, alienation, or the proliferation of election cheating.

(*Table 1—cont.*)

Intentional Harm to Democracy	Unintentional Harm to Democracy

Possible Remedies

Reduce scope of partisan involvement in electoral process by making electoral administration nonpartisan.	Increase capacity through training, institution building, and adequate funding.

Introduce reforms slowly to work out kinks and bugs before large-scale changes are implemented, and to reduce levels of chaos and mismanagement that are sometimes exploited by those who wish to engage in election cheating.

Choose reform strategies and technologies that do not require tight coupling so that the smooth and honest operation of one part of the electoral system is not dependent on the smooth and honest operation of another.

Introduce large-scale changes sequentially to reduce complexity and the likelihood of election error, failure, and manipulation.

Keep elections simple to reduce complexity and the likelihood of election error, failure, and manipulation.

Institutionalize independent audits that assess the overall performance of electoral bodies as well as the integrity and impartiality of financial transactions, hiring decisions, and equipment purchases.

Expose bugs, glitches, bottlenecks, and malfeasance through aggressive investigation by media, civic gadflies, domestic poll watchers, and international observers.

Make voter registration lists available for public inspection well before the election to expose the deliberate or inadvertent purging of legitimate voters.

Allow public inspection of software source code (where electronic voting or counting systems are used) to detect and fix bugs, glitches, and security risks.

Use software-independent vote recounts (where DRE machines are used) either routinely or in the event of suspected machine error, malfunction, or manipulation.

Allow courts or other agents of accountability to take remedial action when incompetence or negligence threatens to compromise the inclusiveness or integrity of the election or when electoral malfeasance is discovered.

Establish a proactive "preclearance" mechanism to safeguard against election error, failure, fraud, and vote depression.

* These remedies are not recommended because of their systemwide effects.

requiring greater transparency with regard to registration lists and software source codes. They can also establish preclearance mechanisms and nonpartisan election bodies.

Depending on the scope of their administrative authority, election officials with a genuine commitment to clean and inclusive elections can implement some of these same changes. They can also conduct pilot tests and evaluation research—if there is minimal danger that this information will be used for partisan vote depression.

Watchdog groups, the media, international monitors, and other civic gadflies with an interest in clean and inclusive elections can pressure lawmakers and election officials to contemplate and implement appropriate safeguards against iatrogenic harm. They can also investigate aggressively the actions of lawmakers and election officials to expose or deter the partisan manipulation of clean election reforms or gross administrative neglect—a task to which other agents of accountability (the courts, prosecutors, auditors) can also contribute.

Civic educators with a genuine commitment to clean and inclusive elections can counteract attempts at vote suppression (by, for instance, helping to make voters' lists easily accessible to the public). They can also be careful to mount voter education campaigns that have been tested and evaluated to prevent surprising and damaging voter responses.

Even partisan operatives with a genuine commitment to clean and inclusive elections have a role to play to the extent that they can choose mobilization strategies that are less demobilizing than others—door-to-door canvassing, for instance, over direct mailing.

Each major stakeholder, in short, can have a role to play if it has the interest and resolve to do so. Of course, levels of interest and resolve vary, depending, among other things, on whether the impending iatrogenic harm is intended. To prevent or minimize unintended harm, lawmakers, election officials, educators, the media, civic groups, and international monitors may well have a shared stake in collaborating. When clean election reform is instead deliberately manipulated by lawmakers, election officials, or partisan operatives, outside agents of accountability must usually take a leading, more confrontational, role.

Trade-offs

There are, then, a number of options and strategies available to prevent or minimize the iatrogenic harm of clean election reform. It should not be forgotten, however, that there are sometimes inevitable trade-offs. The reality of conflicting and competing goals may thus require a careful balancing act that can never be fully or satisfyingly accomplished.

Election administrations must constantly balance the competing demands of neutrality and effectiveness. They must also make difficult trade-offs between independence and accountability. There can also be broader conflicts between the goals of what we might call "integrity" and "access." Enhancing the integrity of elections requires tightening the rules and beefing up the requirements for voting, while expanding access requires removing or lowering barriers that may discourage voters from participating in elections. Thus the kinds of restrictions on voter registration drives today being debated or implemented in many states will in all likelihood both deter partisan workers from submitting fraudulent registration applications and lower registration rates in low-income and minority communities. In Taiwan, reforms intended to increase integrity by reducing vote buying are also reducing access by curtailing the mobilizing activities of grassroots workers.

There are, in addition, trade-offs between holding infrequent large elections and holding frequent small ones. If too many posts are up for election on a single day, the combined elections may become so unwieldy that they fail. If polling for each post is held on a separate date, elections may become so frequent that they generate voter fatigue and abstention. It is thus best to seek the middle ground.

There are also trade-offs involved in conducting evaluation research and pilot tests. As we have seen, knowledge about the behavior of registrants and voters in the hands of democratic-minded lawmakers and election officials can enhance both integrity and access. The same knowledge in the hands of partisans, however, can be used to deny access—to exclude supporters of one's opponents—under the pretext of integrity. In the latter case, it might be best to forgo evaluation research and pilot tests altogether if they are likely to diminish the quality of democracy more than enhance it.

There is, finally, a tension between what we might loosely call "fun" and "constraint." Accounts of elections from earlier eras share with elections I have observed in Senegal and the Philippines something that is largely absent from elections today in America and other relatively "clean" democracies.[33] Not only have levels of blatant cheating and intimidation declined, but something else— call it fun or color—has been bleached from the electoral exercise. To borrow the language of Foucault (1979), cleaner elections have required the imposition of a good deal of *discipline* on voters and local party workers. Consequently, the sense of community; the festivity, carnival atmosphere, and raucousness of election day; and the public and shared excitement have faded. The actual act of voting, for many of us who cast our ballots in cleaner democracies, has been transformed into something of a private errand—something no more shared or exciting than choosing between apples and oranges at the local grocery store. There is no doubt that the long-term process of cleaning up elections—with

---

33. See, for instance, Kishlansky (1986), Reynolds (1988), Garrigou (1992), and Bensel (2004).

its attendant restrictions on drinking, partisan gatherings at polling places, and publicly cast ballots, among other things—is at least partially responsible for making the actual act of voting the disconnected, mundane, and lonely act that it is for many of us today.[34] This may be an inevitable trade-off and one arguably made for the better, but we should not forget what we have lost in the bargain.

When confronted with such trade-offs, it is tempting to tally up the benefits and costs of particular clean election reforms to determine whether enhancements to election integrity gained as a result of the reform were worth any iatrogenic harms that it may have occasioned. Sometimes the question, "was it worth it?"—as it might be posed by someone with a commitment to democratic norms rather than, say, someone bent on winning an election by any means—is easy to answer. When the harm is so great that it completely undermines election integrity and puts into question the basic legitimacy of the election, the answer is clearly no. Consider, for instance, the incorrectly executed computerization of the electoral lists in post-Soviet Georgia, which led in 2003 to the administrative exclusion of up to 15 percent of the electorate. Observers from the Organization for Security and Co-operation in Europe described the failures of electoral administration as "spectacular," postelection protesters took to the streets of the capital, and countries such as the United States concluded that the final results did not accurately reflect the will of the people.[35] In this case, the costs clearly outweighed the benefits.

The question is also easy to answer when the reform significantly bolsters safeguards to voter eligibility, voter insulation, or vote integrity, with few negative side effects. Available evidence suggests that the advent of secret balloting in places like Denmark and Germany, the use of electronic voting machines in the Australian Capital Territory, and the computerization of voter registration in Lesotho were, all things considered, salutary reforms.[36]

It becomes more difficult to answer the question when, as is often the case, we lack basic data to generate even a roughly accurate balance sheet of ben-

34. In the United States in the mid-nineteenth century, many polling places were located in places where liquor was served. As Richard Bensel (2004, 9) noted, "[S]aloons were the most important gathering places for immigrants in the mid-nineteenth century and thus were primary centers for their political mobilization as voters. For this reason, many immigrant political officeholders owned drinking establishments, and, at least in New York, almost nine out of every ten polling places in immigrant neighborhoods were saloons."

35. "Georgia Braces for Elections," BBC News, October 3, 2003; "Observers Condemn Georgia Polls," BBC News, November 3, 2003; "Georgians Brace for Huge Protest," CNN.com, November 21, 2003.

36. Elklit (1983), Suval (1985, 21–36), ACTEC (2002, 2005), SADCPF (n.d., 14–15), and CS (2006 11–13, 29).

efits and costs. Take, as an example, the adoption of optical scan and DRE voting machines in many local jurisdictions in the United States after the 2000 elections. Some people argue that it enhanced the quality of elections by reducing the possibility that votes would be recorded incorrectly, as often happened with the old punch card and lever machines. Other people contend that it harmed the quality of the elections because of all the glitches and possible manipulation to which the new machines are prone.

But as it stands, we have little information about the overall impact of this new voting technology on the accurate recording of votes in subsequent elections. Although there is much anecdotal evidence from local election jurisdictions around the country about votes lost in 2004 as a result of machine malfunction (see, for instance, Carrier 2005), we have no reliable count of the total number of votes lost nationwide. Such a tally is hampered by, among other things, a hodgepodge of state laws across the nation regarding postelection vote count audits (Electionline.org 2007, 12–17). Differing audit procedures and varying audit scopes make compilation of the necessary data impossible.

Statistical analysis of aggregate data is only slightly more illuminating. MIT political scientist Charles Stewart (2006) compared the "residual vote rate" (the percentage of all ballots cast that did not record a vote for the president) in 2000 and 2004 to see whether new technologies improved the accuracy with which votes were recorded and counted. His initial findings suggested that the new technologies did indeed increase ballot accuracy, leading to the "recovery of approximately one million 'lost votes'" (158). But Stewart's further parsing of the statistical evidence revealed that the decline in the residual vote rate may have had other causes. For one thing, there may simply have been fewer voters in 2004 who intentionally did not cast a ballot for a presidential candidate. What looks like increased ballot accuracy may instead have been a lower abstention rate. Alternatively, voters and poll workers may have been more vigilant in 2004, fearing a repeat of the widely publicized horror stories of the 2000 elections. If so, their increased care, regardless of voting technology, would have led to a decline in lost votes. This account would explain why residual vote rates dropped even in jurisdictions using old voting methods. In the final analysis, Stewart could not discount these possibilities and concluded that "people involved in upgrading voting machines cannot take all the credit for reduced residual vote rates in 2004" (166). Indeed, he could not specify how many votes were, in fact, recovered as a direct result of the new technologies. In short, neither election audits nor statistical analysis provides enough information about the 2004 elections for us to know whether the adoption of new voting equipment was worth the iatrogenic harm it inflicted.

The assessment of other reforms around the world introduces more complications still, for sometimes there is no straightforward way to calibrate the disparate costs and benefits of reform. In Taiwan, the 1995 crackdown on vote buying appeared to have been quite effective in insulating voters from undue influence but at the apparent cost of demobilization, especially in local elections. In this case, how do we compare the relative importance of insulation and participation? How much of a decline in vote buying is worth how much of a decline in voter turnout, assuming we could even accurately measure both? Different people, all with a genuine commitment to democracy, might weigh the relative value of insulation and participation differently.

But then again, focusing too narrowly on a balance sheet of benefits and costs may present us with false choices because some trade-offs are less inevitable than they might at first appear. Not all measures designed to promote election integrity, for instance, necessarily restrict voter access. The use of EVMs in India, section 5 of the Voting Rights Act in the United States, and the advent of nonpartisan electoral administration in Canada all enhanced election integrity without raising barriers to voting (though as we saw in chapter 4, it is too early to tell whether EVMs might be generating apathy).

Furthermore, in many instances of iatrogenic harm, the vote depression caused by clean election reform could have been prevented. Had the Democratic Party in nineteenth-century Arkansas not wished to disenfranchise blacks by means of the secret vote, it could have permitted the inclusion of symbols or pictures on the new ballot. This addition would have enabled illiterate citizens to vote without exposing their inability to read or forcing them to rely upon the assistance of suspect precinct judges. Had the ANC in South Africa been more disquieted by the potential disenfranchisement of nonblack voters in the late 1990s, it could have enacted legislation to phase in more slowly the bar-coded ID requirement. It could also have directed home affairs officials to adopt more aggressive measures to get the new IDs into the hands of potential nonblack voters. Had Republican lawmakers in South Dakota been more concerned about the disenfranchising potential of the voter identification requirements they passed into law in the aftermath of Florida 2000, they could have taken more robust protective measures. They could have allowed people to vote if they were known to poll workers, as state Representative Adelstein has proposed. They could also have adopted measures taken by other states. In New Mexico, voters can meet that state's identification requirement not only by showing photo or nonphoto identification but also by providing—verbally—their name, year of birth, and last four digits of their Social Security number. In Montana, the secretary of state established the Voter Verification Service as a means to minimize disenfranchisement. This service enables poll workers to look up an individual's name, date of birth, address, driver's license number, and (partial) Social Security number in state databases as an alternative means of verification. In the June 2004 elections, more than six hundred Montanans were able to vote after having their identity verified by the service.[37] Not all clean election reforms need inevitably result in legal disenfranchisement or other forms of iatrogenic harm.

It should also be recalled that even when there are real trade-offs, some iatrogenic effects of clean election reform might be offset through the introduction of counterbalancing measures. To give but one example, the demobilization occasioned by the drive to reduce vote buying (or the power of local vote-buying agents) might, as we saw in chapter 4, be partially remedied through compulsory voting or nonpartisan door-to-door drives to get out the vote. It would do democracy a disservice, then, to artificially reduce the range of options to a narrow choice between clean elections on the one hand and vote depression or alienation on the other. There are concrete measures that can be taken to make elections both clean and inclusive.

Nevertheless, the limitations of the remedies I proposed in this chapter should also be acknowledged. The whole range of ill and unintended effects of clean election reform discussed in this book should make anyone who contemplates the "reform of reform" sober and cautious. The difficulty encountered by many governments in matching means to ends and in enforcing the rule of law not only makes clean election reform necessary in the first place but also makes reforming the reform process perilous. In addition, some remedies I put forward in this chapter—pilot tests and evaluation research in particular—carry an inherent danger of partisan manipulation. None of the remedies I suggest here are foolproof or likely to be wholly effective.

The mechanics of elections matter. How elections are conducted—how eligible voters make it onto the voter rolls, how voters cast their ballots, and how votes are counted—can fundamentally enhance or detract from the quality of democracy. The conduct of elections determines the degree to which people's preferences are expressed freely, weighed equally, and recorded accurately. The sad irony is that too often tinkering with these mechanics in the name of strengthening the integrity of the exercise damages the very democratic ideals the reforms are intended to promote. This damage can be inflicted by lawmakers, election officials, partisan operatives, or civic educators. Sometimes the damage is intentional, sometimes not. Sometimes the harm is limited to one election,

---

37. "Montana Helps ID-less Voters," *Federal Computer Week,* July 12, 2004.

but sometimes it is chronic and recurring, especially where partisan imbalance or administrative incapacity is an enduring feature of the political landscape. Whatever the case, there are a number of measures that various stakeholders can adopt to prevent or minimize damage. The specific remedies proposed here are, to be sure, fallible. There are, in addition, no cookie-cutter fixes since different contexts require different solutions. Nevertheless, as this discussion has shown, people with a commitment to clean and inclusive elections are not powerless to make reform both effective and benign.

Appendix
Variables and Cases

Stated most simply, my goal in this book is to identify the conditions under which clean election reforms cause damage to democracy. In this appendix, a supplement to chapter 1, I provide additional information about the definition of the two key variables: "clean election reform" and "damage to democracy." I also include a table listing the 122 clean election reforms undertaken from 1991 to 2006 that form the core data set of contemporary reforms I examined for the book. This table, too, summarizes what I could determine about the damage that each of these reforms did, or did not, cause.

Clean Election Reform

A few words are in order to specify the meaning of both "clean" and "reform." *Clean* election reforms are measures designed (in formal appearance at least) to reduce fraud and error in the casting and counting of votes. As I discussed in chapter 1, these reforms aim either to authenticate voter eligibility (to prevent spurious voting), to safeguard voter insulation (to prevent the buying or coercion of voters), or to bolster vote integrity (to prevent the miscounting of votes).

Clean election reform also has a temporal dimension. The focus is on *reform*—on changes to the conduct of elections. It is thus necessary to identify a turning point, a moment when established election procedures are altered to make them less prone to fraud or error. Often such changes are implemented quickly and entirely within one electoral cycle, making it easy to identify such a turning point. There are, however, three types of reform that are hard to categorize.

Pilot tests. Sometimes clean election measures under consideration for implementation are pilot-tested. For this study, I do not count such experiments as instances of reform—unless they subsequently led to plans for full-scale implementation—because of their limited and provisional scope. Thus I exclude from consideration, for instance, the pilot-testing of electronic voting in Panama (1992, 1999), Japan (1999, 2002), and the United Kingdom (2002), since these trials were small in scale and did not lead to a decision to adopt the technology for future use.

Aborted reforms. Sometimes during the process of instituting a reform, problems develop that force reformers to abandon implementation midcourse. Unlike a pilot test, which is a limited and nonbinding experiment, such reforms are adopted, but some difficulty, court order, or unforeseen event compels reformers to halt implementation. For instance, the Irish government, after having pilot-tested electronic voting machines in 2002, decided to roll them out across the country. However, a 2004 report revealed major problems, forcing the government to freeze deployment. I *do* include such aborted reforms for consideration in this study because they constitute attempts at implementation, and those attempts sometimes have consequences for the conduct of elections. I note in table 2 below which reforms were aborted.

Incremental reforms. Sometimes clean election reforms are introduced incrementally over long periods of time and many electoral cycles. In India, for instance, electronic voting was first pilot-tested in 1982 but not fully deployed nationwide until 2004. I also include such incremental reforms for consideration in this study, as long as the first election for which they were partially introduced, or the first election for which they were fully implemented, fell within the 1991 to 2006 time period. For such cases I note in table 2, when applicable, either the initial rollout date or the date of full implementation.

For the purposes of this study, in short, I include aborted and incremental reforms but not pilot tests in the category of reform.

Damage to Democracy

As I discussed in chapter 1, there are three types of "damage" or "harm"—I use these terms synonymously—that clean election reforms might inflict on democracy: vote depression (in the forms of legal disenfranchisement, administrative exclusion, and partisan demobilization), the proliferation of cheating (in either new or established modes), and alienation (whether in the form of popular protest, voter and civic disengagement, or the disaffection of election losers). Among the greatest difficulties in delineating these forms of damage are specifying magnitude and time frame.

Magnitude

How many people need to be alienated, how much participation needs to be depressed, or how much cheating needs to take place for democracy to be considered damaged? That is, what *threshold* of alienation, depression, or prolif-eration constitutes damage?

Certainly we should consider democracy to be harmed if, as a result of the reform, enough damage is done to alter the outcome of an election, undermine the credibility of an election, or significantly compromise the participation of particular groups within the electorate. Using this set of criteria, it is clear that democracy is harmed when hundreds of thousands or millions of people are unable to vote—as happened in Sierra Leone (2002) and the Philippines (2001, 2004); or when election results are bitterly and widely contested, as happened in Zambia (2006) and post-Soviet Georgia (2003); or when the adverse side ef-fects of reform significantly and disproportionately affect members of particu-lar races (South Africa 1999) or linguistic communities (Quebec 1995).

By this set of criteria, harm can also be caused by much lower absolute levels of cheating, depression, or alienation, provided that the electoral race is very close or an electoral district very small. In the Dominican Republic, only about 45,000 people were excluded in 1994 as a result of the manipulated implemen-tation of a new voter registration and identification system—but this level of vote depression was significant enough to affect the outcome of the presidential race, which was decided by 22,281 votes. In the Florida 2000 elections, our best estimate is that a mere 1,100 legitimate voters were excluded as a result of the faulty purge of the voter rolls, a very small number when compared with the exclusion experienced in countries like Sierra Leone, the Philippines, or even the Dominican Republic, but nonetheless large enough to potentially alter the outcome of the unprecedentedly tight U.S. presidential race. Florida was the swing state, and George W. Bush won there by a margin of only 537 votes.

It is not possible, then, to use this set of criteria to establish a fixed and universal baseline amount of cheating, depression, or alienation that constitutes harm. The baseline varies, election to election. For this reason, I did not set any lower limit. As it turns out, the smallest amount of vote depression (the form of harm easiest to quantify) that I discovered was in Florida, with its 1,100 or so excluded voters.

One might object to this way of proceeding on the grounds that it fails to take into account the amount of fraud and error prevented by clean election reform. One could imagine, say, that a new clean election law blocks 100,000 spurious votes from being counted, but in so doing disenfranchises 10,000 legitimate voters. Should this be considered an instance of harm? My answer in this case is yes because it is important to distinguish between the benefits that result from a clean election reform and the harm that it occasions. Only by distinguishing benefits from harm, after all, can we assess trade-offs and determine whether the benefits of a given reform were worth the harm it induced. I take up this issue of trade-offs in chapter 6. The point here is not that 100,000 blocked spurious votes are inconsequential but that we need to determine the magnitude of harm produced to determine whether such an improvement was worth its accompanying costs. In tallying up that balance sheet, it serves no purpose to set, a priori, the minimum amount of depression, alienation, or proliferation that constitutes harm.

Practically speaking, my ability to determine levels of harm was limited. In many cases, I could not find enough information to specify the exact amount of cheating, alienation, or depression that took place as a result of a reform (or the precise amount of fraud and error that was prevented). For some cases, I could make only rough appraisals. For other cases, I could only establish that vote depression, alienation, or the proliferation of cheating had occurred without being able to even roughly estimate their magnitude. In the text I have indicated how precise or imprecise, how certain or uncertain, various estimates are. I have also included summary information about magnitudes of harm in table 2.

There is, finally, one additional complicating issue: what to make of reforms for which observers, scholars, or journalists did not report any resultant harm. In such cases, it may be that no damage was done. But it may also be that damage occurred but went unnoticed. The discovery of harm in Florida 2000 serves as a cautionary tale in this regard. While election officials were conducting the exclusionary purge prior to the elections, it attracted little attention. Only after the elections did investigative reporters and the United States Commission on Civil Rights, among others, take notice. Had the presidential election not been so amazingly close and dramatically important, the exclusion of eligible voters might never have been exposed. To deal with this issue, I distinguish the relatively few cases in which there was credible evidence that no harm occurred (as in the Australian Capital Territory, where electoral authorities conducted comprehensive audits of machine performance after the 2001 and 2004 elections) from the far more ambiguous and numerous cases in which I did not see any mention of harm in assessments of the reform but did not come across any serious investigation that might have uncovered it. In table 2, I mark this distinction by differentiating between "no damage" and "no damage reported."

TIME FRAME

It is also necessary to say a few words about the temporal dimension of damage. How soon after a reform is implemented does harm need to appear for it to be considered an instance of *reform-induced* harm? It is tempting to limit the designation of reform-induced, iatrogenic harm to damage that occurs immediately after the initial implementation of the clean election measure. For most cases under study in this book, I found it easy to apply such a criterion insofar as the iatrogenic harm in those cases appeared during the first election for which the reform was put in place. Sometimes, however, the temporal progression of harm is less straightforward. Four alternate sequences in particular made undesirable the adoption of the first-election rule:

Gradual harm. The harm caused by a new clean election measure sometimes makes itself felt only gradually over a period of several years and several elections as key actors adapt and adjust to the changed electoral environment. For instance, the Australian ballot, adopted in New Jersey in 1892, changed the nature of campaigning during the course of the 1890s, and it was the slow fading of clubs, parades, and rallies that resulted in demobilization. A similar pattern of adjustment occurred in Taiwan after the crackdown on vote buying began in 1995. For such cases, in table 2, I note the date of the initial election during which harm began to appear.

Harm during incremental reform. Reforms are sometimes introduced incrementally, and harm might occur at any time during the rollout process. For example, Belgium deployed electronic voting machines to a restricted number of locations in 1994 and progressively expanded their use in subsequent elections. By the 2003 elections, they were used by 44 percent of the electorate, and it was during those elections that things went logistically wrong; as a result an estimated 10 percent of the electorate in certain locations did not vote (Benoit 2004, 317). In this case, harm came several years after the first machines were introduced but before their full nationwide deployment. For such cases, in table 2, I note both the initial rollout date and the date of the election in which harm occurred.

Latent harm. Dangers of vote depression, alienation, and the proliferation of cheating are sometimes latent within new clean election measures, and actualized only when changed conditions activate some harm-producing feature of the reform. Such changed conditions might include an election of increased complexity. In Venezuela, for instance, no significant problems with the new automated election system were reported during three relatively simple elections and two referendum votes in 1998 and 1999. Only when the system was readied for the far more complicated mega-elections in 2000 did the latent problems become manifest. Changed conditions might also include some transformation of the electorate. The age-disclosure requirement of Chicago's 1885 registration law most acutely resulted in vote depression, as far as I could determine, only after the enfranchisement of women in 1913; France's 1852 ballot disqualification reform appeared to have become especially depressive only when the electorate became more independent in the 1860s and beyond. For such cases, I note in table 2 both the date on which the reform was implemented and the date on which harm was first reported.

Compound harm. Sometimes clean election reforms introduced at different times can interact to produce iatrogenic harm. In Quebec, for instance, the invalidation of valid votes during the 1995 referendum resulted from the interplay of a 1936 reform, which gave parties the right to name poll workers, and the dissemination in 1995 of new and tightened ballot invalidation instructions (to partisan poll workers by party trainers). Although I discuss both reforms in chapter 3, only the 1995 instructions fall within the 1991 to 2006 time frame, so I include them (but not the 1936 reform) in table 2.

Given these various pathways by which harm can develop, I adopted an expansive temporal time frame. That is, I did not impose a statute of limitations on the length of time within which damage had to have occurred for it to be considered a case of iatrogenic harm, as long as I could directly link the causes of harm to the original clean election reform. This decision, to be sure, creates analytic difficulties insofar as almost any instance of harm might ultimately be traced back to some distant reform. Potentially, then, it would become impossible to distinguish harm that results from reform from harm that results from established procedures of electoral administration. This problem notwithstanding, my goal is to investigate why a clean election reform adopted at Time1 sometimes causes damage at Time2, whether the duration between Time1 and Time2 is a month, year, decade, or more. Future researchers, with more refined analytic goals, may well find it necessary to impose more restrictive temporal limits.

As it happens, only three of the thirty-eight instances of harm from the 1991—2006 data set were initially detected *after* the first election for which the reforms were implemented fully (excluding the compound case of Quebec). In each of these three cases—Venezuela, Mexico, and Mercer County, Pennsylvania—harm was reported within six years of full implementation, as can be seen in table 2. The issue of timing was thus more pointed for historical cases of reform in places such as France, Chicago, and New Jersey. If nothing else, these historical cases teach us the importance of incorporating the long view when looking for potential problems caused by reform.

Cases of Clean Election Reform

In table 2 I list the clean reforms undertaken from 1991 to 2006 that constitute the core data set of contemporary reforms for this study. I include information about the nature of each reform, the date of the first election for which it was implemented, what I could determine about any iatrogenic harm that may have resulted, and the agent of that harm, if applicable. Details about how I chose the cases can be found in the Methods and Evidence section of chapter 1.

Table 2.   Clean election reforms, 1991—2006

Country	Date[1]	Clean election reform	Damage[2]	Agent of harm[3]
Albania	2005	Decentralization of voter registration along with door-to-door verification	Possibly depression and proliferation, but evidence inconclusive	Election administrators (if in fact damage occurred)
Antigua and Barbuda	1994	Numbered ballots	Insufficient evidence	—
Antigua and Barbuda	2004	Computerized voter registry with fingerprint and photograph identity cards	Depression (magnitude unknown)	Election administrators
Armenia	1999	Tightened voter registration rules	Depression (100,000 to 200,000 people, 4 to 8% of the voting-age population)	Election administrators
Australia: Australian Capital Territory	2001(a)	Electronic voting machines	No damage	—
Azerbaijan	2005	Applying ink to voters' fingers	No damage reported	—

(*Table 2—cont.*)

Country	Date[1]	Clean election reform	Damage[2]	Agent of harm[3]
Bangladesh	1996	Identity cards, implementation suspended	No damage reported	—
Bangladesh	2001	Computerized voters' list	Insufficient evidence	—
Belgium	1994(a) 2003(c)	Electronic voting machines	Depression (up to 10% of the electorate in some locales)	Election administrators
Bolivia	1993	Tightened voter registration rules	Depression (magnitude unknown)	Lawmakers and possibly election administrators
Brazil	2000	Disqualification of candidates found guilty of vote buying	Insufficient evidence	—
Brazil	2000(b)	Electronic voting machines	No damage reported	—
Brazil	2002	Clean election civic education campaign	Insufficient evidence	—
Cambodia	2003	Clean election civic education campaign	Insufficient evidence	—
Cameroon	1997	Continuous voter registration	Depression (possibly hundreds of thousands of people or more)	Election administrators
Canada: Quebec	1995	Tightened ballot disqualification instructions	Depression (up to 86,500 votes, 1.8% of all ballots cast)	Poll workers and party agents
Canada: Quebec	1996(a) 2005(c)	Electronic voting machines	Depression (thousands of voters)	Election administrators
Canada: Quebec	2003	Tightened voter identification requirements	Insufficient evidence	—

(*Table 2—cont.*)

Country	Date[1]	Clean election reform	Damage[2]	Agent of harm[3]
Costa Rica	1998(a)	Biometric voter identification cards	Insufficient evidence	—
Costa Rica	2002(a)	Electronic voting machines	Insufficient evidence	—
Ecuador	2004(a)	Electronic voting machines	Insufficient evidence	—
Dominican Republic	1994	Voter registration and photo identification card system	Depression (45,000 people, 1% of the voting-age population)	Election administrators
Georgia	2003	Computerized electoral lists	Depression (between 10 and 15% of the electorate) and alienation (widespread protests)	Probably election administrators, but evidence inconclusive
Germany	1999(a)	Electronic voting machines	No damage reported	—
Ghana	2000	Photo voter identification cards, requirement blocked by court	No depression reported. Possibly proliferation, but evidence inconclusive	Election administrators (if in fact damage occurred)
Guinea	1998	Clean election civic education campaign	Insufficient evidence	—
Guyana	1997	Voter identification cards	Depression (magnitude unknown)	Parties, candidates, agents
Guyana	2001	New photo identification cards	Depression (5% of the electorate)	Election administrators
India	2004(b)	Electronic voting machines	Possibly depression, but evidence inconclusive	Parties, candidates, agents (if in fact damage occurred)
Ireland	2002(a)	Electronic voting machines, implementation aborted	Insufficient evidence	—

(*Table 2—cont.*)

Country	Date[1]	Clean election reform	Damage[2]	Agent of harm[3]
Israel	1999	Voter registry purge	Insufficient evidence	—
Italy	1992	Elimination of option to vote for candidates by numbers rather than names	Possibly proliferation, but evidence inconclusive	Parties, candidates, agents (if in fact damage occurred)
Italy	2000	Voter rolls purge	Insufficient evidence	—
Jamaica	1997	Electronic voter registration system, incompletely implemented	Possibly depression and proliferation, but evidence inconclusive	Election administrators (if in fact damage occurred)
Jamaica	1997	Establishment of poll-watching group	Insufficient evidence	—
Kazakhstan	2004(a)	Electronic voting machines	Insufficient evidence	—
Kenya	1992	Secret ballot	No damage reported	—
Kenya	2002	Ballot counting moved to polling stations	No damage reported	—
Kuwait	2006	Establishment of poll-watching group	Insufficient evidence	—
Kyrgyzstan	2000	Electronic vote tabulation and results transmission	Insufficient evidence	—
Kyrgyzstan	2005	Application of ink to voters' fingers	No damage reported	—
Kyrgyzstan	2005	Transparent ballot boxes	Possibly proliferation, but evidence inconclusive	Insufficient evidence
Lesotho	2002	Computerized voter registration database with digital photographs, fingerprints, and signatures of registrants	No damage	—

(*Table 2—cont.*)

Country	Date[1]	Clean election reform	Damage[2]	Agent of harm[3]
Liberia	2005	Poll workers barred from assisting voters	No damage reported	—
Macedonia	1998	Voter identification cards	Depression (thousands of voters) and possibly proliferation	Election administrators
Malawi	1999	Photo identification cards	Depression (magnitude unknown) and alienation (rioting, disaffection of opposition parties)	Lawmakers, election administrators
Malawi	2004	Computerized voter registry	Possibly proliferation, but evidence inconclusive	Insufficient evidence
Malaysia	1999	Establishment of poll-watching group	Insufficient evidence	—
Mali	2002	New voter cards	Depression (up to 40% of registered voters) and proliferation (more than 55,000 cards stolen, an unknown number of which were fraudulently used)	Election administrators
Mauritania	2001	Voter identification cards	Insufficient evidence	—
Mexico	1991	Computerized voter registry	Insufficient evidence	—
Mexico	1994 2000(c)	Photo voter identification cards	Depression (roughly 94,000 votes, equal to 0.25% of all votes cast)	Parties, candidates, agents (not lawmakers)
Mexico	2000	Clean election civic education campaign	Insufficient evidence	—
Morocco	2002	Clean election civic education campaign	Insufficient evidence	—

(*Table 2—cont.*)

Country	Date[1]	Clean election reform	Damage[2]	Agent of harm[3]
Mozambique	2004	Computerized tabulation of results	Possibly proliferation, but evidence inconclusive	Election administrators (if in fact damage occurred)
Mozambique	2004	Parallel vote count	No damage reported	—
Namibia	1999	Publication of voters' lists and ballot serial numbers	Insufficient evidence	—
Nicaragua	1996(a)	Identification cards	Possibly depression, but evidence inconclusive	Election administrators (if in fact damage occurred)
Nicaragua	2001	Election roll verification	Insufficient evidence	—
Nigeria	2003	Computerized voter registry	Depression and proliferation (magnitude unknown)	Election administrators
Pakistan	2002	Computerized national identification cards	Possibly depression and proliferation, but evidence inconclusive	Insufficient evidence
Paraguay	2001(a)	Electronic voting machines	Insufficient evidence	—
Peru	1998(a)	National identity cards	No damage reported	—
Peru	2000	Voter lists made available for inspection prior to election	No damage reported	—
Philippines	1992	Establishment of new poll-watching group	Insufficient evidence	—
Philippines	2001	Clean election civic education campaign	Alienation (disaffection and civic withdrawal, magnitude unknown)	Civic educators

(Table 2—cont.)

Country	Date[1]	Clean election reform	Damage[2]	Agent of harm[3]
Philippines	2001	Continuous voter registration	Depression (as many as 3 to 6 million people, equal to 8 to 16% of registered voters)	Election administrators
Philippines	2004	Centralized voter registration database	Depression (900,000 people, more than 2% of registered voters), proliferation (magnitude unknown), and alienation (scattered demonstrations)	Election administrators
Poland	2002	Electronic vote tabulation and results transmission	No damage reported	—
Romania	2000	New type of voter card	Insufficient evidence	—
Russia	1999	More transparent ballot counting procedures in polling stations	Insufficient evidence	—
Senegal	1993	Elimination of testimonial voter registration	Depression (magnitude unknown)	Election administrators
Senegal	1993	Mandatory use of voting booths	No damage reported	—
Serbia	2000	First-time accreditation of domestic and international observer groups	No damage reported	—
Serbia	2000	Application of ink to voters' fingers	No damage reported	—
Serbia	2000	Transparent ballot boxes	No damage reported	—

(*Table 2—cont.*)

Country	Date[1]	Clean election reform	Damage[2]	Agent of harm[3]
Sierra Leone	2002	Registration with voter photo identification cards	Depression (between 500,000 and 1,000,000 people, equal to between 21 and 42% of registered voters)	Election administrators
Solomon Islands	2006	Single ballot box voting	No damage reported	—
South Africa	1999	Tightened voter registration rules	Depression (best estimate: 1.6 million people, 6% of the voting-age population)	Lawmakers
South Korea	1995 1996(c)	Campaign restrictions	Possibly depression, but evidence inconclusive	Parties, candidates, agents (if in fact damage occurred)
Taiwan	1995(a)	Crackdown on vote buying	Depression (rough estimate: up to 10% decline in turnout between the 1994 and 1997 local elections)	Parties, candidates, agents
Tajikistan	2005	Election monitoring by political party observers	Insufficient evidence	—
Thailand	1995	Anti-vote-buying civic education campaign	Possibly proliferation, but evidence inconclusive	Civic educators (if in fact damage occurred)
Thailand	2000	Elimination of block voting	Insufficient evidence	—
Thailand	2000	Compulsory voting	Insufficient evidence	—
Thailand: Chiang Mai Province	2000	Anti-vote-buying civic education campaign	Proliferation (magnitude unknown)	Civic educators

(*Table 2—cont.*)

Country	Date[1]	Clean election reform	Damage[2]	Agent of harm[3]
Turkey	2002(a)	System for continually updating computerized voter registry	Insufficient evidence	—
Uganda	2006	Transparent ballot boxes	Insufficient evidence	—
Ukraine	2004	Restrictions on absentee voting	Insufficient evidence	—
United States: Alabama	2003	Tightened voter identification requirements	Insufficient evidence	—
United States: Arizona	2006	Tightened voter identification requirements	Depression (2,500 voters, 0.1% of all votes cast)	Lawmakers
United States: California (Orange County)	2004	Electronic voting machines	Depression (7,000 voters, 1.2% of all votes cast)	Election administrators
United States: California (Los Angeles County)	2006	Voter registration database	Depression (1,500 people, equal to 0.04% of registered voters)	Election administrators
United States: Colorado	2004	Tightened voter identification requirements	Insufficient evidence	—
United States: Florida	2000(a)	Voter roll purge, implemented in two-thirds of the state's counties	Depression (best estimate: 1,100 people, equal to 0.01% of registered voters)	Election administrators
United States: Florida (15 counties)	2002	Electronic voting machines	Possibly depression, but evidence inconclusive	Election administrators (if in fact damage occurred)

(Table 2—cont.)

Country	Date[1]	Clean election reform	Damage[2]	Agent of harm[3]
United States: Florida	2006	Voter registration drive restrictions, implementation suspended by court	Insufficient evidence	—
United States: Georgia	2002	Electronic voting machines	Depression (drop in turnout of 0.3 to 0.4% for every 1% of a county's population that was elderly)	Lawmakers
United States: Georgia	2006	Photo voter identification requirement, implementation blocked by court	Possibly depression, but evidence inconclusive	Election administrators (if in fact damage occurred)
United States: Indiana	2006	Photo voter identification requirement	Possibly depression, but evidence inconclusive	Lawmakers (if in fact damage occurred)
United States: Kentucky	2006	Voter roll purge	Depression (8,000 voters, equal to 0.3% of registered voters)	Election administrators
United States: Maryland	2004	Electronic voting machines	Possibly depression, but evidence inconclusive	Election administrators (if in fact damage occurred)
United States: Missouri	2006	Photo voter identification requirement, implementation blocked by court	Possibly depression, but evidence inconclusive	Election administrators (if in fact damage occurred)
United States: Montana	2004	Tightened voter identification requirements	Insufficient evidence	—

(*Table 2—cont.*)

Country	Date[1]	Clean election reform	Damage[2]	Agent of harm[3]
United States: Nevada	2004	Electronic voting machines	Insufficient evidence	—
United States: New Mexico	2006	Tightened voter identification requirements	Possibly proliferation, but evidence inconclusive	Election administrators (if in fact damage occurred)
United States: New York (New York City)	1993	Restrictive voter registration verification procedures	Depression (reportedly thousands of voters)	Election administrators
United States: North Dakota	2004	Tightened voter identification requirements	Insufficient evidence	—
United States: Ohio	2006	Tightened voter identification requirements	Possibly depression, but evidence inconclusive	Lawmakers, election administrators (if in fact damage occurred)
United States: Ohio	2006	Voter registration drive restrictions, implementation suspended by court	Possibly depression, but evidence inconclusive	Lawmakers, election administrators (if in fact damage occurred)
United States: Pennsylvania (Mercer County)	2001 2004(c)	Electronic voting machines	Depression (at least 4,000 votes, 8% of all votes cast)	Election administrators
United States: South Dakota	2004	Photo voter identification requirement	Depression (magnitude unknown)	Lawmakers, election administrators
United States: Washington	2005	Tightened voter identification requirements	Possibly depression, but evidence inconclusive	Election administrators (if in fact damage occurred)

(*Table 2—cont.*)

Country	Date[1]	Clean election reform	Damage[2]	Agent of harm[3]
Venezuela	1998	Updated voter registry	Depression (up to 2 million people, 15% of the voting-age population)	Election administrators
Venezuela	1998 2000(c)	Computerized vote counting and tabulation, electronic results transmission	Depression and proliferation (up to 348,465 votes, 5.3% of the total number of votes cast)	Election administrators
Venezuela	2004(a)	Use of fingerprint reading devices to improve quality of the voter registry	Insufficient evidence	—
Yemen	2003	Voter identification cards	Insufficient evidence	—
Zambia	1996	Decentralized vote counting	Insufficient evidence	—
Zambia	1996	Computerization of voter registry	Depression (rough estimate: 600,000 people, 13% of voting-age population)	Election administrators
Zambia	2001	Anti-vote-buying civic education campaign	Insufficient evidence	—
Zambia	2006	Electronic transmission of election results	Alienation (rioting in Lusaka and other cities); possibly proliferation, but evidence inconclusive	Election administrators
Zimbabwe	2002	Proof-of-residency requirement to vote	Depression (magnitude unknown)	Lawmakers

[1] I provide the date of the first election for which the clean election reform was implemented fully (rather than, say, the date on which the reform was initially passed into law). If the reform was rolled out incrementally, (a) marks the date of the first election for which the reform was pilot-tested or partially implemented, whereas (b) indicates the date of the first election for which the reform was implemented fully. The notation (c) specifies the date of the election for which iatrogenic harm was documented or suspected, if it is different from the date of the first election for which the reform was introduced.

[2] If I found credible evidence that damage occurred, I indicate the form of damage. If I located reports that damage occurred but those reports lacked credible evidence, I note that damage was possible

(*Table 2—cont.*)

"but evidence inconclusive." If I found credible evidence that no damage occurred, I specify that there was "no damage." If I located reports that discussed the implementation of the reform but these reports did not mention any damage, I put down "no damage reported." If I discovered little, mixed, or no information about the consequences of a reform, I note that there was "insufficient evidence."

[3] If there was damage, I list the agent who most directly caused that damage. If I could not discern which agent was responsible, I note that there was "insufficient evidence." If I found only inconclusive evidence that a clean election reform caused damage but I could determine who the agent of harm would be if the reports of harm proved to be accurate, I specify the agent, with the proviso "if in fact damage occurred."

References

ACTEC (Australian Capital Territory Electoral Commission). 2002. "The 2001 ACT Legislative Assembly Election: Electronic Voting and Counting System Review." Canberra.

———. 2005. "ACT Legislative Assembly Election 2004: Electronic Voting and Counting System Review." Canberra.

Afronet. 1999. "Malawi Election Report 1999." Zambia: The Inter-African Network for Human Rights and Development.

AIS (American Information Systems). 1996. "Post Election Report: Republic of the Philippines, Autonomous Region Muslim Mindanao ARMM Pilot Election, September 9, 1996," October 15.

Alejo, Myrna J., Maria Elena P. Rivera, and Noel Inocencio P. Valencia. 1996. [De]scribing Elections: A Study of Elections in the Lifeworld of San Isidro. Quezon City: Institute for Popular Democracy.

Allen, Howard W., and Kay Warren Allen. 1981. "Vote Fraud and Data Reliability." In Analyzing Electoral History: A Guide to the Study of American Voting Behavior, ed. Jerome M. Clubb, William H. Flanigan, and Nancy H. Zingale. Beverly Hills: Sage.

Altschuler, Glenn C., and Stuart M. Blumin. 2000. Rude Republic: Americans and Their Politics in the Nineteenth Century. Princeton: Princeton University Press.

ANAO (Australian National Audit Office). 1998. "Corporate Governance Framework: Australian Electoral Commission." Canberra.

———. 2002. "Integrity of the Electoral Roll: Australian Electoral Commission." Audit Report No. 42, Canberra.

———. 2004. "Integrity of the Electoral Roll—Follow-up Audit: Australian Electoral Commission." Audit Report No. 39, Canberra.

Anderson, Allan. 2000. Zion and Pentecost: The Spirituality and Experience of Pentecostal and Zionist/Apostolic Churches of South Africa. Pretoria: University of South Africa Press.

Anderson, Margaret Lavinia. 2000. Practicing Democracy: Elections and Political Culture in Imperial Germany. Princeton: Princeton University Press.

Ansolabehere, Stephen. 2007. "Access versus Integrity in Voter Identification Requirements." Paper presented at the New York University Law School's Election Law Symposium for the Annual Survey of American Law.

Argersinger, Peter H. 1987. "From Party Tickets to Secret Ballots: The Evolution of the Electoral Process in Maryland During the Gilded Age." *Maryland Historical Magazine* 82(3): 214–55.

——. 1992. "Regulating Democracy: Election Laws and Dakota Politics, 1889–1902." In *Structure, Process, and Party: Essays in American Political History.* Armonk, NY: M. E. Sharpe.

Bacani, Bishop Teodoro C., Jr., D.D. 1992. *Church in Politics.* Manila: Bacani's Press.

Bakary, Tessy, and Susan L. Palmer. 1997. "May 17, 1997 Legislative Elections in Cameroon: Report of the IFES International Observation Mission." Washington, DC: International Foundation for Election Systems.

Baker, Paula. 1984. "The Culture of Politics in the Late Nineteenth Century: Community and Political Behavior in Rural New York." *Journal of Social History* 18 (2): 167–93.

Baland, Jean-Marie, and James A. Robinson. 2007. "How Does Vote Buying Shape the Economy?" In *Elections for Sale: The Causes and Consequences of Vote Buying,* ed. Frederic Charles Schaffer. Boulder: Lynne Rienner.

Bass, Herbert J. 1961. "The Politics of Ballot Reform in New York State, 1888–1890." *New York History* 24 (3): 253–72.

Bautista, Maria Cynthia Rose Banzon. 2001. "People Power 2: 'The Revenge of the Elite on the Masses'?" In *Between Fires: Fifteen Perspectives on the Estrada Crisis,* ed. Amando Doronila. Pasig: Anvil.

BCJ (Brennan Center for Justice). 2006. "Citizens Without Proof: A Survey of Americans' Possession of Documentary Proof of Citizenship and Photo Identification." New York University School of Law, November.

——. 2007. "The New Crackdown on Voter Registration Drives." New York University School of Law, February 7.

BCTF (Brennan Center Task Force on Voting System Security). 2006. "The Machinery of Democracy: Protecting Elections in an Electronic World." Brennan Center for Justice at the New York University School of Law.

Benoit, Kenneth. 2004. "Experience of Electronic Voting Overseas." Appendix 2J of the "First Report of the Commission on Electronic Voting on the Secrecy, Accuracy and Testing of the Chosen Electronic Voting System." Ireland, December 14.

Bensel, Richard Franklin. 2004. *The American Ballot Box in the Mid-Nineteenth Century.* New York: Cambridge University Press.

Bercé, Y.-M. 1969. "Les bulletins nuls, source de la microsociologie électorale." *La Gazette des Archives* 65:75–84.

Bernard, André, and Denis Laforte. 1969. *La législation électorale au Québec, 1790–1967.* Montreal: Sainte-Marie.

Bernas Law Offices. 2002. House of Representatives Complaint for the Impeachment of Commissioner Luzviminda G. Tancangco, May 24.

Boily, Robert. 1970. *La réforme électorale au Québec.* Montreal: Éditions du Jour.

Borra, Resurreccion. 2001. COMELEC Commissioner. Interview with author, Manila, Philippines, March 28.

Bosco, Joseph. 1994. "Faction versus Ideology: Mobilization Strategies in Taiwan's Elections." *China Quarterly* 137:28–62.

Bositis, David A. 2000. "The Black Vote in 2000: A Preliminary Analysis." Washington, DC: Joint Center for Political and Economic Studies, December.

Bourdieu, Pierre. 1984. *Distinction: A Social Critique of the Judgement of Taste.* Cambridge, MA: Harvard University Press.

Boyd, Richard W. 1981. "Decline of U.S. Voter Turnout: Structural Explanations." *American Politics Quarterly* 9: 133–60.

Bratton, Michael. 1999. "Political Participation in a New Democracy: Institutional Considerations from Zambia." *Comparative Political Studies* 32 (5): 549–88.

Brown, Deborah, Eric Moon, and James A. Robinson. 1998. "Taiwan's 1998 Local Elections: Appraising Steps in Democratization." *Asian Survey* 38 (6): 569–84.

Burnell, P. 2003. "The Tripartite Elections in Zambia, December 2001." *Electoral Studies* 22: 325–95.

Burnham, Walter Dean. 1970. *Critical Elections and the Mainspring of American Politics.* New York: Norton.

Butler, Vic, and Joe Baxter. 1998. "Report on Issues in Preparation for the 1999 General Elections in Malawi." International Foundation for Election Systems, February 14.

Buxton, Julia. 2001. *The Failure of Political Reform in Venezuela.* Burlington, VT: Ashgate.

CA (Commission on Audit). 2001a. "Annual Audit Report of the Commission on Elections for Calendar Year 2000." Republic of the Philippines, May 9.

———. 2001b. "Special Audit of the National Precinct Mapping and CVL Verification Project." Republic of the Philippines, November 6.

Callahan, William A. 2000. *Pollwatching, Elections and Civil Society in Southeast Asia.* Burlington, VT: Ashgate.

———. 2002. "The Ideology of Vote Buying and the Democratic Deferral of Political Reform." Paper presented at Trading Political Rights: The Comparative Politics of Vote Buying Conference, MIT, August 26–27.

Callahan, William A., and Duncan McCargo. 1996. "Vote-buying in Thailand's Northeast." *Asian Survey* 36 (4): 376–92.

Carnahan, Robin. 2007. "Voters First: An Examination of the 2006 Midterm Election in Missouri. Report from the Office of Secretary of State to the People of Missouri," Winter.

Carney, Timothy P. 2001. "Katherine Harris Not Responsible for Felon Purges." *Human Event: The National Conservative Weekly,* March 12.

Carrier, Michael A. 2005. "Vote Counting, Technology, and Unintended Consequences." *St. John's Law Review* 79 (3): 645–87.

Carter Center. 1993. "Electoral Reform in Mexico." Occasional Paper Series 4 (1). Atlanta.

———. 1994. "Elections in Mexico: Third Report." Atlanta, August.

———. 2002. "Observing the 2002 Mali Presidential Elections, Final Report." Atlanta, October.

CCR (United States Commission on Civil Rights). 2001. *Voting Irregularities in Florida During the 2000 Presidential Election.* Washington, DC.

———. 2002. "Voting Rights in Florida 2002: Briefing Summary," August.

CDU (Central Depository Unit). 2002. "Ghasia Watch: CDU Report on Electoral Violence in Kenya, January—December 2002." Nairobi, Kenya.

CEV (Commission on Electronic Voting). 2004. "First Report of the Commission on Electronic Voting on the Secrecy, Accuracy, and Testing of the Chosen Electronic Voting System." Ireland.

Chan, Dan. 2003. Senior Special Agent, Investigation Bureau, Ministry of Justice, Republic of China. Interview with author, Taipei, August 12.

Cheng, Kuen-shan, Ye-li Wang, and Yun-tsai Chen. 2000. "Analysis of the Causes of Vote Buying, and the Study of How to Prevent It" [in Chinese]. Taipei: Ministry of Justice.

Chou, William. 2003. "The Experience of Combating Vote Buying in Taiwan." Presentation at the Department of Prosecutorial Affairs, Ministry of Justice, Republic of China, August 12.

Chu, J. J. 1996. "Taiwan: A Fragmented 'Middle' Class in the Making." In *The New Rich in Asia: Mobile Phones, McDonald's and Middle Class Revolution,* ed. Richard Robison and David S. G. Goodman. New York: Routledge.

Chu, Yun-han. 1994. "SNTV and the Evolving Party System in Taiwan." *Chinese Political Science Review* 22: 33–51.

Coalition (Coalition on Homelessness and Housing in Ohio and the League of Women Voters of Ohio). 2005. "Let the People Vote: A Joint Report on Election Reform Activities in Ohio," June 14.

Collier, David, James Mahoney, and Jason Seawright. 2004. "Claiming Too Much: Warnings about Selection Bias." In *Rethinking Social Inquiry: Diverse Tools, Shared Standards,* ed. Henry E. Brady and David Collier.

COMELEC (Commission on Elections). 1996. "Report of the Commission on Elections to the Excellency, President Fidel V. Ramos and to the Congress of the Republic of the Philippines on the Conduct of the September 9, 1996 Elections in the Autonomous Region of Muslim Mindanao."

———. 1999. "Modernization Program of the Comelec: Status Report as of 22 August 1999." Republic of the Philippines.

———. 2000. "National Precinct Mapping and CVL Verification Project: Operations Manual." Republic of the Philippines, March 14.

Compuware. 2003. "Direct Recording Electronic (DRE) Technical Security Assessment." Prepared for the Ohio Secretary of State, November 21.

Converse, Philip. 1972. "Change in the American Electorate." In *The Human Meaning of Social Change,* ed. Angus Campbell and Philip Converse. New York: Russell Sage Foundation.

Cornelius, Wayne A. 2004. "Mobilized Voting in the 2000 Elections: The Changing Efficacy of Vote Buying and Coercion in Mexican Electoral Politics." In *Mexico's Pivotal Democratic Election: Candidates, Voters, and the Presidential Campaign of 2000,* ed. Jorge I. Domínguez and Chappell Lawson. Stanford: Stanford University Press.

Cox, Cathy. 2005. Georgia Secretary of State. Letter to Sonny Purdue, Governor of Georgia, April 8.

Cox, Gary W. 1987. *The Efficient Secret: The Cabinet and the Development of Political Parties in Victorian England.* Cambridge: Cambridge University Press.

Cox, Gary W., and J. Morgan Kousser. 1981. "Turnout and Rural Corruption: New York as a Test Case." *American Journal of Political Science* 25 (4): 646–63.

CS (Commonwealth Secretariat). 2004. "Antigua and Barbuda, General Election, 23 March 2004, the Report of the Commonwealth Expert Team." London.

———. 2006. "Lesotho General Election, 25 May 2002, the Report of the Commonwealth Observer Group." London.

CSER (Committee on Suffrage and Electoral Reforms). 1995. Public Hearing, Iloilo City Session Hall, November 18. Congress of the Philippines, House of Representatives.

———. 1996. "Assessment and Recommendations of the House of Representatives Contingent of the Oversight Committee on the Pilot-testing of a Computerized Election System in the September 1996 ARMM Election." Congress of the Philippines, House of Representatives.

Cullinane, Michael. 1993. "*Burgis* Projects in the Post-Marcos Era." *Pilipinas* 21:74–76.

Davidson, Donetta. 2007. Chair, U.S. Election Assistance Commission. Letter to Dianne Feinstein, Senate Rules and Administration Committee, May 18.

Déloye, Yves, and Olivier Ihl. 1991a. "Des voix pas comme les autres: Votes blancs et votes nuls aux élections législatives de 1881." *Revue Française de Science Politique* 41 (2): 141–70.

———. 1991b. "Légitimité et déviance: L'annulation des votes dans les campagnes de la IIIe République." *Politix* 15:13–24.

Demetriou, Harriet. 2001. Former COMELEC Chair. Interview with author, Makati, Philippines, January 31.

Desamito, Milagros. 2004. Interview on *The World Tonight,* ABS-CBN News Channel, Philippines, May 14.

Desposato, Scott W. 2003. Personal communication, February 13.

———. 2007. "How Does Vote Buying Shape the Legislative Arena?" In *Elections for Sale: The Causes and Consequences of Vote Buying,* ed. Frederic Charles Schaffer. Boulder: Lynne Rienner.

de Villa, Henrietta T. 1992. "Faith and Fire, the PPCRV Way: A Post Election Report of the Parish Pastoral Council for Responsible Voting (PPCRV) to the Catholic Bishops Conference of the Philippines (CBCP) and to the Commission on Elections (COMELEC) 25 July 1992."

DGEQ (Directeur Général des Élections du Québec). 1996. "Rejected Ballot Papers—Unity Rally: Report of the Chief Election Officer. October 30, 1995 Referendum." Sainte-Foy, Quebec.

———. 2006. "Élections municipales de novembre 2005: Rapport d'évaluation des nouveaux mécanismes de votation." Quebec.

Dill, David. 2006. "Making Democracy Transparent." March 7. www.tompaine.com/articles/2006/03/07/making_democracy_transparent.php.

DOJ (United States Department of Justice). 2007a. "About Section 5 of the Voting Rights Act." www.usdoj.gov/crt/voting/sec_5/about.htm. Civil Rights Division, Voting Section.

———. 2007b. "Section 5 Changes by Type and Year Totals." www.usdoj.gov/crt/voting/sec_5/changes.htm. Civil Rights Division, Voting Section.

———. n.d. "Elections Fraud Prosecutions & Convictions, Ballot Access & Voting Integrity Initiative, October 2002–September 2005." Criminal Division, Public Integrity Section.

Domínguez, Jorge I., and James A. McCann. 1996. *Democratizing Mexico: Public Opinion and Electoral Choices.* Baltimore: Johns Hopkins University Press.

Douglas, Mary. 1966. *Purity and Danger: An Analysis of Concepts of Pollution and Taboo.* New York: Praeger.

DPA (Department of Prosecutorial Affairs). 2003. "Vote-buying Cases of Some Important Elections in Taiwan from 1997 to July 2003." Information Sheet. Ministry of Justice, Republic of China.

EAC (United States Election Assistance Commission). 2004a. "U.S. EAC Forms Technical Committee to Create New Voting Standards." News release, June 17.

———. 2004b. "U.S. Election Assistance Commission Releases 861 Million Dollars in Payments to 25 States." News release, June 17.

———. 2005a. "Fiscal Year 2004 Annual Report: Preparing America to Vote," January.

———. 2005b. "Initial Recommendations on Voluntary Voting System Guidelines Delivered to EAC." News release, May 12.

EAC (United States Election Assistance Commission). 2006. "Election Crimes: An Initial Review and Recommendations for Future Study," December.

——. 2007. "Pilot Programs." www.eac.gov/pilot_programs.asp.

Eagleton (Eagleton Institute of Politics and Moritz College of Law). 2006. "Report to the U.S. Election Assistance Commission on Best Practices to Improve Voter Identification Requirements Pursuant to the Help America Vote Act of 2002, Public Law 107–252." Rutgers University and the Ohio State University, June 28.

Eckstein, Harry. 1975. "Case Study and Theory in Political Science." In *Strategies of Inquiry,* ed. by Fred I. Greenstein and Nelson W. Polsby. Reading, MA: Addison-Wesley.

Economist. 1994. "Voter's Darling: India," May 28.

EDS (Election Data Services). 2006. "2006 Voter Equipment Study." Washington, DC, October 2.

Eisenstadt, Todd A. 1999. "Off the Streets and into the Courtrooms: Resolving Postelectoral Conflicts in Mexico." In *The Self-Restraining State: Power and Accountability in New Democracies,* ed. Andreas Schedler, Larry Diamond, and Marc F. Plattner. Boulder: Lynne Rienner.

Electionline.org. 2007. "Case Study: Auditing the Vote." Washington, DC, March.

Elections Canada. 2004. "Elections Canada Reaches Out to Young Electors from Coast to Coast." Press release, February 11.

Election Science Institute. 2006. "DRE Analysis for May 2006 Primary; Cuyahoga County, Ohio," August.

Elklit, Jørgen. 1983. "Mobilization and Partisan Division: Open Voting in Fredericia, Denmark." *Social Science History* 7 (3): 235–66.

——. 2000. Personal communication, June 24.

Enriquez, Virgilio G. 1986. "Kapwa: A Core Concept in Filipino Social Psychology." In *Philippine World View,* ed. Virgilio G. Enriquez. Singapore: Institute of Southeast Asian Studies.

Escobar, Cristina. 2006. "Migration and Citizen Rights: The Mexican Case." *Citizenship Studies* 10 (5): 503–22.

Feldman, Ariel J., J. Alex Halderman, and Edward W. Felten. 2006. "Security Analysis of the Diebold AccuVote-TS Voting Machine." Princeton University, September 13.

Fell, Dafydd. 2002. "Political Advertising in Taiwan: 1989–2001." Unpublished paper, Department of Political Studies, London School of Oriental and African Studies.

Ferté, Charles. 1909. *Le secret du vote.* Montpellier: Imprimerie G. Firmin, Montane et Sicardi.

Fischer, Eric A. 2001. "Voting Technologies in the United States: Overview and Issues for Congress." Congressional Research Services Report for Congress, March 21.

Foucault, Michel. 1979. *Discipline and Punish: The Birth of the Prison.* New York: Vintage.

Frederickson, H. George, and Todd R. LaPorte. 2002. "Airport Security, High Reliability, and the Problem of Rationality." *Public Administration Review* 62:33–43.

Fredman, L. E. 1968. *The Australian Ballot: The Story of an American Reform.* East Lansing: Michigan State University Press.

Frykman, Jonas, and Orvar Löfgren. 1987. *Culture Builders: A Historical Anthropology of Middle-Class Life,* trans. Alan Crozier. New Brunswick, NJ: Rutgers University Press.

Garrigou, Alain. 1988. "Le secret de l'isoloir." *Actes de la Recherche en Sciences Sociales* 71–72: 22–45.

——. 1992. *Le vote et la vertu: Comment les Français sont devenus électeurs.* Paris: Presses de la Fondation Nationale des Sciences Politiques.

Geertz, Clifford. 1983. *Local Knowledge: Further Essays in Interpretive Anthropology.* New York: Basic.

George, Alexander L. 1979. "Case Studies and Theory Development: The Method of Structured, Focused Comparison." In *Diplomacy: New Approaches in History, Theory, and Policy,* ed. Paul Gordon Lauren. New York: Free Press.

Gerber, Alan S., and Donald P. Green. 2000. "The Effects of Canvassing, Telephone Calls, and Direct Mail on Voter Turnout: A Field Experiment." *American Political Science Review* 94 (3): 653–63.

———. 2005. "Correction to Gerber and Green (2000), Replication of Disputed Findings, and Reply to Imai (2005)." *American Political Science Review* 99 (2): 301–13.

Gerring, John. 2001. *Social Science Methodology: A Critical Framework.* New York: Cambridge University Press.

Gilbert, George. 2007. Director of Elections, Guilford County, North Carolina. Testimony before the Subcommittee on Elections of the Committee on House Administration, United States House of Representatives, March 23.

Glancy, Kevin. 2000. "Exposing the Enemy Within." *The Issue* 2 (2): 1–6.

Gloria, Glenda M. 1995. "Makati: One City, Two Worlds." In *Boss: 5 Case Studies of Local Politics in the Philippines,* ed. by Jose F. Lacaba. Pasig: Philippine Center for Investigative Journalism.

Göbel, Christian. 2001. "Towards a Consolidated Democracy? Informal and Formal Institutions in Taiwan's Political Process." Paper presented at the 2001 annual meeting of the American Political Science Association, San Francisco.

Grant, Bruce. 1955. *Fight for a City: The Story of the Urban League Club of Chicago and Its Times, 1880–1955.* Chicago: Rand McNally.

Graves, John William. 1967. "Negro Disfranchisement in Arkansas." *Arkansas Historical Quarterly* 26: 199–225.

Green, Donald P., Alan S. Gerber, and David W. Nickerson. 2002. "Getting Out the Vote in Local Elections: Results from Six Door-to-Door Canvassing Experiments." Unpublished paper, Yale University, May 18.

Green, Donald P., Barry McMillion, and Jennifer K. Smith. 2002. "Professionalization Campaigns and the Secret History of Collective Action Problems." Unpublished paper, Yale University, January 31.

Grofman, Bernard, Lisa Handley, and Richard G. Niemi. 1992. *Minority Representation and the Quest for Voting Equality.* New York: Cambridge University Press.

Guerin, Henriette, Lorenzo Morris, and Pierre Tessier. 1992. "Planning for the 1993 National Elections in Senegal: An Evaluation." Washington, DC: International Foundation for Election Systems.

Guionnet, Christine. 1996. "Élections et apprentissage de la politique: Les élections municipales sous la Monarchie de Juillet." *Revue Française de Science Politique* 46 (4): 555–79.

Gwenani, Dave. 2001. "Election Monitor's Consultative Workshop on Corruption During the Electoral Process Organised by Transparency International—Zambia on July 19." Lusaka.

Hall, Joseph Lorenzo. 2006. "Transparency and Access to Source Code in Electronic Voting." Paper presented at the Electronic Voting Technology Workshop, Vancouver, August 1.

Hamelin, Jean, and Marcel Hamelin. 1962. *Les moeurs électorales dans le Québec de 1791 à nos jours.* Montreal: Éditions du Jour.

HAPC (Home Affairs Portfolio Committee). 1998. Minutes Pertaining to the Discussion of the Electoral Act, July 21, 1998. National Assembly of South Africa.

Harris, Joseph P. 1929. *Registration of Voters in the United States.* Washington, DC: Brookings.

Hasen, Richard L. 2005. "Beyond the Margin of Litigation: Reforming Election Adminis-tration to Avoid Electoral Meltdown." Loyola Law School Legal Studies Research Paper No. 2005–7, March.

———. 2007. "The Fraudulent Fraud Squad: The Incredible, Disappearing American Center for Voting Rights." May 18. www.slate.com/id/2166589/.

Hawes, Gary. 1989. "Aquino and Her Administration: A View from the Countryside." Pacific Affairs 62 (1): 9–28.

Hayduk, Ronald. 2005. Gatekeepers to the Franchise: Shaping Election Administration in New York. DeKalb: Northern Illinois University Press.

Heckelman, Jac C. 1995. "The Effect of the Secret Ballot on Voter Turnout Rates." Public Choice 82 (1–2): 107–24.

Hedman, Eva-Lotta. 1998. "Whose Business Is It Anyway? Free and Fair Elections in the Philippines." Public Policy 2 (3): 145–70.

———. 1999. "Mapping the Movement: NAMFREL in Six Philippine Cities." South East Asia Research 7 (2): 189–214.

Helmore, Leonard Mervyn. 1967. Corrupt and Illegal Practices: A General Survey and a Case Study of an Election Petition. London: Routledge.

Hernández Carrochano, David. 2003. "Los intermediarios en la compra de votos en México." Unpublished paper, FLACSO Mexico.

Hewison, Kevin. 1996. "Emerging Social Forces in Thailand: New Political and Economic Roles." In The New Rich in Asia: Mobile Phones, McDonald's and Middle Class Revolution, ed. Richard Robison and David S. G. Goodman. New York: Routledge.

Hicken, Allen D. 2007a. "How Do Rules and Institutions Encourage Vote Buying?" In Elections for Sale: The Causes and Consequences of Vote Buying, ed. Frederic Charles Schaffer. Boulder: Lynne Rienner.

———. 2007b. "How Effective Are Institutional Reforms?" In Elections for Sale: The Causes and Consequences of Vote Buying, ed. Frederic Charles Schaffer. Boulder: Lynne Rienner.

Highton, Benjamin. 1997. "Easy Registration and Voter Turnout." Journal of Politics 59 (2): 565–575.

Hill, Lisa. 2004. "Compulsory Voting in Australia: A Basis for a 'Best Practice' Regime." Federal Law Review 32 (3): 479–97.

Hill, Lisa, and Jonathan Louth. 2004. "Compulsory Voting Laws and Turnout: Efficacy and Appropriateness." Paper presented at the Australasian Political Studies Association Con-ference, University of Adelaide, September 29—October 1.

Ho, Chin-ming. 1995. "The Vote Buying Phenomenon and Its Effect: An Analysis of the Second Legislative Election in Kaohsiung City" [in Chinese]. Political Science Review 6: 109–44.

Hood, M.V., III, and Charles S. Bullock, III. 2007. "Worth a Thousand Words? An Analysis of Georgia's Voter Identification Statute." Paper presented at the annual meeting of the Southwestern Political Science Association, Albuquerque, March 14–17.

Horng, Guang-sheng. 2003. Deputy Director, Department of Prosecutorial Affairs, Minis-try of Justice, Republic of China. Interview with author, Taipei, August 12.

HSRC (Human Sciences Research Council). 1998a. "The Extent to Which Eligible Voters Are in Possession of SA Identity Documents." Report 1: National Survey, South Africa, July 30.

———. 1998b. "The Extent to Which Eligible Voters Are in Possession of SA Identity Docu-ments." Report 2: Regional Survey, South Africa, August 13.

Hughes, Colin A. 2003. "The Independence of the Commissions: The Legislative Framework and Bureaucratic Reality." In *Realising Democracy: Electoral Law in Australia,* ed. Graeme Orr, Bryan Mercurio, and George Williams. Annandale, Australia: Federation Press.

Huntington, Samuel P. 1991. *The Third Wave: Democratization in the Late Twentieth Century.* Norman: University of Oklahoma Press.

Hursti, Harri. 2006. "Diebold TSx Evaluation." Prepared for Black Box Voting Project, May 11.

IDEA (International Institute for Democracy and Electoral Assistance). n.d. "Report of the Audit and Systems Review of the 2001 Elections Process in Guyana at the Request of the Guyana Elections Commission."

IEC (Independent Electoral Commission). 1994. "Report of the Independent Electoral Commission: The South African Elections of 1994." Johannesburg.

Imai, Kosuke. 2005. "Do Get-Out-the-Vote Calls Reduce Turnout? The Importance of Statistical Methods for Field Experiments." *American Political Science Review* 99 (2): 283–300.

Independent Election Committee. 2005. "Restoring Confidence to Voters: Findings and Recommendations of the Independent Election Committee, Mercer County, Pennsylvania," February 8.

IRI (International Republican Institute). n.d. "Final Report, Election Observation Mission, Republic of Macedonia, Parliamentary Elections, 18 October and 1 November 1998." Washington, DC.

Issacharoff, Samuel. 1992. "Polarized Voting and the Political Process: The Transformation of Voting Rights Jurisprudence." *Michigan Law Review* 90 (7): 1833–91.

———. 2004. "Is Section 5 of the Voting Rights Act a Victim of Its Own Success?" *Columbia Law Review* 104: 1710–31.

Jackman, Robert W., and Ross A. Miller. 1995. "Voter Turnout in the Industrial Democracies During the 1980s." *Comparative Political Studies* 27 (4): 467–92.

Johnson, R. W. 1996. "How Free? How Fair?" In *Launching Democracy in South Africa: The First Open Election, April 1994,* ed. R. W. Johnson and Lawrence Schlemmer. New Haven: Yale University Press.

Jordan, David K. 1977. "A Chinese 'Culture of Elections' or the Decline of Honest Bribery." Unpublished paper, University of California, San Diego.

Kadzamira, Zimani D. 2000. "Management of the Electoral Process during the Second Multi-Party Elections." In *Malawi's Second Democratic Elections: Process, Problems and Prospects,* ed. Martin Ott, Kings M. Phiri, and Nandini Patel. Zomba, Malawi: Kachere Series.

Keene, Barry. 2005. Message posted to "California Insider" weblog of *Sacramento Bee* columnist Daniel Weintraub. February 8. www.sacbee.com/static/weblogs/insider/archives/001754.html.

Kelley, Stanley, Jr., Richard E. Ayres, and William G. Bowen. 1967. "Registration and Voting: Putting First Things First." *American Political Science Review* 61 (2): 359–79.

Key, V. O. 1949. *Southern Politics in State and Nation.* New York: Knopf.

Keyssar, Alexander. 2000. *The Right to Vote: The Contested History of Democracy in the United States.* New York: Basic.

Kim, Jae-on, John R. Petrocik, and Stephen N. Enokson. 1975. "Voter Turnout among the American States: Systemic and Individual Components." *American Political Science Review* 69 (1): 107–23.

King, Gary, Robert O. Keohane, and Sidney Verba. 1994. *Designing Social Inquiry: Scientific Inference in Qualitative Research.* Princeton: Princeton University Press.

Kingsley, Jean-Pierre. 2004. "The Administration of Canada's Independent, Non-Partisan Approach." *Election Law Journal* 3 (3): 406–11.

Kishlansky, Mark A. 1986. *Parliamentary Selection: Social and Political Choice in Early Modern England.* New York: Cambridge University Press.

Kitschelt, Herbert. 2000. "Linkages Between Citizens and Politicians in Democratic Polities." *Comparative Political Studies* 33 (6/7): 845–79.

Knack, Stephen. 1995. "Does 'Motor-Voter' Work? Evidence from State-Level Data." *Journal of Politics* 57 (3): 796–811.

Kohno, Tadayoshi, Adam Stubblefield, Aviel D. Rubin, and Dan S. Wallach. 2003. "Analysis of an Electronic Voting System." Johns Hopkins University Information Security Institute Technical Report TR-2003–19, July 23.

Kornblith, Miriam. 2001. "Confiabilidad y transparencia de las elecciones en Venezuela: Examen de los comicios del 30 de julio de 2000." In *Venezuela en transición: Elecciones y democracia 1998—2000,* ed. José Vicente Carrasquero, Thais Maingon, and Friedrich-Welsch. Caracas: CDB.

———. 2002. "La compra-venta de votos en las elecciones venezolanas." Paper presented at Trading Political Rights: The Comparative Politics of Vote Buying Conference, MIT, August 26–27.

———. 2005. "The Referendum in Venezuela: Elections Versus Democracy." *Journal of Democracy* 16 (1): 124–37.

Kousser, J. Morgan. 1974. *The Shaping of Southern Politics: Suffrage Restriction and the Establishment of the One-Party South, 1880–1910.* New Haven: Yale University Press.

Lancelot, Alain. 1968. *L'Abstentionnisme électoral en France.* Paris: Armand Colin.

Landé, Carl H. 1996. *Post-Marcos Politics: A Geographical and Statistical Analysis of the 1992 Presidential Election.* New York: St. Martin's.

Lantigua, John. 2001. "How the GOP Gamed the System in Florida." *Nation,* April 30.

Laquian, Aprodicio, and Eleanor Laquian. 1998. *Joseph Ejercito "Erap" Estrada: The Centennial President.* Quezon City: College of Public Administration, University of the Philippines.

Lazarte, Jorge. 2003. "Los factores técnico-logísticos y administrativos en la participación electoral." In *Participación y abstención electoral en Bolivia,* ed. Carlos Toranzo Roca. La Paz: Friedrich Ebert Stiftung.

Leuthold, David A. 1997. "Further Steps Toward Democracy: The 1996 National Assembly Elections." *Korea Observer* 28 (1): 1–24.

Levitt, Justin, Wendy R. Weiser, and Ana Muñoz. 2006. "Making the List: Database Matching and Verification Processes for Voter Registration." Brennan Center for Justice, New York University School of Law.

Lijphart, Arend. 1971. "Comparative Politics and the Comparative Method." *American Political Science Review* 65 (3): 682–93.

Liu, I-chou. 1999. "Campaigning in an SNTV System: The Case of the Kuomintang in Taiwan." In *Elections in Japan, Korea, and Taiwan under the Single Non-Transferable Vote: The Comparative Study of an Embedded Institution,* ed. Bernard Grofman, Edwin Winckler, and Brian Woodall. Ann Arbor: University of Michigan Press.

Lodge, Tom. 1999. *Consolidating Democracy: South Africa's Second Popular Election.* Johannesburg: Witwatersrand University Press.

———. 2003. "Voter Abstention in the South African General Election of 1999." *Representation* 39 (2): 105–18.

LoGerfo, James P. 2000. "Beyond Bangkok: The Provincial Middle Class in the 1992 Protests." In *Money and Power in Provincial Thailand,* ed. Ruth McVey. Honolulu: University of Hawaii Press.

López-Pintor, Rafael. 2000. *Electoral Management Bodies as Institutions of Governance.* New York: United Nations Development Programme.

Lujambio, Alonso. 1998. "Mexican Parties and Congressional Politics in the 1990s." In *Governing Mexico: Political Parties and Elections,* ed. Mónica Serrano. London: Institute of Latin American Studies.

Lurie, Karen. 2004. "Vote Hacking." October 29. www.sciencentral.com/articles/view. php3?article_id=218392395&cat=3_4.

Madrid, Raúl L. 2007. "The Indigenous Movement and Democracy in Bolivia." Paper presented at the Prospects for Democracy in Latin America Symposium, University of North Texas, April 5–6.

Maley, Michael. 2001. "The Australian Electoral Commission: Balancing Independence and Accountability." *Representation* 38 (1): 25–30.

Maligner, Bernard. 1986. *Halte à la fraude électorale.* Paris: Économica.

Massicotte, Louis. 2005. "Voter Registration, Voter Identification, Increasing Turnout, Election Administration: A Few Hints from Foreign Experience." Testimony before the U.S. Commission on Federal Election Reform. Rice University, Houston, Texas, June 30.

Massicotte, Louis, André Blais, and Antoine Yoshinaka. 2004. *Establishing the Rules of the Game: Election Laws in Democracies.* Toronto: University of Toronto Press.

Mayfield, Loomis. 1993. "Voting Fraud in Early Twentieth-Century Pittsburgh." *Journal of Interdisciplinary History* 24 (1): 59–84.

MCBE (Montgomery County Board of Elections). 2005. "2004 Presidential General Election Review: Lessons Learned." Maryland.

McCarthy, J. P. 2004. "Test Results of the Powervote/Nedap Electronic Voting System. A Submission to the Commission on Electronic Voting and Counting." Ireland, April 15.

McCormick, Richard P. 1953. *The History of Voting in New Jersey: A Study in the Development of Election Machinery 1664—1911.* New Brunswick, NJ: Rutgers University Press.

McCrary, Peyton. 2003. "Bringing Equality to Power: How the Federal Courts Transformed the Electoral Structure of Southern Politics, 1960–1990." *Journal of Constitutional Law* 5 (4): 665–708.

McGrath, Amy. 1996. *The Frauding of Votes?* Kensington, Australia: Tower House.

MEC (Malawi Electoral Commission). 1999a. "1999 Parliamentary and Presidential Elections Report."

———. 1999b. "International Observers Report: Republic of Malawi's Parliamentary & Presidential Elections, 1999."

Merriam, Charles Edward, and Harold Foote Gosnell. 1924. *Non-voting: Causes and Methods of Control.* Chicago: University of Chicago Press.

Mikkelson, Barbara. 2007. "A Scan of Wealth and Taste." www.snopes.com/business/ alliance/barcode.asp.

Mill, John Stuart. [1861] 1975. "Considerations on Representative Government." In *Three Essays.* New York: Oxford University Press.

Minchin, Nick. 2004. *Senate Hansard,* Commonwealth of Australia, June 24, p. 24594.

Minnite, Lori, and David Callahan. 2003. "Securing the Vote: An Analysis of Election Fraud." New York: Dēmos.

Mitchell, Glenn E., and Christopher Wlezien. 1995. "The Impact of Legal Constraints on Voter Registration, Turnout, and the Composition of the American Electorate." *Political Behavior* 17 (2): 179–202.

Monitor Project. 2001. "The Voter Registration Process." Sierra Leone.

Monsod, Christian. 1997. "Comelec and the 1998 Elections." *Kilosbayan,* June 12.

Moon, Eric P., and James A. Robinson. 1998. "Taiwan's 1997 Local Elections: Appraising Steps in Democratization." *American Journal of Chinese Studies* 5:131–46.

Moynihan, Donald P. 2004. "Building Secure Elections: E-Voting, Security, and Systems Theory." *Public Administration Review* 64 (5): 515–28.

Mulder, Niels. 1997. *Inside Philippine Society: Interpretations of Everyday Life.* Quezon City: New Day.

Mvula, Peter M., and John M. Kadzandira. 1998. "Baseline Study on Civic Education and Voter Apathy: Study Report Submitted to the Public Affairs Committee (PAC)." Zomba, Malawi: University of Malawi, Centre for Social Research.

NCSL (National Conference of State Legislatures). 2003. "Elections Reform Task Force: The States Tackle Election Reform." March 24. www.ncsl.org/programs/legismgt/elect/taskfc/electaskfc.htm.

——. 2004. "The States Tackle Election Reform: Summary of 2003 Legislative Action." May 11. www.ncsl.org/programs/legismgt/elect/taskfc/03billsum.htm.

Ndegwa, Stephen N. 2003. "Kenya: Third Time Lucky?" *Journal of Democracy* 14 (3): 145–58.

NDI (National Democratic Institute for International Affairs). 1991. "An Assessment of the Senegalese Electoral Code: International Delegation Report." Washington, DC.

——. 1994. "Interim Report on the May 16, 1994 Elections in the Dominican Republic." Washington, DC, August 12.

——. 1995. "Pan African Democracy Materials Development Seminar, July 13—16, 1995, Abidjan, Côte d'Ivoire, Seminar Report." Washington, DC.

——. 1996. "Ballot Test Report: A Report on a Series of Eighteen Focus Groups Conducted in Malawi to Test Alternative Balloting Procedures," June.

——. 1999a. "Final Report on the May 30, 1999 Parliamentary Elections in Armenia." Washington, DC.

——. 1999b. "Guinea: Supporting the Democratic Process, September 1998—January 1999." Washington, DC.

——. 2002. "Statement of the National Democratic Institute/The Carter Center Pre-Election Delegation to Nigeria's 2003 Election." Abuja, November 22.

——. 2003a. "Nigeria 2003 Elections." *NDI Election Watch* No. 2 (February 28): 1–2.

——. 2003b. "Preliminary Statement of the National Democratic Institute (NDI) International Election Observer Delegation to Nigeria's April 12 National Assembly Elections." Abuja, April 14.

Neuman, Laura, and Jennifer McCoy. 2001. "Observing Political Change in Venezuela: The Bolivarian Constitution and 2000 Elections." Atlanta: Carter Center.

Noren, Wendy. 2006. County Clerk, Boone County, Missouri. Testimony before the U.S. House of Representatives Committee on House Administration, hearing on noncitizen voting, June 22.

OAS (Organization of American States). 2000. "Final Report of the OAS Electoral Mission in the Bolivarian Republic of Venezuela," December.

Ockey, James. 1999. "Creating the Thai Middle Class." In *Culture and Privilege in Capitalist Asia,* ed. Michael Pinches. New York: Routledge.

Ockey, James. 2000. "The Rise of Local Power in Thailand: Provincial Crime, Elections and the Bureaucracy." In *Money and Power in Provincial Thailand,* ed. Ruth McVey. Honolulu: University of Hawaii Press.

O'Leary, Cornelius. 1962. *The Elimination of Corrupt Practices in British Elections, 1868–1911.* Oxford: Oxford University Press.

Opinion '99. 1998. "Voter Participation in the 1999 Elections." Press release, South Africa, November 10.

——. 1999. "Voter Participation in the 1999 Elections IV." Press release, South Africa, May 28.

Organization of African Unity. 1999. "Report of the Observer Group to Malawi during the Parliamentary and Presidential Elections," June 15.

Orwell, George. [1937] 1958. *The Road to Wigan Pier.* San Diego: Harvest.

OSCE (Organization for Security and Co-operation in Europe). 2006. "Republic of Kazakhstan Presidential Election, 4 December 2005, OSCE/ODIHR Election Observation Mission Final Report." Warsaw: Office for Democratic Institutions and Human Rights, February 21.

——. 2007. "The Netherlands Parliamentary Elections, 22 November 2006, OSCE/ODIHR Election Assessment Mission Report." Warsaw: Office for Democratic Institutions and Human Rights, March 12.

Overton, Spencer. 2007. "Voter Identification." *Michigan Law Review* 105 (4): 631–82.

Pastor, Robert A. 1999. "A Brief History of Electoral Commissions." In *The Self-Restraining State: Power and Accountability in New Democracies,* ed. Andreas Schedler, Larry Diamond, and Marc F. Plattner. Boulder: Lynne Rienner.

——. 2004. "Improving the U.S. Electoral System: Lessons from Canada and Mexico." *Election Law Journal* 3 (3): 584–93.

Pasuk, Phongpaichit, Nualnoi Treerat, Yongyuth Chaiyapong, and Chris Baker. 2000. "Corruption in the Public Sector in Thailand: Perception and Experience of Households." Political Economy Centre, Chulalongkorn University, Bangkok.

Pawłowska, Agnieszka. 2004. "Failures in Large Systems Projects in Poland: Mission [Im]possible?" *Information Polity* 9 (3/4): 167–80.

Perrow, Charles. 1984. *Normal Accidents: Living with High-Risk Technologies.* New York: Basic.

Philippine Center for Investigative Journalism. 2005. "I Report Special Edition: The Queens' Gambits." Quezon City.

Pinches, Michael. 1992. "The Working Class Experience of Shame, Inequality, and People Power in Tatalon, Manila." In *From Marcos to Aquino: Local Perspectives on Political Transition in the Philippines,* ed. Benedict J. Kerkvliet and Resil B. Mojares. Honolulu: University of Hawaii Press.

——. 1996. "The Philippines' New Rich: Capitalist Transformation Amidst Economic Gloom." In *The New Rich in Asia: Mobile Phones, McDonald's and Middle Class Revolution,* ed. Richard Robison and David S. G. Goodman. New York: Routledge.

Pinto-Duschinsky, Michael. 2002. "Financing Politics: A Global View." *Journal of Democracy* 13 (4): 69–86.

Pitkin, Hanna Fenichel. 1972. *Wittgenstein and Justice: On the Significance of Ludwig Wittgenstein for Social and Political Thought.* Berkeley: University of California Press.

Pitts, Michael J. 2005. "Let's Not Call the Whole Thing Off Just Yet: A Response to Samuel Issacharoff's Suggestion to Scuttle Section 5 of the Voting Rights Act." *Nebraska Law Review* 84:605–30.

Piven, Frances Fox, and Richard A. Cloward. 1988. *Why Americans Don't Vote.* New York: Pantheon.

PPCRV (Parish Pastoral Council for Responsible Voting). 1996. "5th Foundation Anniversary Celebration. PPCRV National Conference, October 18–19, 1996. Conference Report." Philippines.

Pulse Asia. 2001. Vote Buying Module in *Ulat ng Bayan* Survey, June 15–16, 2001. Commissioned by Frederic Charles Schaffer. Quezon City, Philippines.

Quinn, Herbert F. 1979. *The Union Nationale: Quebec Nationalism from Duplessis to Lévesque.* 2nd ed. Toronto: University of Toronto Press.

Rakner, Lise, and Lars Svåsand. 2005. "Stuck in Transition: Electoral Processes in Zambia 1991–2001." *Democratization* 12 (1): 85–105.

Ramachandran, R. 2004. "Tried, but Tested?" *Frontline,* February 14–27, 14–20.

Raskin, Jamin. 2005. "Lawful Disenfranchisement: America's Structural Democracy Deficit." *Human Rights* 32 (2): 12–16.

Rawnsley, Gary D. 2003. "An Institutional Approach to Election Campaigning in Taiwan." *Journal of Contemporary China* 12 (37): 765–79.

Red de Veedores. 2001. "Informe mega elecciones 2000." Venezuela, April.

Reynolds, Andrew. 1999. "The Results." In *Election '99: South Africa from Mandela to Mbeki,* ed. Andrew Reynolds. New York: St. Martin's.

Reynolds, John F. 1988. *Testing Democracy: Electoral Behavior and Progressive Reform in New Jersey, 1880–1920.* Chapel Hill: University of North Carolina Press.

Reynolds, John F., and Richard L. McCormick. 1986. "Outlawing 'Treachery': Split Tickets and Ballot Laws in New York and New Jersey, 1880–1910." *Journal of American History* 27 (4): 835–58.

Rezende, Pedro A. D. 2004. "Electronic Voting Systems: Is Brazil Ahead of Its Time?" *Crypto-Bytes* 7 (2): 1–7.

Rigger, Shelley Elizabeth. 1994. "Machine Politics in the New Taiwan: Institutional Reform and Electoral Strategy in the Republic of China on Taiwan." PhD diss., Harvard University.

——. 2002. "Weighing a Shadow: Toward a Technique for Estimating the Effects of Vote-Buying in Taiwan." Paper presented at Trading Political Rights: The Comparative Politics of Vote Buying Conference, MIT, August 26–27.

Roberts, Karlene H. 1990. "Some Characteristics of One Type of High Reliability Organization." *Organization Science* 1 (2): 160–76.

Romero Ballivián, Salvador. 2003. "Análisis de la participación electoral en Bolivia." In *Participación y abstención electoral en Bolivia,* ed. Carlos Toranzo Roca. La Paz: Friedrich Ebert Stiftung.

Rose-Ackerman, Susan. 1999. *Corruption and Government: Causes, Consequences, and Reform.* New York: Cambridge University Press.

Rosello, Ramon N. 2001. Acting COMELEC officer for Las Piñas. Interview with author, Las Piñas, Philippines, March 20.

Roseman, Gary H., Jr., and E. Frank Stephenson. 2005. "The Effect of Voting Technology on Voter Turnout: Do Computers Scare the Elderly?" *Public Choice* 123 (1–2): 39–47.

Rosenstone, Steven J., and Raymond E. Wolfinger. 1978. "The Effects of Registration Laws on Voter Turnout." *American Political Science Review* 72 (1): 22–45.

Rufo, Aries. 2001. "A Church in Limbo: Has the Catholic Church Abandoned Its Flock?" *Newsbreak,* July 4.

Rusk, Jerrold G., and John J. Stucker. 1978. "The Effect of the Southern System of Election Laws on Voting Participation: A Reply to V. O. Key, Jr." In *The History of American Electoral Behavior,* ed. Joel H. Sibley, Allan G. Bogue, and William H. Flanigan. Princeton: Princeton University Press.

SADCPF (Southern African Development Community Parliamentary Forum). 2002. "Zimbabwe Presidential Elections 2002: Observation Mission Report." Windhoek, Namibia.

——. n.d. "Lesotho—2002 National Assembly Elections, Election Observation Mission Report."

Salem, Gérard. 1992. "Crise urbaine et contrôle social à Pikine: Borne-fontaines et clientélisme." *Politique Africaine* 45:21–38.

Saltman, Roy G. 2007. "Assuring Election Integrity with Independent Verification." Unpublished paper, Columbia, MD, March 1.

Samuels, David J. 1999. "Incentives to Cultivate a Party Vote in Candidate-Centric Electoral Systems: Evidence from Brazil." *Comparative Political Studies* 32 (4): 487–518.

Sawer, Marian. 2006. "Damaging Democracy? Early Closure of Electoral Rolls." Democratic Audit of Australia, Australian National University, March.

Schaffer, Frederic Charles. 1998. *Democracy in Translation: Understanding Politics in an Unfamiliar Culture.* Ithaca: Cornell University Press.

——. 2002. "Might Cleaning Up Elections Keep People Away from the Polls? Historical and Comparative Perspectives." *International Political Science Review* 23 (1): 69–84.

——. 2003. "Assessing the Effectiveness of Anti Vote Buying Public Education Ads in the Philippines." Report prepared for the National Citizens' Movement for Free Elections, November 13.

——. 2004. "Vote Buying in East Asia." *Global Corruption Report 2004.* London: Transparency International and Pluto Press.

——. 2007. "Why Study Vote Buying?" In *Elections for Sale: The Causes and Consequences of Vote Buying,* ed. Frederic Charles Schaffer. Boulder: Lynne Rienner.

Schafferer, Christian. 2003. *The Power of the Ballot Box: Political Development and Election Campaigning in Taiwan.* New York: Lexington.

Schedler, Andreas. 1999. "Conceptualizing Accountability." In *The Self-Restraining State: Power and Accountability in New Democracies,* ed. Andreas Schedler, Larry Diamond, and Marc F. Plattner. Boulder: Lynne Rienner.

——. 2002. "The Menu of Manipulation." *Journal of Democracy* 13 (2): 36–50.

Selker, Ted. 2004. "Processes Can Improve Electronic Voting: a Case Study of an Election." Caltech/MIT Voting Technology Project, Paper No. 19, October.

Sennett, Richard, and Jonathan Cobb. 1973. *The Hidden Injuries of Class.* New York: Knopf.

Serebrov, Job, and Tova Wang. 2006. "Voting Fraud and Voter Intimidation: Report to the U.S. Election Assistance Commission on Preliminary Research and Recommendations." Predecisional draft.

Seymour, Charles. 1915. *Electoral Reform in England and Wales: The Development and Operation of the Parliamentary Franchise, 1832–1885.* New Haven: Yale University Press.

Shim, Jae Hoon. 1994. "South Korea. All Change: Political Reforms Set to Shake Up Campaigning." *Far Eastern Economic Review* 157 (11): 20.

Shin, Myungsoon. 1999. "Change and Continuity in South Korean Electoral Politics: An Evaluation of the 15th National Assembly Elections." *Journal of East Asian Affairs* 13 (1): 196–220.

Silberman, Susan L. 2005. "Voter Identification in Indiana: A Demographic Analysis of Impact on Older Indiana Citizens." AARP Knowledge Management, October.

Simon, Donald J. 2005. Testimony before the U.S. Commission on Federal Election Reform. Rice University, Houston, Texas, June 30.

Smith, Daniel A. 2002. "Consolidating Democracy? The Structural Underpinnings of Ghana's 2000 Elections." *Journal of Modern African Affairs* 40 (4): 621–50.

Snook, Scott A. 2000. *Friendly Fire: The Accidental Shootdown of U.S. Black Hawks over Northern Iraq.* Princeton: Princeton University Press.

State of Georgia. 2007. "Voter Verified Paper Audit Trail: Pilot Project Report, SB500 2006 Georgia Accuracy in Elections Act." Office of the Secretary of State, Elections Division, April.

Stewart, Charles III. 2006. "Residual Vote in the 2004 Election." *Election Law Journal* 5 (2): 158–69.

Steyn, Phia. 2002. Personal communication, June 13.

Stokes, Susan C. 2007. "Is Vote Buying Undemocratic?" In *Elections for Sale: The Causes and Consequences of Vote Buying,* ed. Frederic Charles Schaffer. Boulder: Lynne Rienner.

Stuart, Guy. 2004. "Databases, Felons, and Voting: Bias and Partisanship of the Florida Felons List in the 2000 Elections." *Political Science Quarterly* 119 (3): 453–75.

Subramanian, Narendra. 1999. *Ethnicity and Populist Mobilization: Political Parties, Citizens and Democracy in South India.* Delhi: Oxford University Press.

Suval, Stanley. 1985. *Electoral Politics in Wilhelmine Germany.* Chapel Hill: University of North Carolina Press.

Swire, Peter P. 2004. "A Model for When Disclosure Helps Security: What Is Different about Computer and Network Security?" *Journal on Telecommunications and High Technology Law* 3 (1): 163–207.

SWS (Social Weather Stations). 2001. Second Quarter (PR1 & PR2) Survey Sourcebook. Quezon City, Philippines.

———. 2003. Fourth Quarter Survey Sourcebook. Quezon City, Philippines.

———. 2004. Exit Poll, May 10. Quezon City, Philippines.

Tancangco, Luzviminda G. n.d. "The Proposed Registration System: For Better or Worse?" Unpublished paper.

"The Tancangco Report: A Symposium and Peer Review." 1991. Proceedings of the Symposium held on April 3. Organized by the President of the University of the Philippines.

Thompson, Glen. 1997. "Ministering to the Oppressed? Change and the Spiritual Economy of the Faith Movement in Durban during the Late Twentieth-Century." *Journal of Natal and Zulu History* 17:60–98.

Thompson, Nicholas. 2001. "Locking Up the Vote: Disenfranchisement of Former Felons was the Real Crime in Florida." *Washington Monthly,* January/February.

Thornton, Laura. 2000. "Combating Corruption at the Grassroots: The Thailand Experience, 1999–2000." National Democratic Institute for International Affairs.

TIZ (Transparency International—Zambia). 2001. "Press Statement of Election Monitoring Findings on Corruption in the Kabwata Bye Elections," September 15.

Tocqueville, Alexis de. [1893] 1987. *Recollections: The French Revolution of 1848,* ed. J. P. Mayer and A. P. Kerr. New Brunswick, NJ: Transaction.

Toobin, Jeffrey. 2004. "Annals of Law: Poll Position." *New Yorker,* September 20.

Transition Monitoring Group. 1999. "Interim Report on the Presidential Elections Held on Saturday, 27th February 1999." Lagos, Nigeria, March 1.

TrueVoteMD. 2004. "When the Right to Vote Goes Wrong: Maryland Citizens Tell the Story of Election Day 2004," November.

Vengroff, Richard, and Michael Magala. 2001. "Democratic Reform, Transition and Consolidation: Evidence from Senegal's 2000 Presidential Election." *Journal of Modern African Studies* 39 (1): 129–62.

Verified Voting Foundation. 2004. Election Verification Project press conference, November 18. www.verifiedvotingfoundation.org/article.php?id=5331.

VerifiedVoting.Org. n.d. "Electronic Vote Miscounts and Malfunctions in Recent Elections." www.verifiedvoting.org/downloads/resources/documents/ElectronicsInRecentElections.pdf.

Villamor, Ignacio. 1909. *Ley electoral de Filipinas.* Manila: E.C. Estrella.

Wall, Alan, Andrew Ellis, Ayman Ayoub, Carl W. Dundas, Joram Rukambe, and Sara Staino. 2006. *Electoral Management Design: The International IDEA Handbook.* Stockholm: International IDEA.

Wang, Chin-shou. 2001. "The Dilemmas of Clientelism: Electoral Mobilization of Clientelism in Taiwan, 1993." Carolina Papers: Democracy and Human Rights, No. 1. University of North Carolina Center for International Studies.

———. 2004. Personal communication, March 12.

Wang, Chin-shou, and Charles Kurzman. 2007. "Logistics: How to Buy Votes." In *Elections for Sale: The Causes and Consequences of Vote Buying,* ed. Frederic Charles Schaffer. Boulder: Lynne Rienner.

Wanna, John, Christine Ryan, and Chew Ng. 2004. *From Accounting to Accountability: A Centenary History of the Australian National Audit Office.* St. Leonards, Australia: Allen & Unwin.

Wattenberg, Martin P. 2000. "The Decline of Party Mobilization." In *Parties without Partisans: Political Change in Advanced Industrial Democracies,* ed. Russell J. Dalton and Martin P. Wattenberg. New York: Oxford University Press.

Weber, Eugen. 1982. "Comment la Politique Vint aux Paysans: A Second Look at Peasant Politicization." *American Historical Review* 87 (2): 357–89.

Weber, Max. [1919] 1978. "Politics as a Vocation." In *Max Weber: Selections in Translation,* ed. W. G. Runciman. New York: Cambridge University Press.

Wertheimer, Michael A. 2004. "Trusted Agent Report: Diebold AccuVote-TS Voting System." Prepared by RABA Technologies for the Maryland Department of Legislative Services, January 20.

Wiseman, J. A. 2000. "Presidential and Parliamentary Elections in Malawi, 1999." *Electoral Studies* 19:615–46.

Wu, Chung-li, and Chi Huang. 2004. "Politics and Judiciary Verdicts on Vote-Buying Litigation in Taiwan." *Asian Survey* 44 (5): 755–70.

Wu, Chung-li, and Shu-fen Yen. 2000. "An Analysis of Candidate Incentives to Vote Buying" [in Chinese]. *Theory and Politics* 14 (1): 1–21.

Yang, Wen-san. 1994. "Application of the Randomized Response Method: The Estimation of Vote Buying in Taiwan" [in Chinese]. In *The Social Image of Taiwan,* ed. Chin-chun Yi. Taipei: Sun Yat-Sen Institute.

Youngblood, Robert L. 1993. *Marcos against the Church: Economic Development and Political Repression in the Philippines.* Quezon City: New Day.

Index